For The See

MW00527616

Ever since Adam and Eve ate the forbidden fruit in the Garden of Eden, humankind has been perpetually struggling against the forces of Evil.

In *Between Good and Evil*, eminent occultist William Gray will help you take the Dark energies that naturally exist within us all and *transform them into spiritual Light!*

This unique book will take you on a fascinating exploration of the nature of Evil, Satan, and God that will stimulate many important insights. Gray will show you that Evil is a necessary challenge without which we would be unable to grow spiritually. But the raw energy of Evil has often been misunderstood, misused, or repressed, leading to a dangerous imbalance in our consciousness. Therefore, we must learn to control this energy instead of letting it control us.

To achieve such an end, Gray has revived an elaborate, centuries-old magical ritual technique called the *Abramelim Adventure*. By following Gray's step-by-step instructions, you will learn to transmute "Evil" impulses by putting them under the control of Good energies and images. Even if for some reason you are unable to use this ritual, you will find the principles discussed in this multi-faceted book valuable and insightful.

In today's world, it is a vital necessity to recognize, confront, and transform those elements of Evil for which we are responsible. By reading this book, you will have made an important first step in that direction, thus creating more efficiency, love, and success in your life.

About the Author

William G. Gray received much of his early training in the Western Inner Tradition from an associate of Papus. This individual was a Qabbalistic Rosicrucian, and Gray believes that his writings were profoundly influenced by this person's teachings. Later, Gray became a member of the Society of the Inner Light.

His writing career commenced when he completed two projects that Dion Fortune left unfinished at her death. One manuscript became *The Talking Tree*, and the other, *The Magical Mass* (which later became *The Sangreal Sacrament*). However, Israel Regardie's enthusiastic response to the manuscript published as *The Ladder of Lights* provided the impetus for Gray's works to reach the public.

Since that time, Gray has written several books on Western esoteric ceremonialism, devoting particular attention to what he calls the Sangreal concept.

To Write to the Author

We cannot guarantee that every letter written to the author can be answered, but all will be forwarded. Both the author and the publisher appreciate hearing from readers, learning of your enjoyment and benefit from this book. Llewellyn also publishes a bi-monthly news magazine with news and reviews of practical esoteric studies and articles helpful to the student, and some readers' questions and comments to the author may be answered through this magazine's columns if permission to do is included in the original letter. The author sometimes participates in seminars and workshops, and dates and places are announced in *The Llewellyn New Times*. To write to the author, or to ask a question, write to:

William G. Gray
c/o THE LLEWELLYN NEW TIMES
P.O. Box 64383-273, St. Paul, MN 55164-0383, U.S.A.
Please enclose a self-addressed stamped envelope for reply, or $1.00 to cover costs.

LLEWELLYN'S NEW WORLD MAGIC SERIES

The European re-discovery of the "New World" was much more than a geographic confirmation of the "Lands to the West."

For the members of various esoteric groups, America was to be the "New Atlantis," a utopia free of ignorance, superstition, fear and prejudice—incarnating a Great Plan for the spiritual evolution of this planet. Central to the political foundations of this *New Order for the Ages* is the intellectual freedom to pursue knowledge and wisdom unrestrained by the dictates of Church and State, and to publish and speak openly that all the people may grow in wisdom and attainment.

At the very core of this vision is the recognition that each person is responsible for his or her own destiny, and to freely pursue this "Happiness" requires that one throw off domination by "personal devils" of psychic nature, just as the American Colonies rebelled against the despotism of the British King.

We must be free of that which hinders our Vision and obstructs the flowering of the Life Force. For each of us that which obstructs is our *inner* personal Evil, and it is the Great Work of the magician to accept responsibility for that Evil and to transmute its powers into personal Good. Therein lies the secret of spiritual growth.

And with personal transformation comes our enhanced Vision and Power to work with magical responsibility in the outer world and to transmute those Evils resultant from human ignorance and fear, superstition and prejudice. We move forward as we perceive such Evils as originating from within ourselves and as we challenge them in their true nature.

We live in perilous times, but a "New Age" is at hand as the techniques of personal magic are used by more and more people to accept responsibility for Evil, and to redeem it for the Good— for individual growth and success, and for the Good of the planetary life within which we have our being.

New World Magic is visionary, recognizing the role of the individual practitioner in the world in which we live, and accepting the promise of a "New Order for the Ages." It is magic that is psychologically sound and spiritually committed. It is magic that builds upon older traditions in the knowledge that within them are our roots, and it is magic that looks to new understanding to ever expand the potential into which we grow.

New World Magic is for all who want to make a *New World*!

Other Books by William G. Gray

Temple Magic
The Ladder of Lights
Magical Ritual Methods
Inner Traditions of Magic
Seasonal Occult Rituals
The Tree of Evil
The Rollright Ritual
An Outlook on Our Inner Western Way
A Self Made by Magic
The Talking Tree
Western Inner Workings
The Sangreal Sacrament
Concepts of Qabalah
Sangreal Ceremonies and Rituals

Forthcoming

Sangreal Tarot (tentative)
Evoking the Primal Goddess

Llewellyn's New World Magic Series

BETWEEN
GOOD & EVIL
Polarities of Power

by

William G. Gray

1989
Llewellyn Publications
St. Paul, Minnesota, 55164-0383, U.S.A.

International Standard Book Number: 0-87542-273-X
Library of Congress Catalog Number: 88-37510

First Edition, 1989
First Printing, 1989
Second Printing, 1989

Library of Congress Cataloging-in-Publication Data

Gray, William G.
    Between good and evil: polarities of power / William Gray.
       p.   cm.—(Llewellyn's high magick series)
      ISBN 0-87542-273-X
   1. Magic. 2. Good and evil. 3. Spiritual Life. I. Title. II. Series
BF1621.G69   1989
133.4'3--dc19   88-37510
                                               CIP

Cover Art: Lissanne Lake

Produced by Llewellyn Publications
Typography and Art property of Chester-Kent, Inc.

Published by
LLEWELLYN PUBLICATIONS
A Division of Chester-Kent, Inc.
P.O. Box 64383
St. Paul, MN 55164-0383, U.S.A.

Printed in the United States of America

Contents

Contents

Introduction

Since this book presents quite a few concepts that may be unfamiliar to many readers (or at least unfamiliar in the forms they are presented here), it may be as well to clarify those in this introduction. Many misconceptions may be purely semantic, or people may understand the same words in totally different ways. For example, the recent supposition, which is taken for granted, that the word *Witchcraft* means "Craft of the Wise"; it actually derives from the much older meaning of "Craft of the Wicked." Such a mistake can be directly traced to Leland, an American folklorist of the last century, who confused the Old English rootword *wic* with *wit*. This might have been understandable, yet it is now more than regrettable in view of the many blameless and entirely worthwhile people classifying themselves as "Witches" purely because they had not bothered to check the meaning and derivation of that word in accurate etymological dictionaries.*

In the same way, the words *Satan* and *The Devil* usually mean quite different things to different people. In this book they are presented as personifications of all our worst faults and propensities—whatever we need to eliminate from our

---

*I hasten to add that, apart from what I consider to be an ill-chosen word, I have personally found those whom I know to have described themselves as "Witches" or "Wiccans" to be rather wonderful women of very high principles. If their ideas of Witchcraft mean that they are seeking a positive and life-affirming religion accenting the feminine aspect of Deity and working in harmony with Nature's cycles, then I'm all for it, and believe me I love every one of you!

characters, in much the same way as we need to eliminate the waste matter from our bodies. Hence the connection of Satan with excrement. Also it is important to consider that by presenting a picture of all that is Evil in ourselves, Satan at least shows us positively what we should be evolving away *from*. That does provide an invaluable pointer in the direction we ought to be taking, and so the idea that he (or IT) is really "The Other End of God" makes a very valid viewpoint.

The fact that the methodology described in this book is derived from a medieval magical system should in no way discredit this. The majority of psychotherapists today are well aware of the life-altering effects of practical psychodramatics when experienced by properly prepared and sincere people. Whether the original author(s) were equally aware of this is uncertain, although the probability is that he or they did indeed know quite well what was being done. There are too many clues suggestive of this to suppose otherwise. There is also too much hard and meaningful work attached to the actual practice of it for anyone insufficiently sincere in eliminating and controlling their own Evils from the very basis of their beings. Only a totally sincere soul would be likely to attempt it in the first place, and such a fundamental attitude is an absolute essential for the success of any magical endeavor.

It is, or should be, a well-known fact that Drama and what are usually called the Holy Mysteries are more than closely linked together. In other words, religious rituals and pure Theater were once synonymous, and still remain in near relationship, with each other. The psychological effects on human beings taking part in either activity is normally understood by the specialists concerned, and one or the other may well be advised or prescribed as conditioners of consciousness, depending on what might be called for. Perhaps they could be described as calisthenics of consciousness, or exercises of existence. Therefore it is a perfectly reasonable idea to consider psychodramatics as being therapeutic where human behavior is concerned, and psychiatrists are doing this all the time in major or minor ways. Thus if we truly intend to control, alter, or convert our Evil impulses into their opposite energy-projections, a well-designed psychodrama that is angled towards that particular end surely seems a very worthwhile commitment.

Once it was truly said that *the Devil is God as worshipped by wicked people,* and if we promote all that is Evil in ourselves to such a position of prominence, such would indeed be entirely accurate. Our Gods are as we conceive them, and to the extent that we allow such concepts to rule our lives, they become our "Above-Beings," however we name them. For example, the "Sangreal Concept" indicates a belief that in ancient times a very superior race of people made contact with our planet and managed to interbreed with the then *Homo erectus,* thus instilling a new genetic code into our species that subsequently developed into *Homo sapiens.* That gene has been responsible for our evolution ever since, with the end effect of evolving us towards whatever Ultimate we are ever likely to reach as creatures of Cosmos. Since those who became most advanced by this initial impact almost automatically became leaders of their families and tribes, they were assumed to bear this Sangreal, or Royal Blood, factor within themselves, and it then became both their duty and privilege to pass it along among their descendants. Hence all the legends concerning the Holy Grail, sacrifical Sacred Kings, and every other esoteric blood-belief. The fact that Christians and others prefer to symbolize literal blood with wine is purely a refinement of religious practice. In essence it remains what it always was and is likely to remain: a salvation symbol that Sangrealists prefer to see as being the LIGHT within and behind their blood, or that Inner Illumination which is our instinctive

and inherent guide to the Truth of ourselves once we become strong enough to bear it.

So what is a wicked person? That definition comes
from the Icelandic root *wic*, meaning weak in the sense of
being pliable or easily manipulated. So strictly speaking, a
really wicked person implies someone too weak to resist
urges to Evil, or impulses presumed to be sent from the
Devil. Even today we speak of those we consider as being
"bent." That is why it seems so odd or incongruous to a verbal purist when perfectly good and honest people who happen to be paganistically inclined should continue to describe
themselves as "Witches" and refer to their practices as
"Wicca." Strictly speaking again, however, the word *Pagan*
would not be entirely accurate either, since this specifically
meant those who lived in the *pagi*, or rural areas around
Rome. Therefore the word came to be equated with those
whom we would now call country people, or rurals, as distinct from urbanites, or town dwellers. It should surely be
obvious to any intelligent person that the self-styled Wiccans of today are neither more nor less wicked than any
other fellow mortal alive, so why should they continue supposing that description refers to Wisdom, when if that were
truly so the root word would have been either *wit* or *wis*,
instead of *wic*? A few moments spent with a good Anglo-
Saxon or etymological dictionary should convince all except
the most determined doubter on this point. It is surely high
time this was settled beyond all argument by some indisputable authority.

Probably something similar might be said about those
calling themselves "Christians," which is now a generic
term for those claiming to follow the teachings of a religious
leader called "the Christ," meaning the Anointed One in
the sense of being formally or theoretically dedicated to
Deity by the application of a specially consecrated scent
considered to be Holy Oil. In Christ's times this conferred

the honorific title of Sacred King on him, or marked him as someone chosen to be sacrificed on behalf of his particular people. Whether the average self-styled Christian is aware of this or not is very uncertain, but most of them seem content to accept the term *Christian* as a description of their religious beliefs. Of course this has been honored by many centuries of usage and common acceptance, so it is possible that the terms *Wicca* and *Wiccan* could expect the same after an equivalent period. One the whole, however, it would seem advisable that another and more suitable description quite beyond all boundaries of argument or misapprehension be officially adopted by this modern movement of undoubted validity and significance. It might be remembered that it took a long time before the term *Christianity* became a generalization for the many sects and cults claiming allegiance to a common Avatar. Therefore it might take a comparable period for present non-Christian esoteric sectarians to reach agreement among themselves concerning a collective title for their religious inclinations. The only thing that seems certain is that none of the well-meaning ones would willingly call themselves Satanists, especially since they consider their Deity to be one with a distinctly feminine gender, at least as a biological Being, whereas the Satan-concept is conventionally associated with masculine meanings.

Foreword

One of the most annoying and irritating things that can happen to esoteric practitioners during the course of their lives is to be wrongly accused of "Satanism," usually by "reborn" Christians or others of Fundamentalist persuasions. Exactly what Satanism means to such people is never quite clear, but that seems to be about the vilest epithet they can think of. For them, Satanists worship all sorts of animalistic beings, have sex at all angles and orifices, fling blood everywhere, saturate themselves with every sort of dangerous drug, commit murder and mayhem in all directions, and in short practice every possible perversion imaginable (and preferably beyond imagination altogether). Satanists, in fact, are the very wickedest of people who should be treated with antipathy and as much legal persecution as can be contrived by earnest Christians, whose Lord advised them to love their enemies and return Good for Evil.

The chances are that those esoterics suspected of Satanism as understood by the popular press are no more than members of some "Nature Faith," or similar occult organization whose customs and practices are neither better nor worse than those of any average association. They are just a collection of human beings trying to cope with their spiritual natures as best they know how. Because they happen to be doing this in a minority manner makes them a natural target for those of opposite opinions, who associate with what is usually called "The Crowd."

It normally starts at school, like most other human habits. The unusual child being singled out and "picked on" by the conglomerate of the others. This happens in every type of herd, either animal or human: the outcast albino blackbird, the deformed puppy or kitten, the freak fish— whatever may be markedly different from the average member of its species, or any individual that does not conform within definable limits to the standards accepted by the majority of its fellow creatures as being tolerable to live with. It is almost as if the entire species had drawn an imaginary line around their central core and proclaimed that whatever lived inside that circle was friendly and should be treated favorably, while anything outside it must needs be hostile and should be met with antagonism. Such is common herd behavior, and humans are no exception to it, being mostly unable to avoid the attitude.

The concept of Satan as an anti-God is a very old one and mainly grew out of antipathy for the sort of God pious people invented for themselves before trying to inflict it on as many humans as they could. Naturally, antisocial and evilly inclined folk needed a God-concept just as much as their better-natured brethren, and so they eventually chose the character of Satan, Leader of the Opposition as it were, to serve as a symbol for their common cause. If Satan was a rebel against Heaven, then so were they rebels against those of society who claimed Heaven as a rightful reward for their earthly conduct. Simple enmity magnified to a metaphysical level of life. The eternal "us and them" syndrome.

However, Satan did not always represent Evil for itself alone. He is reputed to have been the Archangel Lucifer, or Bearer of Light, which of course means Darkness. Nevertheless, the Light he bore was enough to illuminate the intelligence of humankind with inspiration to seek our own salvation through control of Nature, which we have been doing ever since with increasing success. Eventually Satan was reputedly ejected from Heaven by Archangel Michael, and he has been inhabiting an Underworld place of punishment called Hell ever since. Notwithstanding that, there are many legends concerning his ultimate conversion and restoration to original status at the "End of Everything," when all of us will return to whatever Ultimate we began from. A dedication to this hopeful end suggests the type of Satanism this book is concerned with. Should anyone feel like calling such Neo-Satanism, then let them do so by all means.

Whatever that may be, this book is most certainly not concerned with any adulatory worship of Satan as a Supreme Being or whatsoever of that nature. Its principal objective is recognition of the Satan-concept for what it really is, and consideration of the problems this presents to humankind as we search for spiritual solutions on our Eternal Quest. There are endless stories told of eccentrics attempting to "raise the Devil" some centuries ago, and now that we have finally succeeded in doing just that under the appearance of nuclear energy, it becomes urgently necessary to know what our future relationships therewith are likely to be. This book certainly cannot claim to have all the answers, but it does afford some practical suggestions worth considering from an esoteric viewpoint; for those alone it offers a truly contemporary perspective which should provoke at least some kind of spiritual response that could prove helpful to a still-struggling mass of humankind.

Wm. G. Gray, 1987

Chapter One

THE ANTIFACTOR

Esoteric legends inform us that our entire state of existence came together and continues in being because of an initial Motion, Word, Sonic, Name or other intentional manifestation of energy occurring throughout a condition of preexistence termed *CHAOS,* or *Space,* though normally thought of as Disorder. Qabbalistic legend in particular tells us that our Deity constructed our particular Creation from the ruins of several previous ones, which had run their complete courses for many millions of our years, fallen back into their constituents again, lain dormant for equally prolonged periods, and then became re-created by another awakening Deity. It is a case of the Never-Ending Story. If there is the slightest truth in this theory, it means that everything, including ourselves, is in a constant state of flux or is being taken apart and then put together again by opposite ends of the same Power, working within an inclusive field that tends to disintegrate everything by the sheer fact of its own nature.

This is well shown by the Hindu Trinity of Brahma the Creator, or Anabolic Deity; Vishnu the Preserver, or Maintainer of the Manifest; and Shiva the Destroyer, or Katabolic Deity, all of these being Aspects of the mysterious Parabrahm, or nonactive Deity behind all Deities. It is also typified by the Kether-Chockmah-Binah relationship on the Tree of Life with the Ain-Soph-Aur factor in the background; *but* we have to ask ourselves at this point what would happen if the Brahma-Kether field weakened to an unacceptable degree, and the Ain-Soph-Aur started making closer and stronger relationships with Chockmah-Binah?

That would surely have the effect of absorbing into itself things that were insufficiently prepared and conditioned to make that change properly, because in the correct order of creation, all is supposed to pass through a natural process of progression before reaching a condition when it is ready to meet its next stage beneficially. One might say the same thing about undigested food leaving a body before being absorbed usefully, or for that matter any other incomplete process.

The human usage of nuclear energy, during which matter is being artificially disintegrated at an entirely unnatural rate, is having a similar divisive effect on our spiritual equivalents, which in turn is beginning to show up in our lives and society. So far, a noteworthy instance is the disease AIDS, wherein natural, inherent immunity and resistance to breakup of bodily structures becomes lessened to a point where death takes place prematurely. Equivalents along spiritual lines are also occurring, and one of the indicators is the emergence of "Chaos Magic" in esoteric circles.

Chaos Magic is the exact opposite to Cosmos Magic in that it breaks down Order for the sheer sake of doing so without in any way replacing it with anything better. It is anarchy pure and simple. *De*struction without the slightest attempt at *con*struction. Katalysis without Analysis. Wreckage without Restoration. Negative without Positive. Put in a nutshell, elimination of everything from Existence—if possible. Put in two words: Nuclear Nastiness.

From a Qabbalistic viewpoint this means humankind is negating energy without including correct proportions of Wisdom and Understanding, or putting it through its proper processes of consciousness. Consequently a bad state of imbalance is building up behind what should be the free flow of our Life Force. Instead of receiving it in a purified state, we are meeting it precontaminated with the residual remains of our cloacal consciousness. To put it very crudely, we are getting our own shit flung back in our faces. Just as nuclear waste becomes a dangerous contaminant that will ultimately build up into a worldwide threat against all life on this planet, so will its spiritual equivalent do the same on higher levels. We have simply got to find some effective way of dealing with our corruption before it deals with us— definitely and finally. In fact most of the trouble is that we have *not* tried to deal with it adequately at all.

Everyone knows the results of blocked drains when toilets back up and sewage begins to pour out of a toilet bowl instead of flowing freely down it. The equivalent of that is happening among humanity at present. We are choking ourselves with our own crap. Not only physically, but much more importantly, mentally and spiritually as well. We can literally eat our own excreta once it has been reduced to humus, broken down to constituents, then reused to produce vegetable nutrients, eventually emerging as an eatable product of earth. In the course of nature this takes a definite period of time, which cannot be hastened past maximum rate without endangering the ecology of all the integers involved. The whole process might as well be known as the Ilkla Moor Syndrome, since it entails worms consuming corpses, then ducks devouring the worms, following which the erstwhile friends of the corpses enjoy feasting on the roasted ducks. In Shakespearean terms, a defunct king passing through the guts of a beggar. All perfectly normal, providing it undergoes every stage of its proper progress, but entirely abnormal and hazardous if it does not.

An explosion caused by mechanical or chemical means is quite a natural, if unfortunate, happening. A nuclear explosion is nothing of the kind, because it has to be caused by deliberate interference with basic physical structures of suitable material in such a way as to result in maximum disassociation of constituent atoms and those linked therewith. A "normal" nuclear explosion is in fact a Sun, and the Sun's satellite planets are simply cooling down "spin-offs" on which life as we know it may or may not be possible. Everything depends on the precise balance between the forces favorable to live on all levels. Excess or deficiency of energy applied to critical areas of action will most certainly have a very definite effect on life-factors applying in those areas, and such effects can only be calculated according to the specific level indicated. However, all the apparently discrete levels interconnect with each other and should be considered as a whole rather than a series of unconnnected layers as it were.

For example, the spiritual levels of life connect with the mental and intellectual ones, which in turn conjoin with their psycho-physical counterparts. Nothing can happen anywhere in any Sphere of Existence which does not affect its equal elsewhere to some degree, however slight. For instance, we are affected by the thoughts and mentalities of long-dead humans from past eras by means of their recorded thinkings, either quoted by others or read by us in written form. In the case of recently dead people we can hear their own voices or see their visual appearances as well if we wanted to. So human consciousness *per se* is a very far-reaching field, indeed, with its known shores stretching worldwide over a long period of time.

The brutal fact is that we are slowly dying as a people of this planet, and what we are witnessing are no more than symptoms of advancing age *as a species*. This can be compared with the life of an ordinary human individual. We start dying the moment we are born, but this commences with the maturing process of the reproductive system, which we might call the uphill climb. This is followed by a fairly brief period during which nature intends mating to occur, followed by the next generation being born and brought up to a point when they should be able to care for themselves. From then onwards life goes downhill at a steady pace, which increases with rapidity as it draws to a close. This final period is marked by quite noticeable deterioration that can be detected at first maybe monthly, and at the very end almost moment by moment. The whole of this single life-cycle can be seen as a parallel process on a planetary scale over very many millenia.

Our human race has reached its point of maturity when it must either export its seed to other inhabitable planets or else die out altogether. All the unmistakable signs of decadence and subsequent termination of species are evident around us, albeit at a sufficiently slow rate to allow for at least a brief respite, which might endure for a few more millenia if we make a concerted effort to restore human health both spiritually and socially, affording us enough opportunity for sufficient survival.

Successful bids for material survival are already being made by what can be called the *Internats,* an entirely new breed of people arising from the various World Wars. They owe no loyalty to any political, social, or cultural system except to the source of their wealth and power derived from their overall control of world commodities and the ideology that promotes this. Secure on their remote shelters linked by the most elaborate satellite and computer systems, through which financial and other controls can be constantly imposed on the working world, they can do more or less as they like with it. Wars can be commenced almost anywhere and continued for as long as people are stupid enough to fight and pay for them. Human minds may be manipulated by supplies of drugs and every alternative kind of persuasion. In short, the dream of every dictator has come true at last, and control of the entire commercial world has fallen into the hands of what amounts to a single consortium. That could be a good thing if the conglomerate in question were motivated by beneficent intentions, but on the other hand it could prove worse than fatal for us should the motivation be malicious.

If indeed, as seems probable, the major motivation of our controlling consortium is no more than pure profit for themselves, we are unlikely to be much better or worse off than we are at present. What we should never forget or underestimate is that there will always remain one vital factor that none of our unofficial owners can ever completely and entirely control with one hundred percent certainty. That is our spiritual selves with all our insight, aspirations, and intentions. True, they can, to quite a large extent, be influenced in any desired direction by a carefully calculated media and educational program, but as yet this has a limited field of action and cannot extend to the inner edges of our awareness and individual impulsion. Within ourselves we still have some freedom of faith and choice of consciousness. Whether or not we make as much use of this as we might is entirely another matter.

In the old days of Dualism it would have been a simple matter to decide which spiritual side to support. The Lifeforce was believed to be polarized, one end of Entitized Energy impelling us towards what we called Good, while the opposite incited us in the direction of what we knew as

Evil. The Good end we termed "God" and the Evil end "Satan." Sometimes these were considered entirely separate Entities, and sometimes were seen as the same Being viewed from an opposite angle. From extremely arcane sources, however, neither polarity was advanced as an ideal; but a blend of both into a balanced state of Pure Spirit was believed to be the best course to follow, although the ideal methodology of achieving this was always a point of perpetual argument. We ourselves, so to speak, were roughly equated with the Deity-Devil force-flow. What we might call the True Self, or immortal identity, belonged with Deity, and the other, or Pseudoself, end belonged with the Devil. So we have to realize just precisely what these apparently separate selves amounted to.

The True Self is the identity we were always intended to become at the original inception of our beings—the "Blueprints and Maker's Specifications," as it were, which accompanied the Creative Consciousness at the beginning of everyone. If we think of this as being at the very top of the Tree of Life, as an ultimate ideal to aim at, that will serve for a start. At the bottom of the Tree is the Pseudoself, or what we have made of ourselves by our own efforts because of our evolution, and that of course will vary with every single soul. The connection between these extremities is the Middle Pillar of the Tree, which is influenced by what might be termed the God-goad of the White Pillar and the Devil-drive of the Black one. From the God-goad we derive whatever we need to react with in order to work with Good, and from the Devil-drive we obtain those necessities enabling us to work with Evil. The balance between those two polarities produces our resultant evolution as entities of life-experience.

Why should we need exprience of Evil anyway? Because without enough of it we would be unable to make a free choice of conduct, which converts the energies of Evil into those of Good and then redirects their combined output into the Power of Perfection. The main purpose of our existing at all is to perfect our species into something beyond bodies altogether, so that we become energies of existence ourselves, and that will take time and effort extended for very many incarnations yet. Our principal source of energy is supplied by Life itself, polarized between our Divine and Demonic natures. Everything depends on which way we direct that energy, and whether we make the Devil in ourselves serve the God, or the other way around; or better still, both together serving the Power of Pure Spirit.

It is all a question of force-flow and the direction in which we deliberately circulate our current of consciousness. Moved one way from the Black to the White Pillar and then back to the Middle in an upwards direction, we evolve towards our True Selves and Pure Spirit. Reverse this flow and we shall drive ourselves downwards in the direction of Pseudoself and maximum materiality. Again this issue depends on which ideal motivates and inspires us most. Deity or Devil? Would we prefer worshipping God, Satan, or neither? Serve the ideal of Spirit or its opposite Pseudoself. The choice was entirely optional for us.

The medieval sect of the Cathars presented the picture as a somewhat intriguing legend. They claimed that Satan and Jesus were twin brothers who quarreled so bitterly that their father, God, divided his realms between them and constituted Jesus as the ruler of Heaven, while Satan was granted equal sovereignty over our earth. They were both free to compete for the souls of people, who might choose for themselves which leader they would follow. Whoever attracted the most souls would win in the end, after which the brothers would be reconciled and everybody would live happily together again forever. A nice legend with a lot of fundamental truth in its integrals. The Man-God Figure Jesus stood for our Heavenly quotient, while his brother

Satan represented our purely earthly component, although insufficient attention was directed towards the overall Deity above and beyond them both. The sheer simplicity of this scheme would probably not suit the sophistication of most modern minds, but the working principles are surely accurate enough to encourage closer examination.

The rough theory was that those who followed the teachings of Jesus and idealized him as a Deity would circulate their lifeforces Heavenwards so as to spiritualize themselves toward the True Selves they were meant to become by Creative Consciousness. Conversely, those that followed the dictates of Satan would do just the opposite and direct their lifeforces entirely earthwards so as to maximize their Pseudoselves into synthetic substitutes for the purely spiritual reality they were neglecting at the cost of their ultimate destiny. In point of fact, very few humans followed either God-concept very faithfully, or even knew most of the time which way they were working, so they operated in either direction as they felt inclined, and as a whole evolved into our present condition of civilization through the application of every energy concerned.

Now though many millions of human beings have made official and public religions of their God-beliefs, very few have attempted to do the same for the Satanic side of themselves. Unofficially, Satanism has existed for a very long time, though seldom under that name or as any sort of organization proclaiming its purposes and practices for anyone wishing to join its membership. If an average individual were questioned about Satanism and its factualities, they would probably make wild guesses concerning mysterious "Black Masses" and strange sexual orgies enlivened with drink and drugs. Of the actual basic beliefs behind the Satanist creed of "Evil—be thou my Good," or any of the customs and curiosities developing from this, they could tell nothing at all. They could not even explain how Satanism started, what it really amounted to, or why certain human beings should support it so strongly and what they hoped to gain from it in the end. It is with the hope of clarifying at least some of these problems that the present work has been attempted.

First it should be made perfectly clear that an actual interchange of energy between the Good and Evil principles of Existence is entirely necessary for the process of perfection, which we term *Evolution*, to take place at all. The energy supplied by the activities of Evil provides a valuable force for the furtherance of Good. What is important is the actual determination and direction of its flow. If the energy of Evil is directed towards Good and converted to a corresponding change of polarity, then the humans involved will benefit to the degree they they have advanced their evolution towards their True Self ideal. Should the energies generated by the principle of Good be directed into the course of Evil, however, then the opposite effect occurs, and the Pseudoself will be able to apply the results for its own purposes. So it should be quite clear that the ideal course for well-intentioned people to pursue is to treat Evil solely as a supply-source of energy from its side of life, and then put this through a conversion process so that it alters in character and direction to serve the spiritual ends of evolution instead of the merely material ones.

The worship of Gods, both for Good and Evil reasons, goes back to our earliest days on this earth. We saw them first as invisible Powers instigating and controlling the natural forces that affected us as human beings in all ways. It was therefore vital to make relationships with them as favorable as we could. If the various Gods favored us, all would be well, but if we angered or offended them then we would suffer for our presumptuous behavior. Eventually we evolved the Overgod code of conduct in which one single Superbeing was seen as controlling the entire company of lesser Deities, each with its own specialty or area of responsibility for some specific section of Cosmos, as we had begun to know the order of Creation in which we lived. By approaching this Overgod directly we could cut out all these interveners and deal with the Director rather than with his (or her) "middlemen," so to speak. On the other hand it was only sound common sense to discover the agency most closely connected with whichever interest was being advanced. For instance, it did not seem very practical to approach the Rain God for direct money favors, and so the Money God, Mammon, or Maymoun, from whose name our term *money* derives, was duly declared official guardian of gold and bringer of benefices. He was, and still is, revered under different names as a most desirable Deity whose patronage is welcomed almost universally.

However popular Mammon or his more classical partner Pluto may be, neither of these has the specific quality of Evil attributed to Satan. In fact such *is* his particular quality and the whole meaning of his name. He stands for the antithesis of everything ordered, good, regular, beneficial, or whatever may conform to control by Cosmic Consciousness. His legend says that he was ejected from Heaven for refusing to accept the Will of God as the supreme law of life and to acknowledge humankind as God's masterpiece. As the arch-rebel he was consequently condemned to become the Lord of Hell, where he and his supporting angels could exercise their influence on humans who held similar ideas of argument with the Almighty. The Lucifer legend tells the story nearly enough, if from a one-sided viewpoint only. Originally he seems to have been the brightest of the Heavenly Ones and highly favored by the Greatest of Gods. His beauty and intelligence were unsurpassed, yet the fatal weakness that cost him his position happened to be his personal pride. He disagreed with Deity and resorted to armed rebellion against Divine authority, whereupon Archangel

Michael, leader of the Hosts of Light, engaged Satan-Lucifer in combat, during which conflict an emerald was struck from Satan's crown, which fell to earth and was subsequently fashioned into the Holy Grail. Lucifer himself then followed it in a spectacular burn-out, which is symbolized by the Lightning Flash on the Tree of Life, and in doing so became dull red in color and from thenceforth was known as Satan the Adversary, because he had dared to challenge and defy the dictates of God himself.

On the strength of this familiar story, the Archetype of Satan became a Leader-Figure for some humans who would like to do the same as he is reputed to have done, with a great deal more success. There are, and always have been, many humans who abhor, dislike, and absolutely abominate every idea of a directing Deity. They just do not see why they should submit themselves to any codes of conduct based on such beliefs that might interfere with their own schemes for self-supremacy. They despise the so-called virtues on the grounds that these are nothing but sentimental stupidity and weakness of character. To them, there is only one virtue: getting what they want when they want it, regardless of anyone else's interests. Self-aggrandizement at the cost of everyone's contributions towards that single end.

To a certain extent this is a natural rule of life, since each individual is the result of a single sperm winning the race for one solitary egg from a million and more competitors. From that moment forward, life becomes a competitive battle for self-survival in the midst of a most confusing civilization. Exactly the same drive that resulted in birth from our mother's bodies continues to motivate us through life until its end. How far could our expulsion from a warm and wonderful womb into a cold, hard world be compared with Satan's ejection from Heaven? Anyway, we have the ability to modify and alter the behavior and characteristics of that drive, but otherwise it remains the constant of our consciousness and genius of our genetics from which we must derive the major source of our spiritual structures. If that particular energy that is characteristic of each individual could be expressed as a sonic sequence, it would resonate the "True Name" of that soul which they alone would respond with when it was uttered. That is why names were regarded as being especially sacred and never to be misused or "taken in vain." Our True Names and our basic genetics are identical. WE ARE WHAT WE ARE. When we remember the story of God beginning his or her Being with the utterance of his/her name I AM WHAT I AM, we should see the connection between this mythic event and our own origins.

Once in this world, however, we are faced with a Self search pointing in one of two totally different directions. There is the Quest for our Immortal Identity as our True Selves in unison with the Supreme Spirit, or there is the Quest for our Pseudoselves as inhabitants of this planet alone and limited to its conditions of consciousness and terms of expression. This earth has only a limited life, which we have been using up and exploiting at an ever-increasing rate, especially during the last few centuries. We may have a few thousand years of our time left before we face final extinction, but there can surely be no doubt concerning our eventual absorption into the Absolute as a life-species and the consequent cessation of civilization on this planet. Whether or not humankind as a whole is actively and objectively aware of this, we have known it instinctively for a very long while, and this subjective appreciation of our situation has led to the production of our various religions and philosophies, which attempt to deal with our feelings in connection with our many metaphysical problems.

The general outcome of all this has been the emergence of ethical codes that have conditioned human behavior into specific patterns believed best by those holding them most sacred. They are mainly conduct guides based on simple Do's and Don't's. When the celebrated Rabbi Hillel was approached by a Gentile and told that if he could explain the entire Hebrew Faith while the querent stood on one leg then he would adopt it on the spot, Hillel was reputed to have replied, "Simple. Stand on one leg now." When the man had done so the Rabbi continued, "DO NOT UNTO OTHERS AS YOU WOULD NOT THEY DID UNTO YOU. Now put your foot down." He continued further, "That is our entire Law. All the rest is commentary and pure speculation." In other words, behave towards other humans as you hope they will behave towards you. Everything else was just asking for definitions or behavior or specifying the regulation of conduct. Codification.

Eventually, due to social, cultural, and commercial exchanges among the different peoples of this world, a more or less common code of conduct began to appear that was really no more than was needed for the convenience of all concerned. This arose quite naturally as the result of mutual adjustment during the centuries of association. For example, if a trader became known as a cheat, no one would deal with him. Therefore it paid to uphold the principle of honesty as an ideal, even if it could be cunningly circumvented. Those who pillaged and raped could expect the same treatment in return. To murder anyone invited reprisals from the the victim's family, and possibly started a long trail of feuds wasting lots of lives for no particular purpose that anyone could remember. To tell deliberate untruths meant that similar stories would be returned until no one could be certain of what was accurate and what was not. That made life difficult for everyone, and so it became obvious that some kind of standards would be welcome among the civilized communitites of this world, and in the end these grew from sheer experience of each other. Sufficient wrongs did eventually make a right. It was largely a matter of knowing the rights and wrongs attached to conditions and circumstances. What was right in one country could be wrong in another one, or proper in one place and improper elsewhere. Furthermore, there might be alterations made to any such rulings over several generations, and those had to be known and allowed for.

In the end, this general understanding between humans concerning how they should or should not behave among themselves became known as their *code of morals*. Originally this had no especial sexual significance, and meant no more than whatever was customary for its place and period. A liar was an immoral person, and so was a murderer, thief, or any other offender against the prevalent code of conduct. Today we have restricted the sense of our term morality until it applies almost exclusively to the sexual conduct of human beings, and even there it has a very wide area of interpretation. For example, the Eskimo hospitality of offering the use of one's best wife to an honored guest would not normally be acceptable to most modern Europeans, and yet there are circles among those where a woman might offer herself and be accepted on a personal basis.

In fact, most of the generally accepted sexual standards of our present civilization derive from age-old experience with eugenics and the recognized rules of good health. To take great care of carefully selected sex partners and confine them as much as possible within circles known or believed to be disease-free was really just good, sound sense. We have the terrible lesson of AIDS before us now to demonstrate the point of why so many of the prohibited sex practices of olden times were based on nothing except previous painful experience and observation over many centuries. The Biblical text concerning the sins of the parents being visited on their children for several generations was no moral criticism, but a sober genetic fact. Restrictions were proposed to control sex conduct purely for the protection of our species. Nothing could ever be guaranteed one hundred percent safe, of course, but at least an optimum course of conduct might be worked out and recommended as a reasonable ruling.

Most mystical systems postulate a maximum spiritual state as being one wherein humanity and God merge into each other as One Being, becoming common Consciousness, or Universal Unconsciousness, whichever way one looks at things. They vary considerably in their teachings concerning how such a supreme condition can be achieved, but all are in agreement that humans will have to make a great deal of effort in adapting and modifying themselves before they are likely to be developed enough to unite with Divinity. What really matters is that people should keep this ultimate aim in mind and continue to quest for it throughout their lives in whatever manner they sincerely believe may be best for them. In Western parlance, this Divine Union is spoken of as the Mystical Marriage, which may be taken to mean that it is of a distinctly sexual character, masculine human nature uniting with the Feminine polarity of Deity, while feminine human nature unites with Its Masculine complement. When both reach perfect balance they can then combine with the central principle of pure Power. Since all human beings are theoretically bisexual, with the predominantly physical polarity of overt sex counterbalanced by the subjective polarity of the other, this seems to make individual reltaionships with Deity a matter of somewhat complicated connections. Perhaps this may best be shown by a diagram (Figure 1, page 17).

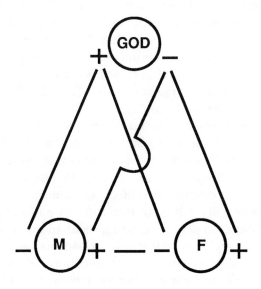

Figure 1

In this we can see a Human-Divine relationship through an idealized circuitry of polarized power. The man's positive side connects with the negative of both his woman and God, while the negative of the woman meets the positive of her male and also of God. This makes sense of the old belief that humans should find a facsimile of their Deity in their sexual partners. Each ought to provide a representation of Divine Life for the other. In the man, the woman should encounter her God, and he in her, his Goddess. We know that in fact this is frequently a very unsatisfactory substitute, yet nevertheless there has to be a vestige, however slight, of this principle in all human sexual partnerships, whether casual or permanent, normal or homosexual. It may even apply in the case of a single soul seeking Divinity in itself, when the masculine and feminine qualities of its own individuality quest for fulfillment through each other. The overall rule is the same as for ordinary magnetism—like poles repel, whereas unlike poles attract. Throughout the entire range of this activity in the whole Universe, it might well be called *Operation SELFSEARCH* wherever it manifests. We are all looking for ourselves in that *SAMESELF* we term "God," whatever we name IT.

Such is the natural order of our esoteric behavior in what we might call our normal condition of Existence. However, this does not suit those whose interests lie in the opposite direction, and it is from them that we may expect to encounter a countercurrent of consciousness that will have the effect of pushing us into contrary paths of performance. That is to say, persuading us to adopt courses of conduct and angles of awareness that lead us away from our unification with the Ultimate Self we really ought to be and towards the Great Artificial Alternative of the SATANSELF.

This is neither more nor less than a substitute Selfstate built up over many millenia by souls and spiritual entities with no inclinations to become what they considered to be subservient fractions of the Great Whole, preferring to set up alternative conditions for themselves that amount to an "anti-God," or an Entity apart from the authentic Deity; whereby they further their Pseudoself interests by feeding them with energies abstracted from all available sources. Since such people are averse to any designated type of Deity, they could truly be called Satanists from a technical viewpoint, because they believe in and pay forms of worship to an Entity of Evil that they have created and sustained with their own consciousness. All our very worst inclinations, most savage behavior, and antisocial impulses have made substantial contributions to the formation of an anti-God Entity influencing us in contra-Cosmic directions.

It must not be supposed for one moment that such a Spirit would present only the old-fashioned image of Evil, typified as a monstrous and misshapen Horror presiding over a fiery pit wherein sinful souls are stewed eternally for the edification of the Elect. Essential Evil can be highly cultured and refined to the highest degree. Cruel and brutal behavior begets a cruel and brutal Satan, whereas a sophisticated and cultured type of consciousness produces a Devil to match every refinement of Evil available for application on any occasion. We design our Devil in accordance with our own grades of Evil. It is simply a question of typification and degree. Both Good and Evil can be considered as relatable, with standard scales varying between extremities of definition; however, these may be graded from minimum to maximum.

Therefore the ancient idea of Hell, or the Abode of the Damned, being graded into specific circles of malefactors would seem to have some distinct truth in it, although probably not as Dante described it. Distinctions would depend entirely on the order of intelligence and degree of development. After all, it has needed our most advanced abilities of awareness to arrive at the most dangerous and destructive energy yet available to humankind: nuclear energy. As we evolved, so did our capacity for killing. First bare hands and claws, then sticks and stones, then arrows and edged weapons, then explosives, then high explosive missiles; and now chemical weaponry plus nuclear destruction and laser technology bring us to an ultimate Megadeath! All Evil, but increasingly advanced and educated Evil. No longer the crude and blunt Evils of our olden times, but their most modern and developed extensions, with a corresponding increase of efficiency and effect. Hell no longer need be horrible in aspect and loathsome to look at. In altered aspects it could seem like most of our modern amenities of an artificial nature. What it cannot do is counterfeit the finer faces of Nature herself: the splendors of Summer, the wonders of the Seasons, the beauties of flowers,

or any of the many miracles we associate with normal Creation. Hell can easily present almost any man-made ambience,
such as splendid restaurants, magnificent theaters, incredible factories, offices and workshops, ateliers of all descriptions. Of course, all kinds of artifical scenery could be
copied easily anough, as with stage or film sets, and there is
no reason why the conventional fire and brimstone back-
grounds should not be available as well, if absolutely insisted on. What is strictly necessary is that all environments
should be appropriate to dedicated Evildoers according to
their characteristics, and those are to be found in all walks of
life.

The decisive question is why would anyone deliberately
select an anti-God to follow instead of the authentic one?
The answer is purely because of the material profit and
advantages to be gained, instead of spiritual status achieved
by efforts and evolution put to that purpose. Of course, a
great many humans do this automatically with no thoughts
of Satan whatever. Their expended energies go into the
general collection of those associated with human activities
and behavior, some of which are detrimental while others
are beneficial to our race in particular. Over the ages,
however, there have developed a specialist breed of beings
who believe that if they serve a Spirit-Entity whose existence is dependent on energies derived from Evil activities,
they will not only be treated well by that Being, but will
receive special privileges for their services. As they see it,
work for the Devil deserves adequate payment, and their
Devil has proved a prompt paymaster. No sensible soul
would work for him willingly otherwise.

During the Middle Ages there was a popular belief that
humans could sell their souls to the Devil in terms of temporary rewards exchanged against eternal servitude in Hell.
A few short years of material pleasure paid for by an everlasting period of pain. One would not think this seemed like

a very good bargain, but there certainly appeared to be some people well prepared to pay the price demanded. Few people might take this very literally today, but the fact remains that the modern equivalent continues in a contemporary fashion. Energy is energy and has to be supplied in every case where specific effects are required. Common sense alone should inform us that no one at all can obtain something for nothing, strictly speaking; and although the soul of an individual is still requested in return for what may be offered, this is needed not so much for purposeless tortures as for practical use as fuel, providing fresh energy that will keep the activities of dedicated Evildoers going for as long as possible. This means that those who intentionally offer themselves to an Entitized Concept of Evil, commonly known as the "Devil," can expect to be expended in the service of that particular Being personified by those who have been clever enough to incorporate themselves with It beyond convenient extrication, modern warfare being an obvious example.

This is a question of what might be called "spiritual solidification," or so integrating a Pseudoself with the incorporative Entity concerned that it becomes virtually part and parcel of that Entity, and to all intents and purposes may be considered as the Being in question. Just as we can "become God" by absorption into the Absolute when we become True Selves, so may we do the diametrical opposite and insinuate our Pseudoselves into the spiritual structure of the Alternative Being associated with the antithesis of Beneficence and Harmony. We can also "become the Devil," providing we are prepared to pay the asking price for ourselves.

In a way, this is not unlike becoming a cancer or an infection of AIDS. The invading organism has a wonderful time while the victim lasts, but in killing that individual it destroys itself in the long run. Nothing is done, however, without deliberate and dedicated intention. Not only does there have to be an intelligent and positive intention in either direction, but this has to be developed and sustained by every means, and furthermore evolved by continuous and constant application. We can no more win our way to Heaven with a few kindly thoughts and casual prayers than we could earn our entry to Hell by means of some wicked words and a bit of bad behavior. The whole of any human being must be conditioned and completely changed structurally into one of the other kind of individual. This takes a great deal of time and energy. By far the great majority of people are neither one thing nor the other, varying between either to whatever degree they may decide on, or may have arrived at by average practice. Very few humans are preponderantly Good or Evil by pure intention only, but reach their current condition through whatever they have been thinking and doing as their normal *modus vivendi*, plus their inherited genetic impulses. This does not mean they cannot be influenced or persuaded to alter themselves by cleverly applied pressures brought to bear for specific reasons.

Nor does that mean anyone is automatically inclined to Good if they claim to be religious, and ostensibly and vocally proclaim their version of God from many odd angles. Their public God could quite well be a private Devil. A "Fundamentalist" Christian who seriously believes that the followers of all alternative religions are doomed at their Creation to the eternal flames of Hell (and an especial treat for him after death would be watching these condemned creatures being consumed by such destructuve burning) is obviously concerned with no sort of God at all, but a distinct Devil of the most vicious kind. Anyone capable of believing that a presumably beneficent Creator could possibly produce the great majority of humankind for the express purpose of sending their souls into a state of eternal torture has a very obviously nasty nature themselves, and does no more than expose this publicly. Yet people of similar persuasions have always existed in all official faiths and creeds, thus strengthening the Devil-concept in the minds of their fellow mortals who meet with them.

Thus it is quite possible to be a practicing Satanist without any of the paraphernalia so beloved by those supposing them necessary. No need for Black Masses or other theoretical trappings openly advertising allegiance to what might be called the "Opposition," since this is precisely what the term *Devil,* or *Diabolus,* means. The common name of Satan derives from several sources, one of these being *Set,* or the Egyptian anti-Deity, and there is a further derivation in the common modern term *Shit,* or excrement normally expelled from the lower end of the body with an objectionable smell and a dislikeable touch. This association of the Devil with dung is at least a fair attempt to convey an opinion of contempt and distaste for an Entity identified with the principle of Evil. Other descriptions vary considerably, from the comical "Old Hornie" to the classical "Asmodeus," the former alluding to the Goat-God and the phallic implication of a male erection, and the latter to a Hebrew-Latin combination meaning a God of waste, desolation, guilt, and utter ruin. It may be significant that one of our most commonly used expletives these days is "Shit!" which amounts to an invitation to the Devil to concern himself with whatever the matter happens to be. Whether people know this consciously or not, the implication is still there all the same. At one time they would have said quite openly, "Oh the Devil take this or that!" Nowadays, with disbelief in the existence of the Devil as an Entity, our current excretory expression makes a suitable modern substitute.

It would be better for those intending to lessen the influence of infernal agencies in our world, who are given to thoughtless employment of the "shit" expletive, to abandon the habit and choose another obscenity instead. This may sound trivial or insignificant, but it is in fact a conscious contributior towards the reduction of Satanic influence on earth. Granted, it would be so small and relatively unimportant as to be almost unnoticeable, but nevertheless it would take place in one self-area, and each has an ultimate part to play in constituting a Grand Total. Perhaps it could be considered as denying entry to one single microbe which might prevent a serious disease from invading someone's body. In any case, it is a useful discipline to practice.

Our current question is: To what extent does Satanism exist in our world of today—what are its effects, philosophy, practices, beliefs, and other incidentals? Can it be called a religion and has it any definite structure, or does it pose any serious threat to other beliefs? Should we take it for granted, or could it be considered as simply another aberration of the human mind to be treated by any practicing psychiatrist, or perhaps in extremity exorcised by a competent cleric. In order to make up our minds on all these points with any clarity, we shall need to consider them very carefully, or else we may be doing no more than occupying our time with foolish fantasies. First let us trace through the general history of Satanism from primitive times up to our present period.

Chapter Two

THE SERPENTINE START

It seems scarcely surprising that the serpent should be so anciently associated with both Evil and cunning, or "Wicked Wisdom." Apart from being killers, the clever camouflage of snakes and their habits of hiding in unsuspected places made them a serious menace to early peoples, with their bare limbs and vulnerable flesh. The snake was that most feared of all creatures, one that could creep close and strike fatally in virtual silence. Furthermore one that was odorless and did not betray its presence by scent. The most acute of human senses were normally useless against it, unless an obvious movement advertised it to the eye, or an audible hiss did the same for the ear, by which time it was often too late to avoid being bitten.

Biblically it was the serpent personification of Satan which informed humankind that the Deity-Figure they had hitherto trusted implicitly was not necessarily to be taken at his word. If they had confidence in themselves and ate of the Tree of Knowledge, they would then learn the difference between Right and Wrong, which would commence their evolutionary climb up the Tree of Life at the apex of which they would be immortal. In other words, humanity learned how to make its own assessments and judgments, plus the decisive isssue of "Yes" or "No," "This" or "That," "One or the Other." So started all human knowledge of life experience without which we could never have arrived at our present position. Be it carefully noted that the Edenic Myth does not credit the Deity with applying such an impetus to his (or her) creations, but the so-called Evil Entity who influenced them to disobey that Deity and act on their own accord. Neither did the serpent pluck the fruit for them; they had to do that for themselves in order to make it authentic as an act of their own intentions, regardless of the serpent's suggestions.

Now a myth does not mean an untruth, but a deep truth presented in such a way that it will appear memorable, interesting, informative, thought-provoking, and what is more, endurable and meaningful to the ordinary intelligent human mind. The Edenic Myth certainly does this for us if it only makes us wonder how far back genetic memory extends, or to what degree we are influenced by our remotest ancestors' awareness, reaching us from their condition of consciousness. No one is likely to rid themselves of several million years conditioning by just a few generations of altered awareness. However civilized and intelligent we may seem on surface levels, it would be well to remember that our primitive and uncultured pre-parentage is always in the background of our beings and may emerge momentarily to embarass or astonish us.

We might suppose that the cells from which our bodies are made are new ones, but they are not. They are old. Extremely old indeed. Their formation may be new, but the fundamental material from which they are built is more than ancient, it is pre-prehistoric. The original atoms and molecules are still being used in a creative process that has evolved every human on earth and continues to repeat the pattern with variations, obviously aiming at an eventual Ultimate that we can only guess at by inspired extrapolation. Locked into our atoms, so to speak, is our entire past with the program that will produce our future, and our only hope of affecting this lies in the eternal NOW through what we have been able to impress into those atoms while we use them for our existence. If we like to think of them as silicon chips to be programmed for succeeding generations, that might be an apt analogy. The question is what do we program them for, and can they be de-programmed subsequently? The only broad-spectrum answer that can be given is that we set them according to our particular prevailing natures, and they are not so much de-programmed as re-programmed by following generations.

This means to say we are living in a constant state of flux that is always changing from one side of a mean point to the other like an alternating electric current, and the whole state might as well be called Life. We interact with this flow according to our peculiarities, leaving our individual impressions in or on it to be reacted with by others adding theirs, then in our turns rejoin the ancestral reservoirs of energy ready for reissuing via the force-flow of repetitive incarnations. Since we are virtually the same old selves recombined and put through the production process again, it need not be surprising so much of everything has a facile feel and a familiar note to it. So-called "new" things and situations are much the same in one century as another, allowing for expressional latitude. Strictly speaking, there is no such thing as a *new* baby, but only another recreated from very old stock indeed. Sometimes one has a momentary impression of this when meeting the gaze of a very young child, noting with surprise a look that seems to be centuries old. As the child grows older, of course, it will lose this strange propensity and adopt a normal juvenile stare.

So we are, at any given instant, living compendiums of everything our predecessors have ever experienced on earth, plus what we may have added to this incredible human heap with our own consciousness. This has mostly amounted to change or modification of some description, which will vary from the infinitesimal to the considerable contribution of some outstanding thinker, designer, or worker with words, schemes, or other means of altering human awareness to noteworthy degrees. Among these could be classed the evident innovators of religions, philosophies, or other thinking systems that have moved the motivations of humankind in definite directions. This would naturally include noticeable artists of every description, or for that matter whosoever has instigated changes of ideology among their contemporaries. All these are cumulative and have resulted in the world civilization we currently experience. So much should be obvious, and yet there are important implications to be considered that account for many of our modern problems and might lead to a clearer understanding of how to handle them.

Once it is adequately realized what a deep and influential effect our past has upon our present, it might be properly appreciated to what extent the power of altering our future lies in our own hands, and with that knowledge could come renewed hope and confidence. It would also help us to sort out the "Goodies" from the "Baddies" of this world and to obtain some contemporary ideas of the "God-Satan" spiritual situations prevailing among people in general. These have always been with us in essence, and only alter in structure over the centuries. For instance, much of what was once expressed religiously is now expressed politically, and all our ideation has done is shift fields from one area to another. The old adage of Karre that "The more things change the more thay stay the same" is a very apt one indeed.

Beginning with the serpentine gift of deciding between Good and Evil, human progress has continued dubiously to its present position. At first, humankind did not see its Gods as specifically Good or Evil, but like themselves, inclined in either direction as their impulses urged them. Whether humans realized such Gods were idealized extensions of themselves as Archetypes is uncertain but highly unlikely. This does not imply that any of those Gods were unreal to the least extent. No concept of consciousness is *unreal*, but it persists in an alternative condition of existence, which we call spiritual. A different kind of reality. A reality that can endure for many centuries, or even indefinitely, if one allows for alteration and evolution. Our Gods are originally our own concepts of esoteric energy, which from our viewpoint are eternal since they are certainly likely to outlast anything of our physical universe. Nevertheless, it is our concepts that evolve and alter as we move from one generation to another.

It scarcely needs to be said that human ideas of Good and Evil varied considerably with different culture beliefs and time periods. What might be Good and right at one point could be Evil and wrong at another, depending on prevailing codes of conduct. Different localities and races chose different and often very conflicting codes, leading to bitter and destructive wars between them. Humans began to set a high enough value on their ideals to kill each other, ostensibly because of their beliefs, but usually for no more than pure profit and acquisition, using the ideals as a plausible excuse. Once humankind learned how to live behind one level of surface expression while acting in reality from much deeper and self-interested motivations, the practice of politics was born and extended itself into most areas of the commercial field, and most organized religion is exactly the same thing extended to spiritual spheres of expression. The simultaneous public proclamation of one ideology and the private practice of oppositional standards is now regarded as reasonably normal behavior, so it would not be impossible now to find humans of a religious bent who publicly worshipped an orthodox God of Good while privately supporting a Satanic Deity they regarded as the secret source of their wealth and social status.

Such an extreme practice of double standards, however, would be relatively rare, though humans originally regarded their Gods as being ambivalent about being approached from whichever angle seemed appropriate. If supernatural intervention was being sought for beneficial reasons, the God was approached from that aspect, but if for malicious ones, then the same Deity would be related with from Its opposite angle. Eventually humans came to view these as separate Beings altogether, classifiable under different reasons. Sooner or later professional theologians from all faiths were inventing and classifying a long list of both Divine and Demonic Names, each with its own specialty subject. In later times the Christians would do the same with equally long lists of Saints. Although this made a fascinating study, the majority of humans seeking religious relationships with supernatural powers felt that was too complicated, and they preferred the more simple and direct approach to the Supreme Source of Good or Evil, God or Satan. One might say they preferred speaking to the organ grinder rather than to the monkey.

In very early times, many of the Evil Ones were considered feminine, presumably because the principal Deities had become patriarchal and thus superiors of a masculine-oriented society. Nevertheless, the "First Fiend" was usually accorded at least honorary membership as one of the male sex, probably from a priestly objection to anyone in a position of absolute authority belonging to what they regarded as an inferior species of human. In other words, just plain old sex-jealousy. They were not prepared to admit that a female could possibly be the Supremo of any Force, not even the Force of Darkness. So although there might be myriads of female Fiends (or should it be Fiendesses?), their executive ability was presumed to be a lot less than that of their masculine colleagues. They had their uses, however, by causing sterility, infant deaths, and tormenting human males with sexual fantasies, plus persecuting people in any way they could think of.

It was commonly believed that Fiends of all descriptions could be persuaded to plague humanity at the behest of anyone with the ability to employ them for that particular purpose. Sometimes such an ability might be acquired, or occasionally inherited, as an inherent faculty causing misfortune to fellow humans by merely looking at them fixedly. A previous Pope, Pius the Ninth, was reputed to have this unwelcome gift, which caused him deep distress. The last occasion it was known to have operated automatically was when the obelisk in St. Peter's Square at Rome was being erected. The Pope happened to be watching the proceedings from a Vatican window, and as he did so one of the steadying ropes slipped, and an unfortunate workman was crushed to death. It was said that the unhappy Pope turned away in deep sorrow and never showed his face in public again, unless absolutely obliged to for ceremonial reasons.

It is more than probable that the real roots of Satanism lie in the basic human desire to injure fellow humans, mostly for reasons of revenge and partly to experience an exhilarating feeling of power over their fate, thus producing a temporary sensation of ego-expansion. This starts with the school bully who feels a lot bigger because he has made a weaker child feel smaller, and it ends with the tycoon who has just absorbed a less well-financed corporation, or the politician who has manipulated some disadvantageous deal on a competitive section of humanity unable to prevent the maneuver. Since it would seem stupid even to a primitive mind to ask spiritual help from a Beneficent Being in such an enterprise, the obvious thing to do would be to appeal to any Evil Agency for assistance. Therefore Evil Spirits would be duly invoked to do whatever dirty deed might be called for. It was realized, however, that a price would have to be paid for their services, and there would be an eventual reckoning to meet in terms of personal pain or some form of retribution. Nevertheless it was hoped that deferment might be obtained or some compromise reached that would at least considerably mitigate the consequences of an original action. Earnest Evildoers are always optimistic on their own behalf.

The chances are that ceremonial Devil-worship began with the concept of Dualism. This very simplistic but practical viewpoint is believed to have been developed by the Medes and Persians with Zoroastrianism, reputed to be the oldest organized religion in the world, which traces its origins back to Stone Age times. They classified their twin Powers into LIGHT, personified as ORMUZD, and DARKNESS, personified as AHRIMAN. Night and Day, the dual phenomena of Life and Movement on this planet. From this in time developed a sect known as the Yezidees, who still exist and officially worship the Devil under the form of a peacock to symbolize his connection with Pride. Their beliefs are very similar to the Cathars in Europe. Both alike saw the Supreme Being as a sort of neutrally beneficent control point, rather like an umpire supervising contenders for the souls of humankind, and personified as Ormuzd-Ahriman, or Jesus-Satan.

This attitude is really the "foot in both camps" theory put into practice. Its devotees see Satan as a Being with enough genuine power in this world to cause endless trouble and difficulties for humanity trying to live peaceably. He is not unlike a touchily tempered ruler who, in a bad mood, would put incoherent people to torture and death simply for the fun of it. There must have been many monarchs of olden days with such characteristics to suggest their Satanic prototype. Luckily for their subjects, they usually had one weak point in common. They were extremely susceptible to fawning flattery or greatly exaggerated praise. Their inflated egos thrived on this to an almost absurd degree. Those who were prepared to pour out the most lavish and fulsome flattery before their ruthless and despotic rulers would not only survive but probably would receive rich rewards and similar compensations for their sycophancy. Therefore if such treatment worked with human horrors, there was every reason to suppose it would do so with spiritual ones. So Satan was seen as a peacock, the very personification of Pride, a major sin.

To a great extent this ambiguous attitude crept into the practice of "Divine Worship," wherein the God of Good is to be approached with "Songs of Praise," informing It of Its own virtues and never daring to suggest the slightest suspicion of any contrary activity. The conventional idea of a typically Christian Heaven wherein such a Deity is eternally surrounded by praise-singers must surely revolt any reasonable soul. Apart from other considerations, the idea of a Supreme Power needing constant assurance from Its own creatures of Its capabilities is not only ridiculous but also derogatory. Such a propensity might be attributable to a Satan-concept, but scarcely to a God believed to be LOVE personified. Perhaps it might be a clear distinction to specify a God of LOVE and a Devil of HATE, although those are both known to be the same feeling reversed.

A certain amount of confusion was caused when new religions superseded old ones and taught that all their previous Gods had now been demoted to Devils and that people should pray accordingly. Really deep-rooted beliefs and customs are not so easily dismissed as that, and pious folk felt that deserting Deities that seemed to have served their needs for many generations would bring bad luck and worse on themselves. This led to a dual standard of obediently offering homage to whichever God was favored by the rulership of a realm, and secretly keeping up old worship customs at private gatherings, or even solitary assignments at former sacred sites. Most of the so-called "Witch Cults" of the Middle Ages were no more than meetings of people who felt it proper to pay some attention to the pre-Christian Deities of fertility and the processes of Nature herself. Such could scarcely be called Devil-worship in the proper sense of the term, since the gatherings were not particularly hate-motivated nor dedicated specifically to Evil, unless in the opinion of those who considered the meetings sinful in themselves.

There were esoteric schools which taught that an essentially Good God had created the Devil for the express purpose of testing humankind in order to improve our spiritual strength, by first exposing ourselves to temptation and then resisting it with all our will power. Sometimes we might fall for the temptation many times in succession, yet not so deeply or quickly on each subsequent occasion, until we finally learned to resist it altogether. This seems comparable to developing first a tolerance and finally an immunity to diseases by building up the needed antibodies after repeated exposures to the virus. Therefore to this school of thought, the Devil not only serves a very useful purpose but also is an important asset in the ecology of Existence. This very practical and sensible viewpoint is set forth in the story of Job in the Bible, where the Devil is described as being an angel or agent of God with a specific task to perform and the authority to carry it out effectively. There is also a lovely little legend to the effect that every time humankind succumbs to temptation, the Devil sheds a tear, since that means his own term of office has been extended just that much further. If humanity ever became perfect, there would be no need for Satan's services, and he could then rejoin his Heavenly companions in Perfect Peace Profound. In the light of this theory, it would seem that Satan is now applying the crucial test to humanity as a whole. Can we learn to live successfully with nuclear energy in this world or not? History alone has the answer in its handbag, so to speak.

Perhaps one of the oddest angles of approach was that of medieval magicians, who presumed it was a good idea to make Demons do their dirty work by invoking Angels with sufficient authority to compel such activity. Exactly why they would assume that an Angel of God would command Demons to obey the whims of human beings is not quite clear, yet such was the supposition, and the grimoires of that period are full of schemes for that plan. At the same time one cannot help thinking that, in effect, such is exactly what we have done with energies that might easily destroy us. If we think of the power in steam and electricity alone, which could quite well consume any human, yet when properly harnessed has contributed vastly to our present civilization—what is this really except a proper control of our Fire and Lightning Demons by the "angelic" part of ourselves? So the basic idea of persuading our "Good" intentions to understand and then exploit energies that would otherwise prove fatal to us is a fundamentally sound one. Nevertheless, it is not part of official Satanism, for there is no intention of worshipping or honoring Evil Spirits in any way, but simply controlling and utilizing them for their energy value.

Another odd yet understandable idea was that Satan might be identified with the "ass-end" of God. The very suggestion that the Deity had such a common and vulgar organ as an anus was a shameful one to be whispered under the breath and hinted at rather than spoken of openly. Nevertheless, the scriptural words were quite clear that humankind had been created and formed in the image and likeness of the Lord, which necessarily implied that God had not only generative organs but also excretory ones as well. If the breath of Life came from the mouth of God, then the blast of death must come from his opposite end, and if Good emerged from his uttered word, then Evil obviously came out of his anus with the excrement. By simple association of opposites, excrement has naturally been connected with nastiness of all kinds—disease, unpleasantness, and shame of every sort. To this day we say that some disliked person is "in bad odor," and hide our excretory activities from each other with embarrassment. The vulgarism "kiss my ass" is meant to be one of utter contempt, yet at one time it signified a clear command to salute the Devil in a traditional way.

This "kiss of infamy," as it was called, was the customary way of offering obeisance to Satan, since it was the direct opposite of a kiss on the cheeks or lips, which is always considered a kiss of honor. Moreover, the risk of receiving a blast of flatulence full in the face during such a salute was a very real and offensive one, which was supposed to be accepted as a special favor. Sometimes the Devil was represented as having another face over his buttocks, but this was taken to mean a backwards-turned face to represent the anus of God being the mouthpiece of the Devil. Everything concerned with Satan had to be taken as the reverse of its equivalent connected with God.

The actual cult of Satanism as presumed by modern people is of relatively recent origin, appearing during the post-Christian era. As the centuries went by, the official Christian Church earned the resentment and antagonism of many members for various reasons: perhaps mostly for its persecutions of non-Christians and its own dissidents, sometimes for the blatant venality of its officials and ministers, occasionally for overbearing dogmatism and dictatorial behavior, and finally, for all the faults that almost any earthly authority imposes on a body of humans over whom it has influence and at least nominal control of conduct codes. Resentment of this caused different reactions among different types of people. Many tried ignoring the Church altogether, and some started rival Churches of alternative character; others attempted reformation of existing religions, while a few developed such a deep and bitter hatred of established religions that nothing would please them except the creation of an entire "counter-religion" devoted to the worship of an anti-God, symbolized by the Spirit of Evil, or Satan. So, strictly speaking, it was the failures and weaknesses of the Christian Church itself that were chiefly responsible for ceremonial Satanism. One might truthfully say that human dissatisfaction with priest-presented Deity encouraged the organization of Devil-worship.

So far as known there has never been an orthodox liturgy of Satanic worship, except insofar as its essential expression consisted of reversing everything possible. From its fundamental creed of "Evil—be thou my Good" to the blasphemous Black Mass with its backwards Lord's Prayer performed by an apostate priest with drugged wine and ergotized black bread, ceremonial Satanism is more or less a complete defiance aimed at insulting and angering a Judeo-Christian Deity and its human followers. The belief that they could do this with impunity, since they saw no evident signs of retribution, convinced sincere Satanists that they were specially supported by friendly Fiends, and the supposition that their activities were seriously interfering with the workings of God's Will inflated their egos enormously. The thought that they could create Chaos amid the operations of Cosmos flattered their vanity to a colossal extent. All they had to do was embark on a program of disarrangement and destabilization of the natural order of thought and action.

For example, if Sun and Light symbolized Good, then they must choose the dark of the Moon for their meetings and conduct their movements in an anti-clockwise direction. If procreation was a command of the Lord, then their seed must be discharged in an opposite manner, such as into the rectum of another male or alternate infertile target. If harmony was pleasing to God they must only utter harsh and discordant sounds. In place of nourishing food and drink, they must ingest health-damaging substances that would upset bodily balance and mental equanimity alike. Instead of doing anything kindly that might induce other humans to think well of them, they should act in a contrary manner with cruelty and deceit so as to attract dislike, distrust, or best of all, plain fear. A combination of all these factors was calculated to attract the Devil's attention and interest at first hand. In other words, they were to behave like modern teenage drug addicts with a tendency to criminal violence.

That, however, would be Satanism on its lowest levels. If people were capable of sufficient self-discipline to express the same principles on more intellectual and cultured planes, they would become advanced accordingly and far more dangerous to fellow humans. Satanism has a hierarchy and aristocracy of its own. A modern exponent of Satanism, Anton LaVey, points out that Satanism has little use for moral weaklings and degenerates who cannot control their own worst propensities. What Satan needs most are those persons capable of channeling their energies into specific courses of conduct that will serve his purposes effectively and efficiently—those who are prepared to pour themselves and all their abilities into the Satanic Cause, which of

course means the overthrow of Cosmos and the establish-
ment of the "Kingdom of Chaos," wherein Satan would
expect to be Supreme, and his strongest supporters would
automatically become the "Chosen Few" of its Administra-
tion.

LaVey is perfectly correct. Anyone supposing that
authentic Satanism is one huge orgy of sexual and other
excesses should think again. Common sense alone should
inform them that such a prodigious expenditure of energy
for insufficient return would accomplish nothing except
sheer purposeless waste. Since Satan has a very definite
purpose (the rulership and control of human life), all the
energy he gets is devoted to pursuit of this aim, and intelligence is called for to direct and process it for that particular purpose. This means that humans of great capability
and qualities have to be recruited into the service of Satan,
and such people are not likely to feel attraction for stupidi-
ties and idle pastimes. Their dedication and discipline has
to be unquestionable and their loyalty beyond the slightest
doubt. Their immediate aim must be that of achieving
efficiency, or maximum output for minimum input, and
whatever their specialty is, it has to be entrusted unreserv-
edly to the service of Satan.

Such characteristics are exactly the same requirements
as those demanded of any professional terrorist, and they
need similar training and conditioning. Though there may
not be any obvious "schools of Satanism" in evidence, the
training and discipline provided by every Armed Service,
or for that matter, an average university or training college,
should be sufficient to provide a competent Satanist for the
field once the initial commitment is made deeply enough.
The rest is a matter of experience and application. Active
and effective Satanists are highly unlikely to proclaim or
even allow their true allegiance to be suspected. Like their
emblem of the serpent, they cleverly camouflage their na-

tures, proceeding quietly and carefully along their courses, doing exactly their designated amount of damage, and, as the efficient agents of Evil they are, always working within the limits of the Satanic Scheme they serve. The higher they rise in the hierarchy, the less likely they are to push themselves into positions where they would have to meet many people, because there is one "giveaway" factor in them that cannot be completely concealed. This is an abnormal feeling of icy cold that is experienced by normal humans coming into close contact with an authentic Son (or Daughter) of Satan.

This strange phenomenon of a supernatural "inner chill" is caused by their intense antipathy to ordinary humans of average good intentions. By contrast, the expert Evildoer seems cold beyond belief. No matter how conventionally correct they may seem, they cannot disguise this side of their natures entirely, and anyone sensing it is almost sure to wonder what is wrong, and will have some shrewd suspicions or warnings of danger in dealing with such an uncanny individual. Another typical characteristic is absence of humor, or the ability to laugh with pure joy. As a rule, a sardonic smile is about the most that may be noticed on their faces, and even that might be infrequent. Though this is not necessarily evidence of Evil by itself, it can prove a confirmatory symptom, and like the hiss of a snake, warn people who would rather not be poisoned to steer well clear of the hisser.

Expert Evildoers are notoriously lacking in feelings for other mortals, nor are their normal feelings confined to controlled channels as, say, doctors and nurses who have to hold theirs in check for the sake of their own sanity. The emotions of carefully conditioned Evildoers are either absent or strangely reversed. A disaster happening to anyone is apt to amuse or please. They cannot love, but only covet or compel. They are not generous, but only calculating and avaricious. They delight in cruelty and suffering to an abnormal degree and are completely indifferent to the effects or damage they might cause by their activities. For example, they will cheerfully profit from the sales of drugs while carefully remaining non-addicts themselves. They view their victims as stupid people deserving all that results from not being able to resist the compulsion of a drug craving, and they justify their profits by remarking that if they themselves did not make them, other operators would instantly take their place. Compassion and sympathy are entirely meaningless words to them, or else they interpret those splendid sentiments as either stupidity or ridiculous weakness and misguided behavior. What ordinary folk would see as a sad deficiency of character, they would only view as a "success at any cost" determination and unshakable strength of mind. What others would call ruthlessness, they would see as sheer power of persistence. Evildoers always explain themselves from opposite angles to ordinary people, and according to their Creed see Evil as their Good.

So if Satan as the Spirit of Evil is the entitized concentration of combined consciousness dedicated to the Devil over the many millenia of humankind's existence, it should be readily appreciated that this is a very real and potent accumulation of energy that is unlikely to be eliminated or neutralized either rapidly or easily. How true it is that the Evil that humans do lives after them, even if the Good they did is not always interred with their bones. How many legacies of hate have been handed down from generation to generation—inherent antipathies ostensibly of race, religion, positions, abilities, or some apparent characteristic, but in reality due to envy, malice, or a deeply seated grudge demanding a ridiculous extension of revenge for no practical purpose whatsoever. We have only to think of historical hatred between specific nations or races to see examples of this everywhere throughout our world. People being penalized because of what their long-dead ancestors did to equally long-dead enemies. Stupid and senseless feuds kept going purely because some humans actually *want* to experience hate, and enjoy harboring it in their hearts. Excuses for Evil are commonly sought for among earth dwellers.

During the Middle Ages and thereafter, most Christians made the Devil an excuse for everything Evil they did. They claimed that they would never have done such dreadful things of their own accord, that it was the wicked Devil who made them do whatever it was. They themselves were good, kind, and innocent people, and it was that old horned horror who induced them to sin so greatly. It was all his fault, so blame him for their beastliness. In fact the Devil was an ideal excuse for many centuries, and his horned aspect made him into the conventional scapegoat on whom the sins of the people might be laid. It also provided them with an Opponent-Figure, against which they could struggle with the help of God and his holy Angels, thus contributing to the ultimate victory of Good over Evil and the eventual Day of Judgment, when God himself was supposed to take over control of our world and hopefully make a better job of running it than any of his creatures had done previously. Opinions differed as to what would happen to the Devil, but they mainly agreed he would meet with an appropriate fate.

The real issue of this situation is that humanity *needs* a moral antagonist to struggle against in order to achieve spiritual growth and development in any direction. This is true of all energies throughout every dimension of Existence. No phenomenon of any description can manifest without its counter-condition to make such manifestation possible. Light demands Darkness, Heat demands Cold, This demands That, and Right cannot exist without Left. One cannot reasonably conceive any kind of beneficent

Deity without postulating an equivalent opposite to validate the concept. A bi-valid Being incorporating both qualities is certainly possible, and the connection between the two can be seen in a number of ways, but both would have to be considered as integral to the same structure, as, say, our two hands and feet belong to the same body. Therefore it would be quite justifiable to alter Voltaire's well-known dictum and say, "If there were no Devil it would be necessary to invent one."

Politicians and playwrights alike realize the basic necessity for enemy-villains. Hate-Figures are essential to stir patriotic or program interest in nationals or audiences. Provide people with a practical focal point for their communal hates and fears, and they will unite in expending energy against it. Hitler knew this very well when he encouraged his nationals to hate and fear Jews, and it was not the first time in human history that Hebrews were made convenient scapegoats for ambitious politicians or fanatical sectarians. What would any novel or play be worth without its villain to hate and hiss? Modern producers of TV dramas are usually careful to include a character specially designed to present a dislikeable personality, one that has some peculiar quality calculated to arouse antipathy in a particular section of a modern audience. This might vary from mannerisms of voice to displays of dress or visual appearance. As a rule, the individual chosen for this function knows perfectly well the reason for his/her appearance, and fulfills it as faithfully as any stage villain. In former times audience and actor alike were well aware of each other's roles and interacted with mutual sentiments. The audience *needed* a Hate-Figure and the actor *needed* appreciation when portraying that type of character. Besides, he/she needed his/her salary, and the audience were paying for the entertainment while the acting was on both sides of the curtain.

In the character of the Devil, the Christian Church probably hoped to offer a metaphysical Hate-Fear Figure that could be used to channel all the adverse energy which would otherwise have been disseminated amongst fellow humans, possibly causing considerable damage. This was not unlike modern psychiatrists who encourage patients to act out their aggressions by beating dummies identified with real humans, who are associated with the real resentments. The only difference between this and the old witch-women who pushed pins into waxen images to curse the persons represented, is the enormous fee demanded by the modern witch-doctor, as contrasted with the modest remuneration requested by the wicked old women. The fact that such psychological relief is only temporary, like masturbation, hardly comes into the picture. Many psychotherapists of our times have simply modernized the principles of old magical techniques, invented an appropriate vocabulary, and applied the results to their patients very profitably.

It could well be that the Christian Church did not go far enough with its psychodramatics of Satanic significance. It was so occupied with glorifying God that it never paid enough attention to dealing with the Devil. Had the Church devised an equal number of ceremonies for the express purpose of confronting and counteracting the concept of Satan, who knows what difference these might have made to our spiritual status in our world of today. It is true that official exorcisms did exist, but those were very rare and more or less of a private nature. Baptism was originally intended as an exorcisory rite, but it was a "one-off" and meant to last a lifetime. When were there ever regular services focused on the "Forces of Darkness," with the specific function of converting their Evil influences into useful energies that would serve the best interests of a hopeful humanity? Perhaps it was hoped that God alone would accomplish this in the fullness of his good time, yet why are there no records of official Christianity at least attempting to assist such a transcendental transmutation with every conceivable effort of their will and imagination? Seeing that the DEVIL arose in themselves, they might have made more of a concerted attempt to cope with it at that same source.

True, they had instituted the Sacrament of Penance, which was their equivalent of the analyst's couch at considerably less cost, but their interpretation of it could scarcely claim to be very satisfactory. Besides which, their belief that the worst of sins could be atoned for by deliberately inflicting pain and discomfort on their own bodies could hardly be taken seriously except by dedicated sado-masochists. Their ideas of compensating for Evil by adding more Evil elsewhere were not very helpful to anyone, nor did they contribute anything very intelligent to the arena of anti-Evil activities. With almost a minimum of imagination they could have contrived a whole series of psycho-dramatic exercises calculated to curb and control the energies of Evil.

Some can be thought of almost immediately: melting a wax image of the Devil and pouring it into a mold representing an angelic figure, while suitable prayers are being said or chanted; reciting a whole collection of prayers and invocations concerned with the alteration of Evil into Good; setting aside special days of meditation devoted to that single end; spending at least an equal amount of time and attentive energy on altering Evil as on advancing Good; organizing intelligent lectures and sermons on the subject, rather than ranting condemnations and senseless attempts to scare souls with bogey-beliefs. There would be no more harm in adopting a personification of Satan, providing people understood the purpose of this as a purely physical focus of concentrated consciousness. An appropriate graphic might well be the familiar mushroom-shaped cloud of an atomic explosion, with the suggestion of a left-profile face in it. That face should present a picture of both exceptional intelligence and malevolent anti-humanness, which would call for a highly skilled artist. There should be a terrifying beauty and danger combined, and the overall impression should convey a complete absence of emotion coupled with a warning of destruction to whoever tries to handle it without adequate protection.

Most people these days are familiar with the dangers from radiation and the warning sign that indicates its presence or likelihood. They know that if they are exposed to a calculable intensity of this hazard they will be liable to develop cancer of a fatal kind. Few would willingly undergo such a risk. The two crude atomic bombs at Hiroshima and Nagasaki in Japan demonstrated clearly and for all time what would happen to humans who were irradiated to such a degree, and since then that type of weapon has been "improved" incredibly. Our whole civilized world must surely be well aware of this. Yet our Devil presents exactly the same risk on a different level. *If the real Satan is the sum total of human Evil, it is bound to ultimately destroy us unless we can bring it under our control and utilize its energy beneficially.* There is an almost exact parallel between the principle of Evil and nuclear energy, which it would be well to consider very carefully.

Both are lethal to humans at sufficient intensity. Both are very insidious and have no obvious immediate effect, so that we tend to remain exposed to them until too late to take any practical precautions, and many people are unaware of what precautions should be taken. Both Evil and radiant energy have long-term effects on human genetics, which we call mutation, or changes for the worse. The physical expression of this results in severe bodily deformity, while the moral effect can cause what geneticists sometimes call the "Bad Seed," or humans born entirely without a sense of obligation to anyone except themselves, and often little

The Serpentine Start / 47

enough of that. Conversely, there might be a badly distorted sense of morality, as in the case of Fundamentalist religions, wherein all other types of belief are considered wrong and drastic measures are proposed against them. This can spread into politics as well, resulting in enmity between alternative systems such as the capitalist and communist. Whatever induces humans to hurt and hate each other can scarcely be classed as anything but Evil, and so attributable to a Satanic source.

On the other hand, without nuclear energy we shall not be able to sustain our contemporary state of civilization on this earth. Our fossil fuel supplies are scarcely inexhaustible, and their eventual end is already calculable. We are literally between the Devil and the deep blue sea. Unless we develop alternative sources of energy within the next century, we shall be finished as a special species of being, and must revert to former conditions of controversy and pursuit of problems. It is quite clearly a case of EITHER/OR in the strongest possible terms. Either we learn how to harness the horrors of Hell and use them to our advantage, or Satan uses us up to fuel his own furnaces, producing power for his particular purposes. If the main rule of Life is "Adapt—or Die," then surely the next on the list ought to be "Use, or be Abused." Life is full of alternatives, beginning with the serpent choice between Good and Evil, but sometimes it can be very difficult to decide which is which.

At least if a reasonably clear concept could be made of a Satan-symbol, and an equally definite one made of its Divine opposite, those might be used as headings, so to speak, for the categories of our consciousness under which could be classified our concepts of Good and Evil, Right and Wrong. For instance, according to Christian thinking, a stylized Satan would stand on top of a column labeled EVIL, while an equally recognizable figure of Jesus would head another entitled GOOD. Each Entity would act as a

Key-concept to whatever the thinker believed should belong with either category. This might not be entirely accurate, but at least it could be practical, because it sorts out the types of thought into definable categories and enables decisions to be made with recognizable terms of reference. Nowadays, when our thinking is so clouded and confused by endless conflicting channels of consciousness, we are apt to become aimless, and only too often are a hesitant mass of mortals groping around for anything holding the slightest hopes of spiritual solidity.

In other words, we have lost our spiritual sense of direction. Where we once had what seemed to be certainty, we now encounter doubt. What formerly appeared definite is now either ambiguous or else untrue. Whatever used to be reliable and dependable may now be considered erroneous or utterly untrustworthy. Perhaps we may be reminded of the unanswered question "What *is* Truth?" Everyone is entitled to say what they think, suppose, or believe it is, but who dares lay down an infallible criterion? It was once said that the only two certainties in Life are death and taxes. All that anyone can honestly say with any degree of accuracy is that in the light of recent research such and such appears to be a satisfactory supposition. Or that in the absence of more detailed information, we have decided to adopt this, that, or the other theory as a working hypothesis. There must always be a provisional area of acceptance, liable to future alteration as a result of preferential evidence or more plausible explanations.

So the sinful old serpent is quite a valid symbol of human progress. In order to go forward it has to take a zigzag path from one side to the other, or an oscillating movement between left and right. Only by combining alternative movements can it make a median one. So with humans. What one would see as a sin against God, another might consider merely a breach of civil laws. Someone else might see the same thing as stupidity and sheer inexperience, while another would view it as a psychological aberration or possibly a social error. Others again might suppose the same behavior perfectly normal or even praiseworthy. Yet it would be the identical God-Satan factor in every variant human that produced these end-opinions. We alternate between the extremism of life in order to experience and evaluate them into a single summary that will serve us and our descendants as a guide to every situation they will encounter. Every human that has ever lived on earth has added a tiny contribution to the whole, but have we reached a point where we can cope with our present challenge, which could be the critical one between Deity and the Devil in ourselves?

Chapter 3

MASSES—BLACK AND WHITE

Ask any average person what they consider the worst thing Satanists are likely to do and they will probably reply, "Their Black Mass, of course." Now why should this reputed rite catch their imaginations more than anything else? Those queried have certainly never attended one, nor most probably have never encountered anyone who has. The majority would not even believe in the efficacy of a normal customary Christian version of the Mass, so what makes an abnormally unusual Satanic one so special and sinister-seeming in their eyes? Where do they get their ideas from and what does the whole notion amount to?

The fabled Black Mass, for which no authentic ritual script has ever been published, despite written references to it and verbatim accounts of its performance, appears to have originated in late medieval France, but the probability is that many previous versions of it had already been practiced for several centuries prior to that by those who, for their private reasons, sought contact with Satan rather than Jesus. They posited very simplistically that if communion could be established with Jesus by means of a religious ritual called a Mass, then it surely must be possible to communicate with Satan by an alternative ritual behavior calculated to attract his interested awareness. If the attention of Jesus could be gained by a symbolic offering of bread and wine representing his body and blood accompanied by a few praise prayers, surely the spirit of his opposite number, Satan, might be summoned by an offering of real blood drawn from a dying human sacrifice, performed in ancient style to an appropriate accompaniment of cacophony and curses. The important thing was that the sacrifice had to be a most unwilling one. Old-time Sacred Kings were commonly sacrificed on altars, but to make this valid it had to be done with the victim's full consent and wholehearted participation. Therefore any human sacrifice to Satan must be one resulting from pure murder and contrary to the victim's intentions.

There were some other inversions to consider as well. If the Old Gods required a young male as the customary sacrifice, then for Satanic acceptance a nubile female was the obvious offering. If pregnant, so much the better, since the life within a life would be included, which increased the value of the offering by that degree. Hence, the celebrant or his deputy would first impregnate the chosen female, or all males present would do so in order to ensure her fecundity as much as possible. The chances are that she would have no advance warning of her impending slaughter and would suppose that her sexual services alone were required for the payment of an enormous fee. Her ensuing brutal murder would thus engender a maximum amount of genuine terror, pain, and intense emotional output. This, combined with the sadistic satisfaction experienced by her killers, was believed to supply enough energy to make Satanic manifestations possible. As an additional sign of their allegiance, they would drink their victim's blood and anoint themselves therewith, also using any urine or excrement she might void during her struggles for survival.

Thus a genuine Black Mass consisted of several very serious crimes, all reckoned to be mortal sins or to cause the death of a soul in terms of Christian thinking. The perpetrators had thus damned themselves to Hell beyond all hope, and so committed themselves to Satan eternally by their concerted action. Since they had all taken part in an illegal activity that could merit capital punishment, they had placed themselves in each other's power so far as the law was concerned, and that made a very solid bond between them. It has long been known that nothing binds people together more closely than a shared secret that must not be revealed to others outside the group, and authentic Satanists certainly had something to hide for fear of their own deaths at the hands of Church and State alike. Though that might not apply today, they could still face long imprisonment as insane persons, which would hardly be an attractive proposition.

However, as belief in the efficacy of the Christian Mass declined with the growth of Protestantism and Nonconformity, the Black Mass altered its shape accordingly, and frequently some unfortunate animal would be slain in the name of Satan and its blood employed in a variety of ways. To this day a survival of the practice persists in the "blooding" of the youngest child at a fox hunt. It is marked on the forehead with the blood of the victim, significantly with the severed stump of the fox's tail, memorializing the "Mark of Cain," reputed as our first recorded murderer, who slew his brother Abel and in consequence was branded by God so that others might avoid him. Blood (normally a chicken's) is also scattered in Voodoo rites with the intention of attracting spirits, though not necessarily Evil ones. Pacts made with the Devil, however, always had to be signed with an individual's own blood in order to authenticate them to the fullest possible extent. In the end it was believed that the use of one's own blood for this purpose constituted an Evil act in itself, which was a mistaken supposition.

Blood *per se* was neither good nor evil, but it was always regarded as individual and personal to an ultimate degree. Blood-brotherhood, or the mingling of blood between two people with slashed wrists, was looked upon as a specially sacred relationship, and to this day that is symbolized at some weddings by the priest binding the wrists of bride and groom briefly together with one end of his stole. The original meaning of our word *blessing* came from the Old English "Bloedsian," meaning to hallow with blood, usually by sprinkling a congregation with blood from a sacrifice on the altar. Today holy water makes a modern substitute. Christians always regard the actual blood of Jesus as the vital factor of their salvation, just as the Jews consider the blood of their own circumcisions to be the special sealing fluid of their covenant with God. One way or another, blood has always been taken as a specially sacred element of our existence. Scriptures said, "the Blood is the Life."

In olden times, when even kings could scarcely sign their names and had to validate state documents with an official seal, it was common for lesser mortals to "make their mark" with a cross witnessed by someone else who could write. For anything of uncommon importance, it was usual to prick the tip of a thumb or finger and smear the cross with their own blood. It might be interesting to compare this with the modern legal practice of affixing a small red wafer to documents on which the client places a forefinger and says, "I deliver this my deed and bond." Bloodsealing was simply a very old way of authenticating legal transactions, especially contracts, so that when the practice of making pacts with Satan developed, people reverted to their primitive custom of signing with blood instead of ink in order to enhance the importance of the occasion. Sometimes the entire terms of the pact would be written in the signatory's blood, although the signature alone was more usual. As a rule the pact contained a "catch clause," which it was hoped might deceive the Devil and obtain his services for nothing, while allowing the signatory to escape scot-free in the end. Nowadays this would amount to the ambiguous statements in the small print, which it is hoped the signatory will not read or study too closely. Who the Satanists supposed taught lawyers their trade in the first place is not in the least clear.

Although there are all kinds of elaborate rituals laid down for making pacts with Satanic spirits, none of them describe exactly how a disembodied being is supposed to append its signature to a physical document. Presumably it was expected to materialize for that precise purpose, although there is no account of any apparition producing more than its own appearance. Poltergeist phenomena has been known since time immemorial, during which all sorts of physical energy has manifested, yet there does not seem to have been an apparent intelligence that could write definite names or information on its own initiative. Yet if the Bible is believed to be the written Word of God as revealed to his or her prophets, where is the equivalent Word of Satan dictated via his disciples, who must be numbered by more than millions?

Some would definitely claim that an ordinary pack of cards was the "Devil's Bible," or for that matter, all gambling devices of any kind. Extremists might interdict all books except the Bible, especially those exalting religions other than theirs. In fact, everyone would point to something in particular that they believed had been compiled or composed for the express purpose of deluding, deceiving, or otherwise leading humans away from whatever they regarded as being "the one and only True Path to Salvation." Such attitudes have probably contributed more to the Satanic Cause than most others, because they engender antipathy and active antagonism among the different branches of humanity, which is surely a Satanic proclivity of its own type. Whatever fosters hatred and misunderstanding among humankind, particularly if it should lead to lethal warfare, can hardly be called anything else than an operation of Satan on earth. Who could possibly be insane enough, except the most fanatical religionist, to believe that war and all its attendant horrors can be connected with the Will of a beneficent Being? Few incidents were more sickening during World Wars I and II than the sight of army chaplains solemnly blessing the weapons of death and destruction while praying to the same God that their compatriot combatants would massacre more than their enemy fellow mortals might slay of them. An all-time classical example was the American Army chaplain during the Vietnam campaign, who exhorted his men to "Go out and kill a gook for God." This could perhaps be compared with the battle cry of the Scottish Covenanters of "Jesus! and NO quarter!"; or maybe with the advice given to troops querying recognition during action against the Cathars at Montsegur: "Kill them all and let God sort their souls out afterwards." Holy hypocrisy has no limits. Why should the Devil bother to work when "men of God" will do it all for him?

One such person was a seventeenth-century apostate priest named Pierre Aupetit, at a village called Fossas in the district of Limousine. He celebrated a Black Mass whereat the words of consecration were reputedly "Beelzebub. Beelzebub. Beelzebub," and the worshippers were served some blackish preparation they had to chew, most likely a psychedelic substance. It was reported that the Devil flew around them in the shape of a butterfly all the while, but after consuming the drugged cake they would have accepted any creature visiting them as an apparition of the Fiend. At any rate, Father Aupetit paid dearly for his Black Masses, being burned at the stake.

The probability is that Satan gets his strongest support from the Christian Church one way or another. Firstly, it believes in him implicitly, and secondly, it has publicized him through the centuries, specifying and particularizing all the qualities and attributes required to make relationships with him of a conscious and unconscious nature. Furthermore, if the Cause of Evil needed human agencies to promulgate its purposes on earth, where could there be a more practical place to plant its clandestine operatives than in its official opposition? Political experience over many millenia has shown that the best place to conceal effective agents is among the ranks of opposing parties, and the most useful of all are those known as "sleepers," who are often planted a long time in advance for the eventual performance of some activity carefully calculated to have specific counter-effects in definite areas. Some may be planted some time before they are born.

A good example of this pre-birth planting was that of a young German couple toward the end of the last century. They emigrated to Britain and produced a daughter there who naturally took British nationality, her parents being naturalized in the normal way, altering their names from Schmidt to Smith. Their daughter grew up to become a practicing member of the Anglican Church and eventually a Sunday School teacher. Little Miss Smith was a modest and somewhat retiring lady living in the area of Aldershot, amongst the heaviest concentration of troops when World War I broke out. She naturally continued with her Christian work, while deploring the Devil's destructive activities in Europe. Among her Sunday School class was an unusually alert lad, who as a Boy Scout in those times was occasionally used as a volunteer messenger by the military. This was the period when the heavily armored tracked vehicles later known as "tanks" were being produced as secretly as possible and were subsequently to play a major part in reversing the advance of the German Army. They got their name from a custom of scrawling a large "TANKS" across their tarpaulined bulk on railway flatbeds in hopes of discouraging any curious viewers. Who would bother to look at common water tanks being transported? They were of no interest to most people. Miss Smith, however, was particularly curious about them, and also paid unusual attention to her pet pupil, inviting him to tea with her and putting a lot of perspicacious questions to him that had nothing to do with Holy Scriptures, but a great deal to do with military matters at the camp he mainly ran messages for, Bovington. The lad could not help wondering why such a nice little old lady, as she seemed to him, should show such a knowledgeable grasp of technical details, and he mentioned this to his father, who put several twos together and informed the authorities, who inaugurated their own inquiries. Later that year Frauline Schmidt was shot for espionage, which was then the prescribed penalty during wartime. Modern sleepers would be most unlikely to make similar mistakes.

The main difficulty with the sleeper scheme is that with every faction of humanity practicing it upon all the others, the resultant confusion is likely to neutralize far more than originally intended. Besides, after many years of conditioning in specific systems, who could confidently guarantee the behavior of any primally indoctrinated individual? Sleepers have their undoubted value, but only insofar as they may maintain loyalty to their initial ideology and are prepared to sacrifice their entire personal preferences for the sake of its supremacy. Otherwise they may constitute a very dangerous double-edged weapon. Nevertheless, an obvious place to store a secret Satanist would be among the ranks of the Christian Church, and the higher that rank the less risk of exposure and expulsion. More than one Pope has been suspected of Satanic interests, and certainly much of papal medieval conduct could be classed as decidedly Devilish. The deliberate cruelties of the Inquisition and official outrages contrary to human decency, and even elementary justice in the name of Christianity, afford ample evidence of both degeneracy and complete misuse of power over people. Since all branches of the Church were clearly guilty of similar behavior, it seemed equally clear that its senior officers had been infiltrated by those who would never have called themselves Satanists by name, but certainly proclaimed themselves so by nature. There is a very true Biblical saying: "By their fruits you shall know them."

For a very long time there have been theological arguments as to whether a bad priest can say a good Mass or not. When, as often enough, it was self-evident that an ordained priest was a thoroughly bad man in himself, the question often arose as to the validity of the sacraments he was administering. Most ordinary people relying on their instincts had serious doubts, but the official Church took an opposite view for obviously administrative reasons. In its judgment, sacraments were valid in themselves, their efficacy lying in their self-sanctity and the faith of their participants. The character and qualities of their administrators had nothing to do with this factor, and therefore a Mass said by the worst of priests would be perfectly valid by virtue of the Church's authorization. If at any time it should withdraw that authorization and suspend or excommunicate him, then any service he conducted would be considered null and void. The Church was perfectly plain and definite on that point. In other words it reserved for itself the authority to decide whether or not the ministry of its appointees was valid, regardless of other people's feelings and opinions, who were in contact with that ministry first-hand.

Though most Christians accepted the official decision, many regarded it as contrary to common sense and basic beliefs. It asked them to believe that a bad man by nature could adequately mediate the Powers of Good purely because the Church allowed him to. That seemed both impossibly presumptuous and contradictory to all they believed of God. They were prepared to allow that the Mass in itself could not be Evil, but it surely could not fulfill its function properly if it were presented by someone whose nature contradicted everything it was supposed to stand for. Anyway, they preferred their priests to be at least halfway representative of the principles they preached about, and not such obvious offenders against the moral codes they purported to uphold. If the Church was prepared to permit evident Evildoers to administer its sacraments, then there was good reason to suspect its leading lights of chicanery, at the very least.

No one can ever be certain or even make a near guess at the number of Satanically inclined officials who have held high office in the Christian Church and who have altered its spiritual structure to suit their outlooks and opinions, or have influenced its essential significance by subtle and sometimes scarcely noticeable variations of meaning towards something altogether different. For example, take the very recent case of translating the official Tridentine Mass into modern English. Here, extremely careful and clever alterations have taken place with original meanings so that different constructions can be put upon once-clear words in another language. One wonders exactly why the Churchmen have done this and what they hope to accomplish by it. Let us take the most important phraseology of the entire script, the words of consecration. They read in the original Latin: *"Hic est einim Calix Sanguinis mei, novi et aeterni Testamenti, mysterium fidei. Qui pro vobis et pro multis effunditur in remissionem peccatorum."* This has been rendered into contemporary English as "This is the Cup of my Blood, the blood of the new and everlasting covenant, the mystery of faith. This blood is to be shed for you and for all men so that sins may be forgiven." Now let us see the difference between what was actually said and the present way of putting it.

The Latin said literally: "Here is indeed the Cup of my Blood, new and eternal testament, mystery of faith which for you and for many will be outpoured for the remission of sins." The first deviation is the translation of "covenant" from *Testamenti*, the latter being a witnessed statement, whereas the former signifies an agreement between different parties. The second variant is " all men" from *multis*, which distinctly means many, yet a limited number nevertheless. Then "remission" does *not* mean forgiveness or the total pardoning of a sinful state, but a reduction, lessening, or improvement of it. Thus by skillful alterations the writers of the modern Mass have extended the range of Christian salvation to include the whole of humanity on earth inclusive of every other religion, whereas Jesus originally only made a mention of "many," or those who intended to follow him. He also did not promise a total pardon of all their sins, but only an improvement of their condition, which might lead to an eventual clearing of it, though not necessarily so. In short he assured his disciples in traditional Sacred King style that he was willing to die for them and many others in order to lessen their karma, but that was all. The modern Roman section of the Church has turned this into a takeover bid for all the souls in the world.

Then take the consecration of the bread. The Latin reads: *". . . ad te Deum Patrum suum omnipotentem, tibi gratias agens, benedixit, fregit, deditque discipulis suis dicens, 'Accipte et manducate ex hoc omnes, hoc est einim corpus meum.'"* The literal Latin should read: "to thee God his almighty father giving thee thanks, he blest, broke, and gave to his disciples saying, 'Take and eat this all of you. Here indeed is my body.'" The modern version goes: "To you his almighty father he gave you thanks and praise. He broke the bread, gave it to his disciples and said, 'Take this and eat it all of you, this is my body.'" The main variation here is the careful omission of the word *blest*, and although Jesus did give thanks, there is no specific mention of praise. Now why should this be? The blessing of bread was a normal and customary Jewish procedure that all present would have been familiar with. The usual formula was "Blessed art thou O Lord our God King of the Universe who bringest forth bread from the earth." Why should it be made to seem as if Jesus would have offered his friends bread wihout having first pronounced the traditional blessing? The only possible implication seems to be that he considered his substitution of bread for the old-time offer of his own body as a Sacred King sacrifice blessing enough.

Additionally, in the previous version of the Latin Mass, when each communicant had the bread placed in their mouths by the priest, it was accompanied with words that signified, "May the body of our Lord Jesus Christ preserve your soul to eternal life." In the modern English Mass this well-wishing phrase is omitted altogether and replaced by a brusque "The body of Christ." Just that and no more. No mention of an immortal soul. A simple statement that could mean whatever might be wanted. The Church itself has been frequently referred to as the Body of Christ in this world. Could it be that? It might be. Or is it a hint that the modern Church does not particularly believe in immortal souls but is too polite to say so specifically? At all events, by a minimum of arguable alterations, the official Roman Church has effectively suppressed the once-mystical meaning of a formerly powerful esoteric ritual.

In early times, of course, the Sacred Victim would have been literally cooked and eaten by the congregation that witnessed his or her offering. That was the old-type testament and mystery of faith mentioned. Later a sacrificial lamb was paid for by the participants, slain and cooked by the priests, then eaten by the buyers as they would once have eaten a human being. An animal had been substituted for a human, hence the description of Jesus as the Lamb of God. He in turn substituted common bread for his own body as a new type of witnessed testament, but not a covenant of any kind except insofar as those present agreed it was a good idea. By his day a natural revulsion to eating human flesh had arisen amongst civilized people, and extreme horror was recorded by Roman writers when incidents of starving humans eating children were noted at the siege of Jerusalem. Two thousand years later, German concentration camp attendants would record equal horror at inmates consuming portions of their companions' corpses for food. Sacred Victims, however, were a special exception because they meant themselves to be eaten.

There is a faint trace of this savior substitute remaining among the Welsh people in relatively modern times by the largely rural survival of "sin eating." Before burial, a small saucer with bread, salt, and a little silver money in it would be placed on the breast of a corpse, and the services of a man called a "sin-eater" would be requested. That person volunteered to take the sins of the departed on his own soul, in token of which he dipped the bread in the salt and ate it, pocketing the money for his fee. This idea of human sins being transferable is a very old one, tracing back to early scape-goat days when a goat with red wool around its horns would be ceremonially loaded with the sins of an entire community and then driven out into the desert, where it would eventually perish of starvation. The red wool was partly reminiscent of a Victim's blood, and it also was used to warn off hunters who might kill and eat it, in which case they would absorb all the sins it was carrying in addition to their own. Though it was never an actual dogma of the Church, there was a definite belief among professional soldiers that if a man was dying and no priest were available, his confession could be validly made to a comrade who would subsequently confide it to a legitimate priest and receive absolution in his ex-comrade's name. Until he could do this, however, the full burden of those sins lay on his own shoulders, so it called for the strongest sense of friendship to accept such a spiritual risk. There was a similar supposition among European mercenaries that in case of an imminent death, a little earth pushed into the mouth of a dying man counted as a substitute sacrament. Though there is no Church authority for this belief whatsoever, it was held as an article of faith by most of the Christian military. It was most probably a remnant from very primitive times of a final appeal to the Earth-Mother on behalf of a stricken comrade.

Nowadays there is a tendency in the official Christian Church to "de-mythologize" its former tenets and dogmas by glossing over controversial issues and explaining its so-called supernatural structure in terms agreeable to logic and science. Jesus was only a miracle worker in the sense that his contemporaries did not understand how he produced his reputed effects. His switching water for wine at Cana could easily have been done with the help of accomplices, his "healing" marvels by straightforward psychology and hypnotic suggestion. Raising Lazarus from the dead was pure collusion with relatives, and his survival after three hours of crucifixion was either a result of pseudo-death in a semi-trance state and recovery in a secluded tomb while undergoing resuscitation treatment, or else the substitution of a look-alike. All kinds of plausible theories are advanced and very pertinent questions raised, but with a lack of any more reliable evidence than accounts written two or three centuries after his death, there can scarcely be anything more than educated guesses made. In fact, there may never have been a historical Jesus that existed as an individual human being, and some moderns believe this to be the case.

His era was a very well-documented one, with quite a number of books written by writers and historians in several different languages. Why did none of these have anything to say about Jesus, and why did the few passages in Josephus purporting to mention him prove to be forgeries inserted at a considerably later period? In fact, was "Jesus the Son of God" a purely invented character based on the personality of a young Essene preacher who was eventually crucified for political reasons? And that his followers survived him to build up stories that have since become a major social and cultural force amounting to a religion in this world? All the God-legends connected with Jesus had already existed in his days. The Virgin Birth, the Divine King system, the miraculous episodes, the death-survival. They were almost a compendium of events reputed to have happened to other Avatars of the past. Then the bulk of the moral and ethical teachings attributed to Jesus was reasonably well known by his time. For example, there is a chapter in the Chinese classic *Tao Teh Ching*, written several centuries previously, that is almost word for word the celebrated "Sermon on the Mount." To sum up, was Christianity simply a condensation and compilation of what were considered the best points of other religions? A recent Pope has given it as his opinion that it really would not matter very much if Jesus had never lived on earth at all, because the beliefs and behavioral doctrines that have developed around his name *do* exist and are still exerting a considerable influence on Western civilization.

Such would appear to be perfectly true. Faiths and

beliefs are genuine in and as themselves, whatever they may be based on. They alter and adapt or even change completely over the centuries as they persist, but once beliefs have been formed firmly enough in human awareness, they will achieve sufficient reality to affect our lives by the behavior patterns they engender or encourage, especially through the effects they exert on our genetics. Children are, after all, products of their parents' thinking just as much as their mating. The fact that in later life they may disagree with this and form oppositional opinions of their own simply means that their parents have provided them with something to oppose, and so have given the groundwork for such change of outlook. The point is that if Christianity had not been passed from one generation to another, it would not have survived in any form until modern times, and the same can be said for Satanism. Satan has never been associated with any specific human Figure like Jesus, but has been frequently linked with those who have achieved notoriety because of their bad behavior or military madness. Genghis Khan, Alexander Borgia, and Adolph Hitler have all personified Satan in the minds of very many humans. More would postulate that there is a degree of Satan in every soul with Evil proclivities, and they would be theoretically correct. So who, if anyone, is passing on traditions of Satanism to their offspring, or how does it continue in being?

Here we have to differentiate between Satanism as an organized religion and Satanism as an inherited instinct, which is a far more deadly form of it, and could be called the "real thing" in contradistinction to its more flamboyant and theatrical expressions of externalism. In order to practice Black Masses, Chaos Magic, and similar means of making contact with the Satanic Spirit, practitioners must necessarily demonstrate emotions and a considerable amount of feeling, albeit of hates and antagonisms aimed against specific spiritual targets. Deeply committed Satanists do not display such emotions, for the simple reason that they cannot. Their Satanism is seldom of the ceremonial kind, because ceremonies and rituals are always *effects* of essentially egoistic characteristics, and never the *causes* of them. Real Satanists are neither moved nor impressed by ceremonies which to them would seem like cabaret shows.

There have been many rumors of worldwide "Black Brotherhoods" and clandestine "Black Lodges" working all kinds of Evil against hapless humanity. These conjure up pictures of sinister black-robed people practicing their wicked "nameless rites" before an image of a villainous-looking Goat-God brandishing an upside-down crucifix, or whatever worse vision can be called to mind. Perhaps that might have been plausible several centuries back, and it could even be true today in a limited number of cases, but a much more accurate guess would be to imagine the atmosphere of a board meeting or company conference at some super-luxury milieu, where human destinies were being decided by their commercial and political controllers. The most prosperous and successful-seeming people determining the fate of their fellow mortals with completely callous calculation. An entire efficiency of Evil collected around their computers to examine the expediency factor of all the problems posed.

One could classify human Satanists into four distinct categories as follows: First, the ordinary part-timer or simple sinner who is not particularly Evil but merely has what might be termed a "mean streak" running through him (or her), which inclines him/her to antisocial conduct of an unpleasant kind, involving cruelty and abnormal behavior such as bestiality and child abuse. Second, the "interested" class, who are willing to participate in ceremonials reputed to be Satanic in character, yet do not infringe limits imposed by law to a very great extent. There could be conduct that might be found in common sex clubs but with a Satanic angle, such as urinating or defecating on crucifixes, kissing the bare buttocks of a demonically dressed man, singing pornographic hymns, viewing blue movies of an explicit nature, mutually masturbating to appropriate music and so forth. Nothing much worse than that. Third, the "initiates," who are sufficiently dedicated to participate in every detail of the real Black Mass with enthusiasm and enjoyment, while undergoing instruction and training in the technical details of superior Satanism and educated Evil. Before passing from this to the next grade, they would have to pass proficiency tests in all categories of Evil activities, including those of the most intelligent kind. Fourth, the "Supersinners," who are above all lower levels of bad behavior. Officially they would not even break a by-law, let alone a statutory one. They mainly belong to the controlling classes— professional people such as politicians, financiers, industrialists, scientists, and the like. Additionally, those with an ability to influence human thinking and feeling would be recruited. Artists of all types, including musicians and writers, media people and preachers. Every possible expert on manipulating the minds of humankind so that these may be moved in any desired direction.

Such Fourth-grade Satanists are the Elite of Evil, who utilize and control the energy generated by the former three classes. They are the intelligentsia, so to speak, who have smaller and more intimate circles within their own company. From these the main commencing control extends throughout the remainder of the ranks, directing the energy-flows towards whatever target may be selected by the "Governing Council." They are the Officer Class of the Satanic Cause on earth, so there is no need for them to practice the crude types of Evil worked so well by their social inferiors. Their contribution is far more deadly and dangerous because it is so subtle and highly sophisticated. If all were snakes, the comparison would be that while the primary classes either missed their mark altogether or injected their poison into bodily tissues, the Elite Ones hit the bloodstream directly every time, and so were the most lethal of the serpentine breed. By no means is every sort of snake fatal, and many are perfectly harmless, but these in particular could be termed the kraits, cobras, mambas, and fer-de-lances of their species, and so to be treated as highly privileged persons.

No conflict can be continued without the necessary expenditure of energy, demanding sources of supply that even the most experienced officer can only direct as, where, and when he considers necessary. Such responses derive immediately from the natural Evildoers of this world, who are possibly unaware of how their energies are being tapped and collected for furtherance of the "Celestial Struggle" between the Forces of Light and Darkness. What they do not realize is that all our life-activities utilize, modify, and then emit specific types of energy. It is just as if every living creature were a receiving and transmitting apparatus for radiant energy operating over a wide spectrum of frequencies. We are always intaking, altering, and outputting this continual force-flow, which we are actually capable of controlling with our consciousness if we only would understand and put that process into practice.

Just as we are living in an earth-ambience of electromagnetic energy, which is generated by every radio and TV station in this world and which carries the results of consciousness, constructing all the programs there are, so do we exist in a sort of sea composed purely of consciousness itself, which contains every single thought in the minds of all humankind. Exactly as the radio programs can exist in separation from each other because of their variations in frequency, so does human thinking and feeling classify into types and strengths of consciousness according to its characteristics. Every single soul radiates this energy around and within itself, circulating the currents constantly. The physical brain alone will do this electromagnetically, which can be measured by an encephalograph, but we are talking about far finer forms of energy than electrical ones. Just because we have not yet invented a machine capable of indicating the invisible influence of intelligence itself does not mean that these energies do not exist or do not have any effect on us in consequence.

They have far more effect on us for good or ill than we might care to admit. Politicians in particular are always concerned with what is called their "public image" and public opinion, which in reality is the general consensus of human thinking in the overall area of socioeconomics. The same applies to every organizer of whatever humans are likely to expend their life-energies on, and all of them are anxious to captivate human consciousness for their particular fields. What might be thought of as the "Presiding Powers" of both Good and Evil alike are no exception. Each has developed its own expertise for collecting and channeling supplies of energy from human sources into their respective Causes. In former times there were far fewer methods of doing this than there are today, but the basic principles remain unchanged. It is simply selective accumulation, not unlike the process of charging a car battery or, for that matter, saving up a bank account.

It was an old belief that holy men (or women) could accumulate their "Mountain of Merit" by prayers, meditations, and pious thoughts. When they died, this could be used to assure them of a certain length of time in Heaven, then when their credit was finally exhausted they had to reincarnate in order to earn more merit. There was a comparable belief in some sections of the Christian Church that the minor sins of a soul piled up in a "Mountain of Demerits," which had to be paid for by so many years of our time spent in Purgatory, or a place of punishment from whence they would be released into Heaven when their allotted term of chastisement was completed. A related belief was that special souls had earned far more merit than was necessary for their individual salvation, so this meant that all the ownerless merit was, so to speak, floating around awaiting claimants. The Church naturally claimed custodianship of this spiritual fund and allowed their members to have a share in it by reciting formula prayers or performing special pilgrimages and penances. This idea became known as the controversial "Doctrine of Indulgences," which theoretically enabled people to liberate themselves from Purgatory either through payment or by performing the prescribed practices. Popes decided the conditions attached to specific formulae, as for example Pius the Ninth decreed a plenary, or total, Indulgence for the recitation of a short prayer before a crucifix. It may be remembered, he was the Pope with a reputedly Evil Eye.

Moreover, an Indulgence might be applied on behalf of any departed soul presumed to be in Purgatory, or it might be put to the credit of all sufferers in general. All it needed was a stated direction by the performer or a formal Act of Intention. The fundamental principle was that esoteric energy could be stored and directed for specific purposes much as money might be banked and withdrawn by whoever had the authority for signing checks. So far we have been speaking of merits applied for beneficial purposes, but if there is any substance in the broad hypothesis at all, then its opposite has to be true, and the same process can be used to promote the ends of Evil as well. It is purely a question of intention and application. If the Church of Christ on earth can lay claim to the merits of humankind and distribute these as it sees fit, then surely the Hierarchy of Hell has an equal right to their demerits and the authority to place these wherever they would serve some nefarious purpose.

Legend says that the Emerald which fell to earth with Lucifer and became the Holy Grail that held the "Holy Blood" of our salvation was named the Stone of Exile to indicate its Heavenly origin, and also to hint at our remote ancestral connections with a superior sort of people from a far-off planet, which has long since perished forever. Whether their prototypes arrived here by some physical form of spaceship or as a very special type of virus, we cannot know for certain, but it is evident that a most unusual event of some kind occurred in human history to change the human race from *Homo erectus* to *Homo sapiens*. Esoteric teaching is to the effect that this dramatic stride in human evolution was due to the introduction of fresh and foreign genetics from these "Star-People" by cross-breeding with our animalistic ancestors, whose descendants developed into the people we are today.

Such is the Sangreal story, or the beginning of "Blood Royal" among the species that commenced our civilization, evolved us into our contemporary condition, and that will ultimately lead us away from this world altogether to continue in some other part of the Galaxy. The Never-Ending Story of our survival. Be it specially noted it was Satan who "fell" to earth as a result of war in his own world, and he has presumably carried on the conflict among humankind ever since. It most certainly is the Satanic Spirit in us that encourages war, inspires our inventiveness in that pursuit, and makes the most profit from it in every sense. Yet however horrific wars may have been, something of value to humanity has usually emerged from them, such as tremendous advances in medicine and surgery, techniques that can be applied in other fields, and altered outlooks leading to great social changes among the combatants concerned. We are again reminded of the lines in Goethe's *Faust* when he queries the character of Mephistopheles and is told, "I am. . . part of that power, misunderstood, which always Evil wills, yet ever worketh Good." Whether the Good that comes from wars is worth the price paid in human suffering is always arguable.

It is interesting to observe that the Stone of Exile is supposed to be an emerald. The color green has always been associated with the Holy Grail, and of course is the color of the vegetable kingdom, besides being the optical opposite of red, the color of blood that Satan was said to have assumed after arriving on earth, subsequently turning black. Then in the Hermetic Tradition the entire principles of magic were said to have been engraved on an emerald tablet by Hermes using a diamond point. This was reputed to have been found by Alexander the Great in the Great Pyramid of Giza, which was highly unlikely historically, yet significant mythologically, since the symbolism points to the military conqueror of the then civilized world holding the secret key of arcane knowledge in his hands while being unable to use it through lack of understanding. Green again is the generally accepted sign of Peace, and its combination with the red of blood in the Holy Grail concept surely signifies a perfectly balanced condition in which our inclinations towards war and peace both blend into a harmless harmony. It also indicates that if humans ever hope to hold Satan in check, they had better find that Stone before he does.

It must be admitted that the Satan-concept has grown very considerably in extent and importance during the last few centuries. Some might even say that it has reached a maximum degree of maturity during the present era, though of course not under that title. Nevertheless, whatever humans regard as their chief source of Evil and a major Anti-factor in their lives is automatically their Satan-concept, however they term it. There are millions of Communists for whom the greatest Evil is called Capitalism, and equally millions of Capitalists who regard Communism in the same light. Millions more view a variety of socioeconomic factors with similar suspicions, which all amount to the same thing. So it is really just a question of semantics. In earlier times Satan was not widely regarded as being a great deal more than a mischievous Spirit and troublemaker, who was scarcely the equal of the Beneficent Being who kept all Cosmos in control with an authoritarian hand. For the last several centuries the Satan-concept has been growing in stature and significance, while the Deity-Figure has been shrinking and becoming of less importance to the mass of humankind almost every day. The two Powers seem virtually even in the estimation of the average modern mortal. The time seems to be approaching when more conscious attention will be paid to Satan under all sorts of different descriptions than is presently being paid to the Deity under another diversity of names. What effect is this likely to have on our lives should that happen?

To try and extrapolate that, we would have to look back on our world when so many of our minds were occupied with Deity and all the supporting subjects connected therewith. Were we actually better people? History in fact says NO, although that would be a qualified estimate. What modern society would tolerate the dirt, disease, poverty, and other factors that were not only considered quite normal but also believed permissible by the inscrutable "Will of God"? The more we suffered on earth, the happier we should be in Heaven. The Goodness of God and the Wickedness of the Devil decided how everything should be, and it was not for humankind to interfere with the workings of Providence. Such were the general beliefs of the period, which were fortunately transcended by many individual minds that eventually exerted a combined effect throughout the mass of humankind.

Such pioneering souls balanced God against the Devil, and cancelling one with the other in their consciousness, they went ahead as if those were both combined or fused into a single Force, which provided them with Power for their own purposes. They did this by simple reversal of polarities between the opposite Powers, so that the Devil's positive became for them a negative and so altered to a positive of God, which meant the "Yes" of the Devil became a "No" from their concept of God, and they themselves chose which to act upon. This meant that whatever their worst instincts (or the Devil in them) incited them to do, they deliberately inhibited or negated, and whatever the same impulse told them not to do they took as a positive injunction to perform if they could. Which was the reason that most of the Ten Commandments were given in negatives, and why Jesus gave the often unwelcome advice to love one's enemies and to return Good for Evil, thus reversing normal inclinations.

Following this procedure, it worked out that although they were nowhere nearly as Good as God might have hoped, neither were they anywhere as bad as Satan meant them to be. In other words, they were directing their own destinies as they believed best, and progressed along a line somewhere between the two extremes. They were becoming what we now regard as average human beings, aiming at neither Hell nor Heaven, but at an ordinary earthly existence based on their own resources and what they could make this earth produce. Unhappily, it remains a basic truth that *the love of money* IS the root of all Evil, meaning that sheer overpowering desire for what money can buy in terms of power, position, luxury, and the services of every available human specialist. Whoever was capable of exploiting our earth for the sake of making the most money could make the world work for them, and them alone. Whether they realized until fairly recently the ultimate price that would have to be paid is doubtful, but there is an old proverb that says, "Give the Devil his due," which also signifies "pay him what is owed to him," and Satan is now presenting us with the biggest bill for his services that we have ever faced. We owe him more than we thought possible.

Chapter 4

SIN OR PSYCHOLOGY

From time immemorial humans have thought of God and Heaven as being somewhere above their heads, and the Devil in Hell down beneath their feet in the bowels of the earth. The sophisticated Greeks considered Pluto, the Dark God of wealth, to exist in the Underworld because that was literally where all the wealth came from in the form of minerals and jewels, which they used as currency. We might say the same today of coal, oil, and other valuable products extracted from the earth. Ideas of Hell-Fire obviously originated from volcanoes, and the destructive demons were most probably race-memories of prehistoric monsters. To this day we associate Good with Heaven, or "up there," because of inherited memories of our long-lost "starhome," and Bad with Hell, or "down there," deep in the earth where we had to dig for prosperity and technical progress.

77

Philosophers noting this connection commented that God in his infinite wisdom had hidden the harmful things away from the sight of humans in the darkness, yet brought beneficial things to light above the ground where they might easily be seen and handled. Though this is only theoretically true, it put forward a valid point insofar as the products we cultivate above ground have principally contributed to our benefit in the way of food, clothing, homes, medicines, and the like, while what we have mined from deep below ground, such as fossil fuels and minerals, may have brought us short-term benefits; but they have also supplied us with the means of making worse and worse wars until we are now in the nuclear age with what could be called the ultimate weapon straight out of Satan's locker, and that is by no means the end of the story.

By this time, the various accounts of poisonous pollution in our atmosphere by chemical wastes and by-products plus the genetic effects of factors that did not exist until our present period of history should be widely known to any average person of intelligence with access to a public library. All these evils have been extremely well documented and set out for anyone to read who has the slightest interest in the future of our race or of this world as a whole. The findings are beyond denial, and the facts being pushed in our faces make alarming reading. Unless humanity becomes willing to cooperate amongst itself on a worldwide scale, organizing some practical scheme for coping with the contaminants it has produced, we and our world will eventually perish from the long-term effects of those poisons. Otherwise we have only two choices: Do we die quickly because of nuclear war, or slowly because we have poisoned our planet? We have literally come to the crunch where at last there is the Devil to pay.

The old belief that we could sell ourselves to Satan for seven years' prosperity after which period our souls were his to burn is becoming literally true. Yet the interesting point is that it is not the actual raw materials we have dug from the earth that are doing the damage, but what they have produced because of our processing them. For instance, coal is only fossilized wood that has become carbon and of itself does nothing harmful to us. By burning it in open grates, that same coal produces lethal gas and suffocating sulphur fumes. Again by adding lead derivatives to gasoline we have added poisons to the atmosphere that affect the human brain, especially those of growing children, and that particularly affect crowded cities, where traffic is concentrated. It is our vehicles that discharge this dangerous contaminant, and gasoline itself would pose no problems otherwise. Since our scientists and engineers are mainly responsible for our technical troubles, it should surely be their job to devise systems capable of clearing them. On the other hand, those experts would not have applied their skills and services without the inducement of financial and social rewards. So in the end it devolves on the wealthy of this world to offer the richest rewards to those able to plan the most practical projects for liberating us from the lethality of our own greeds and venalities. One might as well say delivering us from the Devil if possible. Satan is not going to relinquish his rights without a supreme struggle, nor is he likely to be banished with some casual brandishings of a crucifix and a few Latin formulae. Only stage or storybook Satans cringe before humans calling on their Gods. Those names mean absolutely nothing to a *real* Satan. What genuinely impresses him is the spiritual stand taken by humans who sincerely try to resist or reverse the energies he directs against them.

It would be an exaggeration to say that Satan admires any human creature with the courage and conviction to oppose his intentions and say so to his face as it were, but such an idea does supply some notion of the spiritual situation implied. It is perfectly possible to have some respect for a worthy opponent while at the same time attempting his (or her) destruction with all the force at one's command. History is full of incidents illustrating this point, especially among the so-called "savage" fighters. Many of the Cossack tribes had the tradition that if they found a helpless and wounded enemy, they were bound to take him into their homes, nurse him back to health if they could, then give him a horse, weapons, and about half a day's start. At the end of that time some of their young men would ride after him as hard as they could and try to catch and kill him if possible. Satan might not be as chivalrous as that, but he does respect those souls who are prepared to resist him, especially those who are determined to die in their attempts to break free from his clutches. It has long been a belief that Satan was not permitted to push humankind past the maximum limit of his resistance, and the classic story illustrating this is told in the Biblical tale of Job.

In this story a prosperous and blameless man is deliberately given into the complete power of Satan by God himself, solely for the purpose of demonstrating human fidelity to the Divine Ideal. It is almost as if God is throwing out a challenge to Satan purely in order to prove which of them has the greatest influence on conditioned human consciousness. The interesting point to this tale is that Satan is classed among the "Sons of God" who present themselves regularly to their Divine Father for consultation and exchange of information. It is most probable that it was from this imaginative tale that the Cathars obtained their ideas of Jesus and Satan being twin brothers. At all events, with the full permission of God, Satan does his worst allowed limit with poor old Job, depriving him of health and wealth, and yet *still* the wretched man continues to praise God and display the most amazing patience and fortitude. His three philosophizing friends sit with him in the depths of his ruin and regale him with one platitude after another, which Job takes as part of the God-sent affliction. In the end, however, having proved his point, God reproves those tiresome three and restores Job to perfect health with twice his former prosperity.

Biblical scholars classify this story as a fictional presentation of the spiritual principles underlying the nature of our bi-polar Lifeforce. It is essentially illustrative of how human minds work when confronted with opposing energies of Good and Evil, both operating as arbiters of experiences from which a soul emerges in ultimate triumph, providing it remains true to its basic beliefs in the efficacy of Beneficence versus Malignity. But the story does not tell us what might have happened had Satan been allowed a completely free hand with his choice of afflictions. Which agrees with the postulation that Satan is only permitted to test us up to our maximum degree of resistance, and that means we would have to exert energy for a somewhat extended period in order to transcend his trials altogether. Making those efforts, however, often needs just a little bit more push than most humans are willing to exert, or the extra energy gets spent in such a way that it converts back to Evil quite easily.

For example, suppose someone is well aware of Satanic suggestions and decides to defeat these by joining a religious sect. Suppose this sect has such strict rulings that the new member soon becomes mean-minded, intolerant, unkind, narrow-viewed, and develops a lot of similar propensities that are very far from the usual Christian ethic and much closer to Satanic principles, such as hating humanity and refusing to forgive enemies or to tolerate anyone who does not share the same restrictive opinions. Thus in avoiding some Satanic traits at one end of the behavior scale, they fall right into another set at the other. Becoming a nominal Christian is no assurance of developing non-Satanic incli-

nations, and in some cases it is almost a declaration of Demonic direction. One has only to consider the diabolical
cruelties of the Inquisition or the fiendish fanaticism of the
Covenanters to see indisputable cases of Evil in the guise of
God-worship. Authoritarian religion has contributed more
to the cause of authentic Satanism than a multitude of Black
Masses. Wherever deliberate cruelty and suffering are inflicted on fellow mortals or animals, Satan will always present a smiling face of approval.

Of course there is always the question of capability to
be considered when contributions to Satan are estimated
from his supporters. A great many extremely Evil activities
are completely beyond the scope of average mortals; yet
within their limits and because of their combined mass-
effect, they can still extend the empire of Evil to an appreciable degree. Someone who may not be able to commit
murder literally could effectively "kill" another person's
character with carefully worked out words. They might not
have the connections to perpetrate elaborate financial frauds,
yet they could still steal some poor person's purse with
vitally important pennies in it. Most people would agree
that it is far more dishonest to rob a poor person of pennies
than a multimillionaire of a few thousand dollars. The
criterion is the degree of damage inflicted, which should be
obvious to anyone taking the factor of relativity into account.
Thus a large number of souls contributing a small amount
of Evil each would total more than a very few each offering a
great deal. Nevertheless, a significant number of Satanically
inclined souls acting in concert can "trigger off" chains of
Evil energy amongst humankind that might not have commenced otherwise.

There is a well-known Scots proverb: "many a mickle
makes a muckle," or a lot of little things become one very
big one, and this is true in all fields of action, besides being a
fundamental law of energy where or however applied. This

means to say that unless there were a large proportion of people prepared to permit a small amount of Evil each, the minority of expert directors would not be able to apply it as they had intended, and the total amount of Evil in our world would lessen dramatically. The same is true of Good as an energy. The mass of humankind supply the raw material, so to speak, while the experts of processing and application turn it into finished products. For example, suppose a major war is to be an end-result. First the contenders have to be chosen a long time in advance and the Satanic experts placed exactly where they can best bring this about.

First these Malignants will destabilize the relationships between the chosen humans as fast as possible, doing everything feasible to create suspicion and enmity between them. Race, religion, and politics mixed with economics are the usual levers moved to create an atmosphere of hate and antipathy for as long as can be. At this stage those involved resemble Japanese Sumo wrestlers making threatening moves at each other as they circle around waiting for the most advantageous openings. Everything depends on working up a maximum head of pressure during this initial preparation, on which the end-result so often depends. Alliances must be consolidated and supplies assured. Money must be moved to safe places and credit arrangements made. Armaments have to be designed, manufactured, and stockpiled. Above all, the people who will mainly suffer have to be motivated deeply enough to endure whatever horror is likely to be thrown at them during the course of the conflict. It is well known that the most important ingredient of a war is a curious commodity called morale. Without it, no politician could continue a war for more than a few days. Formerly morale was something more or less confined to the fighting services, but nowadays it applies equally to the bulk of the civilian populace who will have to endure the privations and sufferings wars inflict on them. Once their morale breaks down they will insist on surrender on almost any terms.

In view of this and the side issues involved, wars are no longer an exclusively politico-military matter but include every factor connected with human behavior on earth. Psychological warfare was developed into a specialization during World Wars I and II, and computerization will most certainly be a major issue in any future conflict. The one-time augers and soothsayers who formed an essential part of the Roman armed forces and played such an important role in their victories have now become technologists and scientists, manipulating machines that are the modern version of an ancient *lituus*, or divining scepter. Most of all, the former financiers who invested in warfare and made such vast profits out of it have now become enormous institutional concerns with interests all around the world. They could not fail to be the final winner in every war that human beings are likely to have on this earth.

Once the initial and expert Evildoers are properly placed and prepared, each pursues his or her specialized function. In our times apart from previous instabilities we have to take drug addiction into account, which in large enough proportions makes a serious problem for any civil authority, linked as it is with crimes of violence and robbery. Additionally, terrorism, under the disguise of nationalistic idealism, has become an international industry funded from many sources, and its active agents trained by qualified instructors earning extremely high salaries. A single well-trained terrorist can cause incredible trouble when intelligently directed at the right time against a correct target. It may not be as easy as it once was to trigger off a war by the assassination of a major political or religious figure, but invasion of territory by armed aggressors will usually provoke replies that can be relied on to erupt along increasingly dangerous lines until the hoped for conflagration occurs.

When that disaster happens, the task of the Malignants is to keep the conflict going for as long as possible so that the maximum of money is made from it by their backers. The Benevolents will naturally try to ensure that the ill winds of war will blow *some* Good for humankind one way or another. When we think of all the gains made by surgery alone due to warfare, plus scientific advances in nearly all fields, we have to admit that wars can sometimes help as well as hinder human progress. The point is, however, that wars would be impossible if the majority of mortals refused to fight each other purely for the benefit of their political or other leaders. They must agree to hate and hurt their fellow mortals in the first place, and therefore the Evils in themselves have to multiply and combine until the flashpoint is reached where it can all be exploded by the experts. In a way, it is not unlike the critical mass of a nuclear warhead. It cannot explode until it actually becomes that mass, but on the other hand it needs the correct mechanism to complete the process, and human intelligence has been the means of designing this. So with the mass of humankind providing all the energy and the Master-Malignants supplying the expertise, Satan gets served as he undoubtedly expects. Frequently and faithfully.

It was chiefly to release these inner pressures of Evil that the early Christian Church commenced the custom of confessing one's sins to a priest, elevating it into their Sacrament of Penance, or At-one-ment between the penitent and their God. Its basic purpose was to make the penitent realize just how much energy he or she had been donating to Satan, and they would then determine (or intend) to improve themselves accordingly for the future. What really mattered was the sincerity of their behavior-altering intentions, and depending on this, the Sacrament was valid or not. The original purpose behind it was to induce people to practice regular course-corrections throughout their lives and so make some changes for the better. In the end, as one might expect, familiarity bred contempt, and its real meaning was misunderstood by both priests and laity alike until it became no more than a mere formality, which did little good worth considering.

The earlier Church took "sins" very seriously and classified them into two categories, mortal and venial. The mortal ones were so called because they were believed to kill the soul, and they consisted of really serious things like murder, arson, sacrilege, armed robbery, rape, and so forth. Venial sins, like telling small lies and petty thefts, were not supposed to kill the soul, but they were considered to damage it according to the degree and duration of the sin in question. These were more or less the sort of sins most people commit almost without thinking about them, but when added up to a life total they could amount to an impressive figure in terms of Satanic supplies. Now in Christian thinking, all sins had two elements attached to them. First, they were an offense against God that incurred a specific amount of guilt on the part of the sinner, and secondly came the consequences, which had to be compensated for in order to neutralize them. This was the Christian version of Karma, where each act of humankind automatically invokes its equal and opposite energy in order to bring the lifestate of everyone back into balance and harmony. From a Christian viewpoint, only the "guilt" of a sin would be forgiven through the Sacrament of Penance, but its consequences would still have to be paid for by whatever means God deemed most expedient or appropriate.

The Scriptural definition of "sin" traces from the interesting Greek word *harmatia*, which was an archery expression meaning to miss the mark, or to go wrong by failing one's purpose. In the Old Testament the Hebrew word ChTA also signifies not to hit the target, and so by implication to sin or go astray. So both terms agree with each other on the point of wrongdoing in the view of God being failure of expected achievement rather than the actual commission of an offense agasint the Almighty himself; yet the subsequent doctrinal interpretation of sin became exactly that: an offense against the Goodness of God, which merited guilt on the part of an offender. Originally the word *gylt* meant a money fine for some specific crime, or in other words, the price to be paid for it. So an admission of guilt signified an acknowledgement of one's debt due to Deity as a result of disregarding Its laws.

In the case of instructed Christians, who had been taught the technical differences between right and wrong, their sins were considered far more serious than those of others because they had been committed with knowledge of the offense they would give God, and therefore must have been done deliberately, which made their sins a great deal worse than those of uninstructed Pagans, for example. It was really for this class of soul that the Sacrament of Penance was instituted. The belief was that they did not confess their sins to any priest, but to God alone, who "heard" them through the ears of the priest, who was there to witness and also act as an adviser to help them through difficult passages. The penitents would acknowledge their wrongdoing, admit their guilt, ask sincerely for reconcilement with their Deity, and then await the issue with hopeful confidence. Here it was the duty of the priest to consult the God within himself concerning what he had heard, and then pronounce whatever real or symbolic penance that Deity deemed necessary to remit the guilt of the admitted offences.

The psychological value of this exercise is quite considerable. Properly carried out, it is a constant catharsis of the soul that keeps it in good working relationship with the Life Spirit. Its process has been likened to a boy who has broken a window with a ball in some spot where he has been specifically forbidden to play. So feeling guilty and knowing that he deserves punishment, he approaches his father, admits what he has done, says he is sorry and will try not to offend in the future, and then awaits judgment. The father lectures the boy on the wrongs of his disobedience, and then tells him that because he was honest enough to acknowledge his fault freely, there will be no blame attached, nor paternal anger, *but he will still have to pay for that window out of his pocket money.* This analogy is not a bad one, since it emphasizes the Parent-Child relationship between Deity and humanity, plus simplifies all the principles involved.

Eventually, as it happened, quite a large section of the Christian Church objected to the presence of a priest in these proceedings, believing that they should approach the Deity directly and arrange their own affairs with purely private prayer. Had they been competent enough to assess their spiritual status accurately and estimate their guilt more or less correctly, this would have worked quite well. Unfortunately, humans do tend to exaggerate their activities in all directions with increasingly wide margins of error, which a medieval story illustrates perfectly:

It seems that a certain wealthy man became so overburdened with a sense of sin, he decided nothing less than a public penance would expiate it. So he hired the whole local cathedral, bishop and all, to serve this purpose, and appointed a day for the action. When the time came, there he was—clothed in sackcloth and ashes, barefoot, stripped to the waist, carrying a seven-pound penitential candle as he processed up the aisle amid a huge congregation with a full choir of monks chanting behind him, who occasionally applied a ceremonial scourge to his bared back. When he got to the altar and stepped in front of the robed Bishop, in full view of everyone with all their attention focused on him intently, he groaned, and casting his eyes upwards said in stricken tones audible to all, "O may God forgive me, for I am the most wicked man this world has ever known!" At this, there was a sudden flash and explosion, then with a terrible smell of sulphur Satan himself appeared in a most irritated mood, roaring at everyone, "Don't any of you believe him. He's nothing but a stupid and conceited little fool!" After which home-truth Satan vanished as quickly as he appeared. Some lies are just too much for even the reputed father of them, especially when they make him look ridiculous in the eyes of his official enemies.

One of the easiest ways of magnifying self-importance to virtually absurd degrees is by increasing one's sense of guilt out of all proportion to a sin's true estimate. The idea of a minuscule human being having the ability to anger or disturb a Creative Force that has the power to construct entire Universes is literally mind-boggling. There seemed so little to do in fact. Some bad behavior in the way of being nasty to one's neighbor or stealing a little petty cash seemed to upset this God to a totally disproportionate extent. Therefore, what an importance a soul that could produce such an effect on the Almighty must have. Many a medieval soul, and maybe a small proportion of modern ones, achieved their maximum sense of self-identity by overstressing the importance of their sins and exaggerating the interest in their affairs shown by such prodigious Powers as God and Satan alike. The greater their sense of guilt and the more blameworthy they considered themselves, then the bigger they must be in the eyes of Eternal Energy. This is factually the most gigantic ego-boost possible, and modern youngsters who depend on drugs, chemical stimulants, and similar excitants can never imagine the thrills that came from a cultivated sense of sin in former times.

When it was wicked to play card games, not attend Church on Sundays, blaspheme, or otherwise contravene the puritanical codes of current conduct, the slightest deviation from the "straight and narrow" provided people with a wonderful sense of wickedness that increased their sense of self-importance to an incredible extent. To them, both God and Satan were frightening Figures threatening doom and destruction for any infringement of the rules their brand of religion laid down. They might know quite well that other branches of Christianity were not nearly so strict, but they looked on those as being damned anyway. There is an apocryphal tale of a Scots minister describing the fate of sinners to his fascinated flock and saying, "Aye, there ye'll be ma brethren, wi' the fires o' Hell flaming all around ye and suffering for yer sins in the maist awfu' agony, so ye'll be weeping and wailin' and crying to the Laird sayin', 'Laird, Laird, we didna ken, we didna ken.' And then the Laird in His infinite maircy will look down on ye all from above and say, 'Aye, Well ye ken the noo!'"

The Scots in particular have always had considerable respect for Satan, whom they call almost affectionately "Auld Hornie" in memory of their Pagan past. Since their Calvinistic doctrine of predestination dooms a large proportion of humanity to Hell anyway, they obviously hope to make the best possible relations in advance with the Lord thereof. In their beliefs it is not he that condemns them to eternal damnation, but the Deity who decides the fate of every soul. So if they have to go to Hell in obedience to God's Will, they might as well endure it as stoically as possible. Their general standpoint is that Satan simply does the job for which God appointed him, and if their ultimate association is inevitable, then there is no more to be said. A type of fatalism that does not admit any argument or disagreement with it. Their rigidly inflexible God made Satan for his (or her) inscrutable purposes, and who were humans to challenge or dispute that? They could not accept that their concepts of God and Satan alike were projections of their own peculiarities into appreciable Images they could relate with and to.

The most basic emotions of humanity are Love and Hate, or attraction and repulsion. We want to move towards or away from anyone or anything. So we conceive the God we need to Love, and the Devil we are supposed to Hate, both being opposite ends of ourselves and the Lifeforce we have to relate with in order to exist at all. There is a Scriptural text that says, "The fear of the Lord is the beginning of Wisdom," but originally the word *fear* meant to respect and set a great value on, or treat as being extremely important. So we really ought to fear or respect both God and Satan together, because they are the most important metaphysical relationship points of our lives. One is the Spirit of all the Love and Good that every human being has ever had or ever will experience, and the other is the opposite end of that same Spirit comprising the Hates and Evils we also share amongst us. However, it is important to realize that neither God nor Satan originated with us, however much we may have contributed to their construction on this earth. All we have done is to formalize with our awareness the natural energies they are, whether in this world or anywhere else throughout the whole of Existence. We have only interpreted them with our limited intelligence, coming to comprehend something of them through the millenia; and as our experience of them alters, so apparently do they, although it is really ourselves advancing enough to perceive those Powers from a different and, hopefully, higher angle of observation.

Nevertheless, since we have personified those Powers, so they in turn have motivated us. The Deity, beneficently, and Satan, maliciously. As we evolve, so should we steer ourselves centrally on a balanced course, between the two extremes that will eventually produce the type of people we were meant to be from our beginning: beings whose bodies are built from pure energy, who are capable of existing in a different condition of consciousness altogether from what we know at present. In contrast with our contemporary set of circumstances, we shall be "as Gods" ourselves. That, of course, is assuming we have not exhausted or destroyed the resources of our planet first. Before that happens, however, we should have exported our species to another planet and begun breeding there so as to continue our climb up the Tree of Life towards an ultimate perfection, which we are still very far from reaching after several millions of our years. As our evolution advances so does it accelerate, and during the past few decades we have made more technical progress than we have made for as many previous centuries. Should that rate continue, it is anyone's guess where we may stand by the end of the next century. Perhaps it might be of interest to remember that the word *evolve* consists of *evol* (Evil), the reverse of which is *love*, the two main factors behind the phenomena of intelligent LIFE.

Concentrating on either Deism or Satanism *exclusively* does not take us very far up the Ladder of Life. Entirely by itself, Satanism would bring out the very worst in us in every way, although it would produce enormous energy and a tremendous drive as well as a keenly sharpened intellect and intensified sense of cunning. Pure Deism, on the other hand, would increase an awareness of spirituality very considerably and would encourage our finest characteristics, although it might also lead to sectarianism and the negative qualities of not actually doing Evil being mistaken for positive Good. Also, we should not confuse the practice of any religion *per se* with the adoption of Deism or Satanism as a way of life. Any individual who is intentionally living by his or her worst motivations while deliberately inflicting disadvantages and sufferings on others for the sake of their own temporary gains is a practicing Satanist, whether they believe in Satan as a Being or not. Conversely, whoever attempts to help fellow mortals and develops oneself with one's best qualities is a practicing Deist whether he or she believes in any kind of an intelligent God or not. Most ordinary humans behave in both ways at different times of their lives, and it is simply a question of which type of behavior happens to be predominant as to how they could be classified.

Many a human being must have wondered what life would be like if all the energy and enthusiasm aroused by Satan in their souls could be converted into an equivalent amount of energy to serve the purposes of God instead. One previous writer not only asked that question of himself, but also worked out his scheme for putting that process into practice. This was the unknown author of the Abramelim (sometimes spelled "Abramelin") magical system, which purports to control Demons with the aid of what was termed a Holy Guardian Angel. The general idea was to spend six whole months of preparation in character-altering exercises and then invoke this Guardian Angel—which in fact was the operator's own conscience and "Better Self"—and with its assistance invite all the Devils and Demons to come and take an oath of obedience that they would work for the magician as the Angel directed. All the Devils had to be called by name, and a full description of their characters was given. Each Demon was some specific human fault or deficiency of nature, and the whole operation was factually a brilliant piece of psychodramatic psychology, as sound in principle today as it was when it became conceived in the fifteenth century.

Most modern Wesoterics are at least familiar with the text, although very few indeed have practiced it in detail as it was laid down in the original book because of the complicated conditions insisted on—specifying the type of person, proper place and season, together with all the accessories and sundries necessary to the success of the operation. There are endless warnings that unless the entire list can be made available and will indeed be scrupulously complied with, it would be best not to commence proceedings in the first place. Again and again it is stressed that commitment to the complete course must not only be totally sincere but also dedicated and constant. Once begun it has to be finished without interruption unless for the most serious reasons, such as severe illness or family misfortunes of maximum magnitude, in which case the whole process must be recommenced the following year.

The idea of a Holy Guardian Angel, or attendant spirit attached to every human, encouraging it to think kindly thoughts and do good deeds in order to make it worthy of Heaven at physical death, is a very old one, and so too is the matching Demon suggesting Evil thoughts and acts. Not infrequently the Good Angel was thought of as belonging to the opposite sex of its human charge, while the Bad one would be of the same sex. Carl Jung was familiar with these concepts and called them the Anima (female) and Animus (male), although he saw them as a kind of alter ego. He came to believe that his own Anima frequently informed him of the facts behind the condition of his most puzzling patients. Whether or not Jung was unfamiliar with the Abramelim thesis is very uncertain, but the probability is that he was, since it had been published in his lifetime.

So to begin with, whoever wants to put this Abramelim system into practice must be someone willing to personalize and contact consciously their own Holy Guardian Angel, or the best side of their own nature, and then with its help summon and contact the very worst of themselves in the shape of various Fiends, with the object of commanding the Fiendish Energies to serve the Angelic side of themselves. That is to say, make Satan work for God instead of himself. All this implies that such a soul is already prepared to make the necessary changes that will put this process into at least the commencement of practice, and has most probably done much of the preliminary development already. In other words, it is telling itself: *"I have come of age spiritually and grown beyond Angels or Devils. From this point forward I will direct myself as the Angelic side of my nature suggests, but I will obtain the necessary energy to do so from the side of myself that would otherwise have been Devilish. Hitherto this may have been an instinctive and almost unconscious process in myself, but from now on I shall take charge of it myself intentionally and consciously. I shall use the symbology of Angels and Devils as a convenience of my consciousness and shall continue to use ceremonialism as a perfectly practical means of coordinating everything in my awareness, but these will have fresh and much more modern meanings for me, however ancient they may be in actuality. So with updated understanding in the language of today, I will work the Rite of old Abramelim as I think it should be done in this century."* In other words, an old magical practice is converted into a present-day psychodrama for the same basic purpose: the subjection of Evil to the service of Good and then neutralizing the resultant energy back into the original Ocean of spiritual supply.

With that same process we would also be working pure spiritual Alchemy, or the achievement of something that does not later lead into gold but changes the worst of Evils into the best of Goods, by reversal of polarity in the activating Power. Since theoretically energy is energy pure and simple, and only intention motivates that energy for Good, Evil, or any intermediate purpose, the same energy that empowers a brutal murder might equally well be applied to saving a life or to some corresponding benefit to one's fellow human. All that would be needed would be change of motivation, but nothing is likely to do that except the strongest intervention of something we once called "Conscience," or "Knowing with Knowing." It is dictionary-defined as a moral sense of knowing the difference between Right and Wrong, or discerning Good from Evil.

Scripturally, the ability that made us like Gods and involved Satan so intimately with our affairs.

Broader interpretations of conscience might be argued indefinitely. Some would say it was meaningless except in the mind of whoever presumed possession of one, in which case it could be described as an "elastic" conscience. Others might say it was purely a matter of which code of ethics was accepted by followers who might make certain specifics right for them yet wrong in the eyes of others. Conscience seems to be a very ambiguous faculty that humans either have or have not, and all we can fairly say is that it amounts to one's own self-estimate according to whatever ethical standards may be taken as a general or particular guide to living. Beyond grading such standards as almost absent or very "low," an average number or "normal," some additional ones amounting to "high" and "extremely high," we cannot grade conscience into closer classifications. It does not follow, however, that the more numerous and rigid our standards are, the better types of people we shall be.

If some literal standards are sought, against which to compare and measure those of any individual, one could scarcely do better than use the Holy Tree of Life. This postulates ten definite degrees, or Principles, that are all attainable by human beings to some degree, and together they comprise a most practical Life-Standard to set for anyone intending to make something worthwhile of themselves and the lives they experience on this earth. They have the somewhat unusual property of being timeless and applicable to both sexes, whereas the Ten Commandments have a definitely masculine slant. Take the one concerning observation of the Sabbath: "The seventh day is the Sabbath of the Lord thy God. In it thou shalt not do any work, thou, nor thy son, nor thy daughter, thy manservant nor thy maidservant, nor thy cattle, nor thy stranger that is within thy gates." What about the man's *wife*? She apparently is not forbidden to work on the sacred Sabbath, unless of course she is included with the cattle. In fact, the Sabbath would seem to be the one day of the week when the wretched woman has to wait on her entire family, house guests, animals, and all, including her own servants. Although very few would take this commandment as literally as that, the omission of the maternal member of a family group should be carefully noted by those accepting the Mosaic Commandments as a standard of behavior. Moses selected and adapted them from the forty commandments imposed on the Egyptians as a standard of good social and ethical conduct. The ten Concepts of the Tree of Life are inclusive of the commandments and cover the whole of human behavior regardless of sex, religion, or social status. Moreover, they specify the spiritual principles motivating the best possible courses to follow by any human who means to make the most of themselves in the direction of Divinity.

So we can take it that anyone who already has developed, or who is in the process of developing, a conscience, must necessarily be a soul with the intention of improving itself and of sublimating its own Satan into something superior and more valuable than self-destructive dross. To accomplish this, it will obviously need some satisfactory methodology that is seldom available from the customary religious sources. So supposing someone were magically inclined in our modern world and wanted to try out the old Abramelim system, how would they work this in a contemporary manner so as to obtain at least a shadow of success from the experiment? Let us consider how this might be done, and commence by examining some salient factors of the original instructions.

Chapter Five

ABRAMELIM UPDATED

The entire Abramelim ritual is really a confrontation between both spiritual ends of oneself, and a conscious dedication of one's Devil self to one's Deity self while the two extremities are linked to the natural energies they express through the medium of the operator. In the original version a great many conditions and obligations were laid upon this individual in order to enhance and impress upon him or her the singular importance and solemnity of the occasion. These could well be duplicated today, even if they varied somewhat in accordance with our times. First an upper and lower age limit is advised. This was somewhere between twenty-five and fifty. Although this might be arbitrary today, the essential requirement is that the operator must be old enough to understand what this operation is all about, yet not too old for its purpose to have much value for him or her or anyone concerned. In earlier centuries it was estimated that by fifty a man's children should be grown up and independent enough not to interfere with the process. Provided that non-interference from one's family can be depended on during the entire operation, such a condition should suffice in our times.

Good physical health was insisted on, and that is as valid now as it was then. Poor health of body or brain is a guarantee of trouble in a psychological experience of this kind, and the reasons should be obvious. Disease of any kind is an unbalancing and discordancy of one's physical and mental energies, and should this happen beyond a certain degree, any normal human being will be quite unable to cope with the stresses and strains imposed by the course of conduct demanded. Though this might not apply with minor problems such as a common cold, sprained ankle or the like, the health rule would certainly disqualify or seriously disadvantage anyone suffering from a systemic illness or chronic disability affecting the balance of body and mind. It would be well to bear in mind that a successful Abramelim ceremony should be a life-altering experience, yet an unsuccessful one would be a positive disaster of a major kind. Could it be imagined what would occur if instead of an Angelic triumph over the Devilish side of one's nature the reverse happened? Suppose that instead of making oneself into a better type of being by undergoing the Abramelim Experience, something went wrong and a hitherto reasonable human being became a Demon-dominated individual governed by the nastiest side of its nature? Many stories are told of sinners being converted into saints somewhat rapidly, but it is equally possible for the opposite effect to take place, and the only possible safeguard against that event is to take all proper precautions against the possibilities that either suggest themselves or are advised by persons of previous experience in that particular field. The faculty of a sound mind in a healthy body is an absolute prerequisite in the Abramelim area of action, and those with any doubt about their own condition would be well advised to leave it severely alone, because it can be a "make or break" ordeal.

Assuming good health prevails and there is reasonable hope of carrying out the enterprise, the next step is ensuring self-sequestration from adverse living conditions and influences as far as possible. Short of monastic or hermetic seclusion, this presents a maximum difficulty to most moderns. Nevertheless, it is essential to eventual success that the optimum suitable situation be created for its achievement, and that appears to demand considerable self-discipline, freedom from material worries, ample opportunity for prayer and meditation, sympathetic surroundings, avoidance of antipathetic people and influences, plus peaceful and harmonious working atmospheres. How this ideal condition is to be achieved short of considerable independent means and status we are not told. Given an average type of congenial employment plus few family or social commitments, it could be simulated by avoiding close contact with casual acquaintances as far as possible; by refraining from exposure to all news media, including TV, radio, magazines and newspapers; and by isolating oneself from external influences as far as practical, within one's own home with the cooperation of one's close family members. This might not be ideal, but at least it would be a fair attempt to comply with conditions laid down for good results with the very best reasons.

This whole idea of self-insulation from mundane affairs as far as possible for a definite period is to virtually enforce confrontation with one's best and worst characteristics, which are frequently masked by contacts with other humans. In a way this is similar to the feared yet most effective of prison punishments—solitary confinement. Kept in a small and darkened cell on a minimum diet and prevented from contact with anyone except themselves, a prisoner is thrown up against his or her most intimate thoughts, with often painful yet remarkable results. Very few men or women emerge from "solitary" in the same spirit they entered it, and all experiments in psychological laboratories with what are called "sense deprivation" sessions have demonstrated their character-altering effects. Voluntary seclusion and isolation from close human contacts show similar results, as in monastic life. The nearest most people can get to this state, as a rule, is a simulation of it in their own homes. Not ideal, but at least a good imitation that could be acceptable to a Cosmic Intelligence.

For the purpose of such a retreat, a period of six months was specified, lasting from Easter till September, which still seems practical in view of European climactic conditions and seasonal significance from Equinox to Equinox. Also a special personal Temple was planned as an ideal place for the performance of the Rite itself. Although it was designed as a sort of wooden hut, with a central altar of conventional shape having convenient cupboards for keeping accessories in, it could quite well be a prefabricated garden shed if space is available. Otherwise a spare room may be set aside, especially if it can be stripped of furniture. At all events it has to be a confined space wherein one can be alone with one's thoughts and that, preferably, will not be entered by anyone else during the prescribed period. Perhaps a loft might be converted for the purpose, or a built-on house section added, if allowable. At any rate, some kind of a private retreat place is absolutely necessary for the production of an Abramelim ritual, since it helps emphasize the individual nature of the enterprise.

The original text stressed the importance of a clean wooden interior and floor with an absolute minimum of furniture for this little Temple, but nowadays this would apply to most rooms kept clean by modern methods, and apart from the altar-cupboard in the middle, there seems no reason why a comfortable chair and a prie-dieu plus a book-case with a flat top should not prove practical; or some significant symbol such as a crucifix, Tree of Life, or whatever sums up the individual's Life-Faith might be displayed on one wall. Appropriate flowers and plants could be helpful, too. Even though our houses are lit by electricity these days, there should still be some living flame present at all prayer sessions held in this Temple. Preferably that should come from a lamp hanging above the altar, or maybe from a menorah on a stand by the South wall. Perhaps both. On the altar itself is the censer, from which the burned offering of incense arises frequently to remind the devotee of ancient customs persisting in pursuit of the same God, which has been sought under varying names and descriptions during the many millenia of our earth occupation. It is not suggested for a single second that any hallucinogenic substances should be burned. Nothing but straightforward incense, which can be obtained from any church supplier or occult shop.

In our times we have the advantage of tape-recorded music or videos to assist our reflective meditations, and a selection of these should be most carefully chosen and used at discretion. It seems obvious that such tapes must have individual appeal for the operator and should invoke appropriate moods in his/her mental and emotional makeup. Color changes by means of electric light selections are certainly possible, but these are mainly mood-modifiers and have to be regulated with extreme caution and complete certainty of effect. The needs of individuals will here again determine the selection, but in general all light changes should be gradual rather than rapid, moving upwards from the red end of the spectrum through the orange, pausing longest at the central yellow, then going through the green and blue, then via the violet back to red again. Should any special frequency be needed, it can be held for as long as required, but it is not advisable to hold either red or blue for too long a period, because red alone is likely to raise aggressive feelings, while blue for the same length of time could be depressive. Yellow on its own, however, has an equalizing effect of normality, which can be continued without noted effects in either direction.

The original writer of the Abramelim system, under the pseudonym of Abraham the Jew, strongly advised against women being allowed to embark on it unless they were virgins, but we can surely overlook this technicality in our times except to remark that they should be subject to the same obligations as their male confreres. If they should be responsible for the upbringing of children, care of elderly relatives, or some similar charge upon their capabilities, they can scarcely be expected to stop such valuable services for the sake of undergoing a psychodramatic experience that could well be deferred until some time later in life when time and opportunity might allow. Deliberately setting aside reasonable responsibilities towards fellow creatures in favor of personal spiritual ambitions will automatically render those ambitions fruitless and unattainable. This applies to both men and women alike. Obligations we owe each other should always take priority over those we think might be preferable elsewhere. Anyone supposing it would be more meritorious to meditate and pray for an hour in a Temple than to spend the same time attending a sick relative in their time of need should think otherwise. Which is the more important? To invite oneself before a Temple Presence of God, or Invite that Presence into the Temple of oneself as an act of service to a fellow mortal? There should scarcely be any argument about that point.

So the question of male or female suitability for the Abramelim Experience need not arise in our days except as to the suitability that is supposedly the same for everyone.

Assuming such to have been fulfilled up to the present point, what would be the next necessity? We are told that there should be a special costume for wearing in the Temple precincts. Need we do this nowadays? It is actually advisable to do this because it helps to emphasize the "specialness" of the occasion. Correct costuming for each specialized acitivity of our lives does assist the furtherance of that particular effort. Imagine what would happen if anyone attempted to swim in full evening dress, put out a fire in a bathing costume, or run races in a diving suit. Visualize any activity with participants wearing the most unsuitable clothing imaginable, and then state categorically why there should *not* be any proper costume for facilitating the practice of religious performances. With Western esotericism in modern times, the customary wear is a habit or hooded cassock girdled at the waist with an ordinary tasseled cord. There can be in whatever symbolic colors seem suitable for the occasion, which for Abramelim purposes would appear to be variable according to which section was being worked. Say for the first two months a black habit with white girdle, for the second period a white one with a black girdle, and for the last section a white habit with a golden or yellow girdle. That would symbolize first a state of non-knowledge bounded by hope, then a condition of pure intentions bounded by knowledge of what not to do, and lastly the same state bounded only by aspiration towards the Highest Holiness of all. At the absolutely final stage of Spirit Summoning, whatever ornaments may be considered proper can be worn, such as headdress, ring, or pectoral, signifying authority and spiritual status.

Having duly assembled all the material means of conducting the Abramelim Experience, the operator was next advised how to conduct its spiritual components. Part of this entailed abstinence from sexual intercourse during the previous four months, and we are bound to ask ourselves whether this should still apply. The natural answer is only with the full agreement and consent of one's normal sex partner. There should certainly be no casual or meaningless mating done purely for the sake of relief from bodily tensions. Only couplings caused by sheer love and joy of intimate companionship with a truly beloved being could possibly be permissible during this entire six-month period, and of course the old ban on menstruating women being allowed to share a marriage bed need not be taken seriously in our society today. In previous eras this was purely because of the belief that female menstrual blood carried a curse and would contaminate all it touched, and therefore a woman was considered unclean during her periods and accordingly slept apart from her mate at those times. It was supposed to be a lethal curse if a girl having her first period ran completely around anyone's house while dripping her blood all the way. She would have to be stark naked so that her blood fell on the bare ground. This was believed to cause sterility and death to the house owner.

So far we are more or less in agreement with the original Abramelim process, with the exception of some modifications in accordance with modernity. Now we have to see what should be done with each section of the complete six-month course of action. For the first two months a simple morning and evening prayer session was suggested, lasting about an hour on each occasion. It was especially important that the prayers should not be standardized ritual ones but come directly from the heart and soul of the suppliant on a direct Human-to-God relationship. Any form of language could be used, and words need not be chosen carefully so long as they expressed exactly what was in the mind and intentions of the speaker. Even crude phraseology or folk obscenities would be permissible, providing these were normally used by the utterer in order to emphasize or put some particular point over in the plainest terms possible. That was what really mattered. Absolute clarity and sincerity of meaning. Nothing should be concealed, excused, or euphemized. Simply stated and abided by. Nothing more.

Such a procedure is still to be recommended, providing it is done with this realization: Let it be accepted that each of us consists roughly of an Upper, Middle, and Lower self, the Upper being the best of us and closest to our concepts of Deity, the Middle being the ordinary everyday self we present to other people, while the Lower expresses the nastiest side of our natures and is therefore closest to our Devil-concepts. Maybe we might think of these as our Nice, Normal, and Naughty selves, or perhaps the Overself, Centerself, and Underself. Naturally they all blend into a Single-self, but the important thing is to see the triple condition as a three-point conception of one's own character from different yet related angles. However the state is seen, or by whatever terms it may be characterized, it has to be thought of as "The Best of Me, the Middle Me, and the Worst of Me." All can be thought of as sections of Self, like head, trunk and limbs, or any other bodily items of identity.

Having settled this triplicity question satisfactorily, it should now be determined that from henceforth all intelligent communications will be between the normal Centerself and either of its other extremities. That is to say if a Deity-concept is being invoked, the energy exchange will be from Centerself to Overself, but if a Devil-concept is addressed this will be reversed from Centerself to Underself. As an additional aid to imagination it could be directed for the former forwards and upwards, while for the latter backwards and downwards. This is purely to emphasize the contradistinction between the two ends of entity and to give symbolic meaning to the process in a rational manner.

So the proceedings might be started by the Centerself as a prayer to the Eternal Energy (represented by the Overself of the entity). After putting incense in the censer and visualizing the prayers ascending like the smoke, the suppliant could say something like:

"Listen to me O Lord of Life present in every person. I am going to evolve until I link up with you in reality and become one with your Being. I know that may take me millions of our years and countless incarnations of all kinds, but that is what I mean to do no matter how long it takes me. To reach you I shall have to expend a lot more energy than I normally have, and so I am embarking on my present plan: to procure the additional energy I need directly from the Devil—to employ those forces in my nature that have been called Evil, which alienate me from you and enslave my soul for their own purposes, so making me into fuel for the Devil's dynamos, providing him with power for working whatever wickedness he wants.

"All I need is to learn how to catch, convert, and then place all that power at your disposal, so that instead of causing Evil it will only inspire Good from me and for all my fellow-beings sharing it with me. Otherwise, I need to know in order to make the Devil work for Deity instead of himself, and I realize this must begin by altering my own nature for this particular purpose. Just show me how to make the Middle part of myself into a converter that will accept all the impulses to Evil that Satan sends me, and how to alter their character while retaining their energy so that they will serve you in myself."

Anything of this nature will do for opening the complete six-month sessions of the Abramelim Experience. The main thing is that once it has officially commenced it must be continued until the very end, whatever its eventual issue may be. That is extremely important. It is the amount of regular attention put into the proceedings that provide its power and efficacy. Unless it is seriously treated as a major life-altering episode with every expectation of its ultimate success, it cannot be anything else except a waste of time and resources. Literally, it is a course in correct conduct and ideal behavior so that the best side of oneself is afforded a chance to practice its control over spiritual situations. So it should be approached in the same spirit as if an important interview or vital examination were being prepared for. That in fact is the case, and maybe it could prove the most important of anyone's life, and in particular one which no one attempting it *dare* fail for fear of the consequences.

So throughout the whole process there should be a strong sense of gravity and responsibility in relation to what is going on. There need be no undue lack of confidence or uncertainty concerning eventual results, yet on the other hand there must be a singular feeling of committal to an absolutely vital undertaking of maximum importance: the voluntary dedication of oneself to the Cause of Cosmos, using the Deity side of one's nature empowered by the Devil-driven energies of the other. How often have we seen some natural force in action and thought," If only that amount of energy had been put to better use it could have done such and such for us!'" As for example, an enormous lightning bolt expending enough electricity to light a small town for a week. So with the energy going into Good or Evil actions. The force spent on the commission of a crime could have accomplished some alternative of value for a whole community. It is all a question of motivation and intention, which are for us alone to decide. With the Abramelim Operation, humans positively place their path on a line leading directly to Divinity.

Quite apart from any prayers or meditations during the first two months, conventional "good works" are enjoined on an operator, and these are highly advisable and should be conducted in terms of our times. We must all be familiar with the words "Faith without works is dead," and that has always been found very good counsel. The good works suggested then were mainly alms to the poor, which we may largely disregard nowadays, although if individual and deserving cases are known personally, those might certainly be supported. Mere check donations to official charities will very seldom reach anywhere near the stated beneficiaries, being mostly swallowed up by their collector's expense accounts or private pockets. There are many other types of charity in need of attention, and it might be well to remember the adage about charity beginning at home before giving money to total strangers while one's own family remain in need of care or kindness. They always deserve first consideration. Still, no opportunity of doing the proverbial good deed a day should be neglected when it presents itself.

During the second two months, usually June and July, the same procedures are to be followed except that prayer and meditation periods are somewhat prolonged and more intense. Nowadays there is no reason why appropriate music should not be played or suitable books studied. The incense is to be kept going at intervals, and so may be mild physical exercises such as chest expansions and body bending. Extreme forms of exercise, like weight-lifting and push-ups, must be avoided. Isometrics are ideal to adopt in these circumstances, while pranayama practices need not be forgotten. Scarce need to say that both smoking and drinking alcoholic beverages are strictly prohibited in the Temple, although mineral waters and fruit juices are perfectly permissible should thirst become pressing. Food, however, is not to be taken into the Temple at any time. In the original script of the ritual, great stress was laid on personal cleanliness, but no more than would be quite normal in our times.

There is considerable stress placed on the necessity for confession of personal sins at intervals during the Rite, and the reason for this is to consciously acknowledge and most of all try to understand one's own faults and failings, be-

cause those form the basis of a subsequent Devil-relation-
ship with Deity. Unless one's worst propensities can be
specified and called into mind quite clearly, there is nothing
much that can be done about them. It is the identifying and
pinpointing of every Evil characteristic in the makeup of
each human individual that is of the utmost importance in
altering them into beneficial influences. Therefore, the old
custom of examining one's conscience and confessing or
plainly acknowledging one's weakest and most offensive
propensities is of the greatest value if accurately assessed or
estimated. The Delphic injunction to KNOW THYSELF
applied to every attribute of one's individuality whether
Good or Bad, for all of us are an odd mixture of both and
need awareness from every angle. It is very important to
see such imperfections as clearly as we can, and much of the
second period might well be devoted to this purpose.

After all, there is not any real point in trying to conceal
or gloss over individual fallibilities from one's own awareness. Self-deception is purposeless when the objective is
self-knowledge. So several sessions might be spent in pinpointing one's very worst characteristics, both verbally and
on paper. It could be worthwhile to compile a carefully
thought out fault list, and so document all findings about
oneself something along these lines:

Specific Fault	Frequency	Intensity	Remarks
Thinking ill of others	2-4 per day	2-6	*often self-related*
Ill-wishing	1-4 per week	1-8	*sometimes lethal*
Ill-temper	6-12 per week	1-7	*depends on mood*
Refusal to see myself in the wrong	2-15 per month	1-10	*fear of loss of face and self-im-portance*
Self-interests always first	very frequently	9-10	*believe greatest fault*

And so forth until nothing else can be thought of. The frequency and intensity columns, of course, are much of a rough guess in order to calculate the seriousness of the failing. The remarks are recorded purely as personal opinions and as an assessment of the characteristic being examined.

Formerly such a list would have been called an examination of conscience and its headings termed sins, which gave a lot of offense to an Almighty and Omnipresent God and therefore needed sincere repentance and pleas for mercy from the sinner. Nowadays we are far more apt to call them character deficiencies, discussing them with an expensive psychiatrist who is likely to condone them and explain that they are probably due to early childhood behavior patterns such as bedwetting or repressive toilet training. Here, however, we shall be equating them with specific Demons that we are attempting to control with intensive energy. Whichever they may be, that would certainly be a good thing to do in the interests of any individual concerned, and if a psychodrama can accomplish what a psychiatrist may not, then it should definitely be taken seriously.

If there is any difficulty deciding where to start, it could be as well to do so with the Seven Deadly Sins, and these were Pride, Anger, Envy, Lust, Gluttony, Avarice, and Sloth. It should be specially noted that these are all very closely connected with the principle of Self, three being concerned with Expression, three with Acquisition, and one with Inaction. Sometimes Envy is called Covetousness. At all events Pride occupies the first position, and it was said to be the cardinal sin by which the Devil fell from Heaven. It is essentially the acme of selfishness and insists on the exaltation of Self above every other consideration. It is capable of sacrificing anything or anyone in the cause of self-interest and is utterly ruthless in its action. It will allow nothing to stand in its way that can possibly be circumvented or destroyed if necessary. It invents or postulates all kinds of excuses for its preservation—personal, family, or political honor for example, or anything likely to afford justification for its employment and expansion. Thus it encourages untruths and avoidance of conduct codes likely to impose restrictions on its impulses. It is most frequently Pride that opens the door for other types of misconduct.

Anger argues unreasoning violence and disregard of cooler counsel. It is emotional instability on a grand scale and frequently instigated by Pride. It clouds clear thinking and is a serious unbalance of mental and spiritual energies, allowing disruptive forces to upset and damage the entire equilibrium of any Selfstate. Anger is degeneration into a state of wild disruption that accomplishes nothing but harm throughout one's entire being. It is an absolute waste of otherwise valuable energy and indicates someone of irrational behavior and unpredictable conduct, and it also identifies someone who can be easily manipulated by others able to exploit this wasteful weakness.

Envy (or Covetousness) is a condition of being dissatisfied with one's own state because of comparison with those who appear more favored by fate than oneself, while at the same time not making any particular effort to obtain such supposed favors by fair and honest means. It is a form of jealousy, implying criticism of Cosmos for not providing such supplies regardless of merits or deserts. Worst of all maybe, it is one of those insidious states that continues gnawing away at one's soul until deterioration and erosion eventually weaken it to increasingly serious degrees so that it becomes damaged beyond reclamation and ultimately perishes entirely. It should be seen very well why Envy was called a deadly sin.

Lust means a lot more than over-preoccupation with sexual affairs. It is an overwhelming passion for egoistic aggrandizement absolutely regardless of results or of anyone else's feelings. A compulsive condition of "must have it at any price," which impels one towards whatever Evil may be needed to guarantee personal gain. Lust implies complete disregard for other humans, provided the personal appetite for possession is temporarily satisfied. Genuine Lust is the continual aggravation of the egoistic impulse in anyone, which constantly calls for more and more in an insatiable urge for expansion.

Gluttony is again much more than a matter of overeating. It is an old adage that people often dig their own graves with their teeth, and Gluttony is an extension of this principle into spiritual dimensions. A good example of it is found with animalcula, which constantly force food into themselves until they literally burst with the pressure and so become food for other organisms. Sheer, stupid, suicidal self-destruction by following a natural instinct to eat far beyond its utmost extremity. No opportunity is allowed for digestion and excretion, but food is piled on food until it destroys its recipient by disease or similar systemic problems. Had an adequate cycle of digestion and excretion been included in the food program, no troubles would have occurred. All this can happen on spiritual levels, too, and it is here in particular that we should try to safeguard ourselves against this particular sin.

Avarice, as the dictionary defines it, implies not only an excessive love of gain but also a miserly and mean-minded intention of holding on to possessions without the slightest intention of ever doing any good with them. An avaricious person is by nature an uncharitable one, oblivious of his or her neighbor's needs and purely concerned with his/her own acquisitions. All take and no give. This also applies in spiritual dimensions as well—when people refuse to offer support to others after having received it themselves. Avarice is not confined to material ownership, but the principle of it applies to spiritual advantages not shared with others who might be very glad of the opportunity.

Sloth is possibly the most serious sin of the lot except Pride. It signifies deliberate inaction where the provision of positive power is called for—refusal to supply needed and available activity when such might bring benefits both to self and to other souls. This is real spiritual laziness and indifference that damages a soul by default and impoverishes it through intentional rejection of opportunities for doing some necessary service in the Cosmic Cause. It applies in the case of delay and tardiness, where swift and decisive interventions are demanded, and is a refusal to recognize responsibilities in all affairs pertaining to human welfare and duties to Deity alike. Sloth is an aversion to expenditure of energy on behalf of other beings and an avoidance of offering aid to those who may need it urgently. It constantly seeks excuses for such nonintervention or for procrastination with one's own spiritual development, and altogether it deprives whoever practices it of many advantages that might otherwise be well earned.

Looking over the Seven Deadly Sins, it should be evident that they are really all one: extensions of extreme self-interest to the exclusion of every other consideration. It is their extremity and obsessional nature that constitutes the sin in the first place. Thinking about them carefully, it will be found we actually *need* a small percentage of each one in order to make any real progress possible. We must have a modicum of Pride to provide an incentive for living, enough Anger to make us indignant at all the Evils we see people suffering, enough Envy to incite us to emulate those who succeed with the labor of living, a little Lust to send us in search of what we should be looking for, just a soupçon of Gluttony to give us a taste for the indigestible things of life, sufficient Avarice to make us take care of our profits through human experience, and finally some cautious Sloth to make us pause and think things out rather than rush in carelessly and ruin everything by rash interference.

In other words, it is the uncontrolled excess of such human propensities that constitutes the sin or character fault concerned. If they are kept to controlled and calculated proportions, that percentage of them would actually count as virtues. It all depends on what controls which. That is why the Devil is often shown as a species of goat, an animal that was extremely useful and valuable if kept in full control by its owner, but a wantonly destructive beast if allowed to wander around at will—multiplying itself and eating up the environment in all directions. The whole of the Abramelim Adventure is to assert authority over the Demonic part of ourselves by means of an elaborate and influential psychodrama, and so it is essential to know exactly what that nature consists of. Hence the two full months spent on estimating and assessing it accurately will be very well spent indeed.

A tape recorder can be a great help here. Listening to oneself enumerating and detailing all the character faults observed and studied in one's own psyche can have a most salutary effect. It would also be as well to take note of what others believe are the worst personal traits. Usually close personal friends and especially spouses are only too willing to mention these, though allowances have to be made for their theories and exaggerations. Nevertheless, if a consensus of opinions seems to agree, the chances are in favor of accuracy and a careful note can be made to that effect. Obviously, those people who have known anyone intimately and for a long time, with the possible exception of mothers, are likely to make the most accurate estimates. Mothers are the least likely to find serious faults with their progeny, and that fact must always be allowed for.

It could be a good idea to write out a classified list of one's self-found feelings and read through it quickly on each occasion the Temple is visited. Sometimes an unexpected weakness may be discovered in that way. It might also be advisable to change the tape from time to time as such alterations are made. What is important is that by the end of the second two months the Abramelim adventurer should become very clearly aware of all his or her worst propensities and have them condensed down to definite headings and categories. Those familiar with the Qabbalistic Tradition might equate them with the Tree of Life system, thus confining them within a 1 to 10 scale. The earlier Christian Church had a standard method of viewing sins in relation to God, one's neighbor, or oneself. It was based on the Ten Commandments and is phrased as follows:

In relation to God

1. Have I omitted morning or evening prayers or neglected to make my daily examination of conscience? Have I prayed negligently or allowed willful distractions?
2. Have I spoken irreverently of God and holy things? Have I taken his (or her) name in vain or told untruths?
3. Have I omitted my duty through human respect or interests?
4. Have I been zealous for God's honor, virtue, justice, or truth, and reproved those who acted otherwise?
5. Have I resigned my will to God in troubles, necessities, or sickness?
6. Have I resisted thoughts of infidelity, distrust, or presumption?

In relation to my neighbor

1. Have I disobeyed my superiors or spoken against them?
2. Have I been impatient when told of my faults and made no efforts to correct them?

3. Have I offended anyone or given way to hatred, jealousy, or revenge?
4. Have I made rash judgments or spread false reports about my neighbors?
5. Have I caused discord or misunderstanding between neighbors?
6. Have I taken pleasure in vexing, mortifying, or provoking them?
7. Have I been excessive in reprimanding those under my care or negligent in giving them just reproof?
8. Have I borne with their oversights and imperfections and given good counsel?
9. Have I been solicitous for those under my charge and done my best for them?

In relation to myself

1. Have I been obstinate in following my own will in matters that are dangerous, indifferent, or scandalous?
2. Have I taken pleasure in hearing myself praised, or acted from vanity or pride?
3. Have I overindulged myself in Sloth or yielded to sensuality or impurity?
4. Has my conversation been edifying or have I been proud and troublesome?
5. Have I spent too much time in recreation at the expense of my devotions?
6. Have I yielded to intemperance, rage, impatience, or jealousy?

Many might disagree entirely with such a list and prefer one with a purely psychological background, but however the job is done, the end result has to be a neat and orderly presentation of all faults found, with one's own character related to whichever system seems preferable. The Abramelimist is quite at liberty to invent his own system if he or she prefers. Anything is allowable, providing that by the end of the fourth month a complete self-assessment is firmly impressed into the consciousness. Only when this is satisfactorily done may the operator turn attention for the last two months to the more pleasant attempt of trying to make contact with the better part of him/herself personified as his Holy Guardian Angel, or HGA.

Few instructions are given in the original script for this, apart from frequent prayers and reading edifying material, but in our times considerably more might be added. The whole tone of the Temple may become a lot brighter and more colorful by the provision of flowers and a different incense of more pleasant perfume, plus an inspiring picture or so on the walls. The music might be stylistically altered to convey cheerful and confident impressions of beneficence and well-being. Everything reasonable should be done to emphasize the change of focus from bottom to top end of oneself. Every altruistic and philanthropic instinct in the individual concerned has to be highlighted and stressed as strongly as possible. Talk-tapes that stress the presence of Deity in human beings and the attainments possible to those making earnest efforts in a Divine direction should be listened to. All the accents must be heavily laid on upliftment and beliefs that the Abramelim Adventure is designed to teach the art of commanding the Devil-side of ourselves to serve Deity by supplying the required energy to do so. Nothing less will be acceptable.

As the time gets closer to the climactic events of these proceedings, the original script advises the practitioner to obtain the services of a clairvoyant or mediumistic boy-child of approximately six, seven, or perhaps eight years old, who must not be a relative, and he should be carefully instructed in his duties beforehand. He is supposed to wear a veil of semitransparent white silk and should watch for any sign of the Angel appearing in writing on a highly polished silver plate some six inches square placed on the altar. As soon as the child becomes aware of any presence except themselves in the Temple, he is then to notify the invocant, who should be praying on his or her hands and knees or prostrate with face on the floor and veiled with black silk. Confirmation of the Angelic presence completes the child's duties, after which he is sent home. The operator should then leave and lock the Temple until the following morning.

In our times, the employment of a child for mediumistic purposes is quite unnecessary and even inadvisable. Probably the black veil could prove useful as a psychological adjunct for inhibiting the sense of sight throughout the initial stages of the ceremonial climax, and so might be the silver scrying mirror for inducing subsequent hypno-visual experiences, but both should be considered purely optional. What really matters is that the operator should steadily become more and more aware of a nobler side to his or her nature that is quite capable of redirecting the Life-energies within him/herself from their lowest to their highest forms of expression possible. By a species of spiritual alchemy, he or she is proposing to transmute the coarse lead of his or her lower nature to the finest gold of his/her highest being. Six months of his/her life are being devoted to this most magnificent of aims, and those are far too precious to risk their loss at the last moment through carelessness or other mismanagement.

Having spent the last two months in prayer and in doing good deeds in the assurance of an Angelic Higher Self, the time must surely arrive when the anticipated Day of Angelic Action is definitely decided on. When this comes, all close friends and relative must be warned that the practitioner will be incommunicado for a few days, and every reasonable precaution must be taken against intrusion or interference from any possible source. During the whole six months a careful diet should have been adhered to, and for the final two weeks or so a near fast maintained, though fruits and fluids are allowable as needed. All food should have been salt-free, and of course a nonsmoking regime observed. Should wine be taken at all, it has to be of the lightest table variety and limited to maybe a glassful.

When the actual day dawns, the Abramelimist should rise early, wash very thoroughly, and assuming ceremonial costume, enter the Temple, kindle the lamp and censer, switch on background music and visual effects if required, and then address the Creative Consciousness something as follows:

"I am not talking to the human side of me, but to that Greater Being of Whom I am but a minimal fraction. I am trying to make a better human creature out of myself so that your Infinite Identity will also be improved to that extent. Therefore I am attempting here to become more clearly conscious of my superior spiritual self which can come into closest contact with you. So I am asking you to increase my awareness not only of that selfstate, but most especially with it, so that I shall know for certain what you mean inside my mind and with my limited intelligence. Let me feel and experience the actuality of my connection with you, so that this becomes as an advisory Angel guiding me in the golden way of goodness and guarding me against all adversaries and Satanically set snares. I will wait with patience while you work with Power inside my individuality."

Whereupon the speaker should sit or kneel and concentrate on increasing a sense of Overself and the reality of its Angelic nature. To some extent this is accomplished in a comparable fashion as an actor would create a characterization before expressing it on stage. One has to imagine the sort of being which, if tempted towards some malicious course of action, would say in effect: "Thank you very much for your offer. Now let us take the energy you are proposing to employ for that purpose and put it into altogether dif-

122 / Between Good and Evil

ferent uses for much better and more kindly actions." This might be said with a gentle smile at the thought of Demons being exploited for Divine doings, yet that would be nothing more than plain justice, since such was exactly what they would have done with Divine energy had they succeeded with their original proposition. Guardian Angels have to be intelligent and knowledgeable beings quite capable of coping with Demonic entities of equal or sometimes superior intelligence.

All the old and time-honored techniques of "God Assumption" can be used here. In ancient Temple practice a trained priest or priestess would be taught to "Assume the God" (or Goddess) by characterizing the Deity invoked in the hope that Its reality would indeed "possess" them to the extent of uttering Its guidance through their mouths, impressing Its nature into their beings for the benefit of worshippers awaiting such contacts. To this day the custom persists, with mediums intending to present the personality of some dead relative, or with the Christian practice of intentional communion with the actual Spirit of Jesus Christ. This Angelic Assumption is only a variation of the same practice for a similar purpose, and so may be made by the same means assisted by any modern improvements.

In the old days, "Personifying the God" was relatively simple. Each Deity had a characteristic appearance, manners, and appropriate accouterments. For example, in Egypt, any priestess wishing to produce Bast had only to put on a cat mask, carry a basket in one hand and a sistrum in the other, speak with a meowing voice while moving in a feline style, and everyone would recognize Bast immediately. All Gods and Goddesses each had their own particular specialities. Here, however, we are dealing not so much with externalities as with invisible and internal qualities that are nevertheless perceptible to those encountering them on Inner levels of Life. So they have to be made evident by presentation of personality, style of speech, tone of voice, and maybe movement and body behavior. All these have to be altered even subtly or suggestively in some way that will characterize one's individual Guardian Angel.

During many previous meditations the prevailing thought should have been: "What would my Holy Guardian Angel look like if it were perceptible to my sight?" and a clear picture built up piece by piece in the mind. Reasons should have been worked out for everything. Why the hair and eye coloring should be as they are, or the face male or female. All the different mannerisms and vocal peculiarities ought to have been observed and accounted for, while every single one of them must be imitable by the Abramelimist. In other words, a workable Telesmic Image made of the sort of self that is aimed at as an alter ego of Angelic potential, which sums up and surpasses every good quality and ability of the operator.

After all, this is something we are doing subconsciously all our lives. Building up the sort of personality we present to others as an aspect of our Real Selves, which we conceal behind this screen for our own purposes. Humans very seldom show very much of this Real Self to each other, or even acknowledge it to themselves if they can avoid doing so. What is more, they may develop several different personalities for presentation to different circles. The family person can be very different from the professional one, and another may be reserved for ordinary social occasions. It may take many years to manufacture sufficient personalities to suit all the areas of their appearance or to blend them into a common consortium for universal acceptance. Here the practitioner is being asked to produce an idealized image of the Self he or she would wish to be on Angelic levels of life, and then "assume it" to the closest state of identity possible.

For us, identities are associated with names, and it is

extremely important that our HGA identities should have some special and appropriate name to be invoked or addressed by when being related with consciously. Preferably this name should be communicated to the inquirer by the Angel itself. This could occur during the early stages of the ceremony or be thought of and bestowed on its Image by the adventurer at any later stage of the proceedings. Perhaps it could come from a flash of inspiration or a direct contact with the "Spirit World" from whence such Telesmics derive. At all events it has to come from *somewhere* to provide the closest possible connection between the individual and the ideal image identifying him (or her). Once known, that name has to be closely guarded and communicated to no other living creature whatsoever, being used only for the purpose of summoning the Intelligence it properly belongs to.

If there is some specific appurtenance that is uniquely associated with the character being created, then it should be provided and used accordingly. For example, as most of the Egyptian Gods are pictured as holding some implement indicative of their nature, so might an HGA have a similar symbol such as a lamp (for enlightenment), a magnetic compass (for guidance), or whatever portrays its most important characteristic. This could be a plain staff (for support), but whatever it is, the object should be practically or symbolically available during the ceremony and used in a believable way. A conventional staff is usually of plain ash or almond wood some six feet high or measured to the top of the operator's head, and it is normally kept in the South quarter of the Temple, stuck upright in some special holder.

Should an artist be capable of painting an idealized portrait of the Angelic face required, be willing and able to do so, that would indeed be a valuable accessory to hang on the West wall of the Temple for unveiling at the right moment. Failing this, the operator's own face—suitably made up with costume to match—could be photographed in full color and size to be hung there instead. This is not an essential refinement at all, but more in the way of being a luxury addition to an adequate Temple. A substitute for this would be a plain mirror permitting full facial view when unveiled. Under no circumstances should any costume for this purpose be depicted with wings or unsuitable additions of any kind.

Assuming the ritual has progressed to the point where the HGA is being personified by the operator and the moment for identification has arrived (which can only be decided by the operator when everything feels exactly right for the happening), a bell or gong should be sounded very firmly and deeply (any family or others likely to hear it should be warned in advance) and the chosen or revealed name of the HGA intoned loudly several times, and an open invitation made to come and make itself manifest in its offered vehicle, i.e., the operator's own body. The mirror or picture should be unveiled and viewed, and a transference should be steadily imagined as taking place between the represented external Image and its interior reality, which is being built up by the exchange of consciousness between the Image and its Abramelimistic acceptor. Free gestures of welcome and embrace may be made while the various characteristics of the HGA are adopted one by one. First the stance and gait, then the general movement, and lastly the voice and speech, which should vary a fair degree from the normal tone used. It is suggested that the Angelic voice be somewhat lower and slower than the one in common use, and even a slight touch of an accent could be permissible, although this must be one admired by the operator.

When the operator is in the character of the Abramelimist, he or she must be addressed by some familiar name that only someone very close to him or her would employ, and this ought to be the very first word the personified

HGA utters audibly. The operator responds with his or her own voice, answering the HGA by name and giving some conventional greeting, to which a reply is received in characterized style. This initial attempt at communication with one's "Better Self" should not be kept going too long, and once the operator is satisfied that contact has definitely been established between his/her ordinary level of life and the best side of him/herself, further development of the contact should be left for the following day. After a period of meditation on what has passed, the Temple should be closed for the remainder of the day, with the lamp left burning.

It is necessary to explain here that creating an entirely false and secondary personality is definitely *not* the purpose of this ritualized "Angel Assumption." The idea is to focus and give meaning to something that is already there in the operator and only calling for more open and conscious expression. In one sense it is a genetic inheritance from our farthest past being concentrated for guidance in our present position, and hopefully for our future as well. The entire purpose of this elaborate and long-lasting ritual is to enhance the value of such a Self-side by giving it a definite form of expression and a means of communication. Very often small children invent imaginary playmates who influence them a great deal with what they supposedly say. They are actually projections of the child's intelligence into fields not normally open to them. The Abramelim process we are concerned with here is an advanced extension of exactly the same childhood game played in a very adult manner.

Now we come to a somewhat tricky problem. What if the "Higher Self," HGA, or whatever else the superior part of anyone may be called, should justify the Jungian theory and be of the opposite sexual nature to that of its human hosts? The Anima and Animus postulation of Jung's was scarcely a new one in his day, and stories of Guardian Angels having sexual characteristics opposite to their charges are of great antiquity. Every human soul should have qualities generally found in the opposite sex. For example, males are usually predominant in physically expressive traits, such as brutality or bravery, magnanimity or meanness, etc., while females specialize in psychically evident ones such as cleverness or cunning, intuition or indifference, although such is not an exact criterion. Nevertheless, it seems relatively certain that specific faults are either typically masculine or feminine, and since we need correction in our opposite directions it is most likely that the HGA of any human would be biased towards the complementary sex of our worst and most prevalent faults.

Thus the thing to do when summing up the fault list during the preceding part of the ceremony is to make an educated guess at the probable sex of the invited HGA. For instance, a male full of typically masculine faults will definitely *need* a feminine HGA to act as his "Better Self," while a female with equally feminine faults would need a masculine type of HGA in her case. Conversely, if the situation were reversed and it were the male showing up feminine weaknesses, a masculine Animus would be the answer there. So a major value of the time spent on faultfinding during the earlier stages of the Abramelim Adventure is to assist in determining which sex the HGA should be.

In the event of this being the opposite sex to the Abramelimist, there would be no need to arrange a sort of transvestite act, but the supporting symbols might be altered to a cup or bowl instead of a staff, a lighter tone of voice employed, another scent substituted, and a more suitable style of mannerisms adopted. So the final decision as to whether a male or female type of HGA is most appropriate must definitely be made before the assumption of its form is attempted.

After initial contact has been made with the HGA and a little practice gained, there may be a very odd sense of "otherness" experienced in relation to the HGA and oneself. While being perfectly aware that all the verbal communications spoken with an assumed voice are coming through one's own brain and mouth, it will seem that these words are really being inspired from another source entirely, and one is simply acting as a "relay" for them. At first it will probably be difficult to keep consciousness "tuned" to the correct harmonic, but with persistence this will eventually improve and clarify. *One especial point must be emphatically warned against:* Under no circumstances should the operator demand answers to purely material questions, such as how large sums of money are to be gained, when anyone is likely to die, how to make vast profits in the business world, and similar queries. Such inquiries would break the tenuous contact forthwith by their very nature, since they do not come from the purely spiritual part of oneself but solely from the lower side of a human being, which the entire Abramelim Experience is intended to transcend. Thus the very asking of purely material questions would be in itself a complete denial of the entire principles on which this ritual is based in the first place.

Therefore, this highly important section of what might be called "Getting to Know Your Guardian Angel" has to be taken in a very understanding spirit. Its central theme must be confined to the topic of dealing with Demons, or the control of the Lower Self by the Higher Self. These two will necessarily meet in the Centerself, which mediates them both and acts as a kind of transformer through which the massive low-tension energies of the Demons can be converted into the specialized high-tension currents needed by Angelic agencies for their spiritual purposes. Thoughts concerning this process should be carefully considered and queried during this preliminary discussion with the HGA (or one's Overself) and the ordinary Centerself. Both these aspects of the same individual should appear as distinct and autonomous beings with their own stories to tell.

This is accomplished by Centerself doing most of the talking, though a good deal of the time is taken up by listening in silence to what the HGA is communicating. The method is to start audibly and vocally as that character and then lower the volume until the voice becomes fainter and almost inaudible, while simultaneously becoming correspondingly louder in the head so that as the spoken word ceases, the mentally heard message continues at the same level. Some practice will be needed at this, but it can be developed until there is no longer any necessity to commence aloud, though a few audible words occasionally are advisable. Notes should be taken of salient points arising during such meditations, and it is also important to use the designated names of the HGA and the Abramelimist fairly frequently so as to impress them both on the Centerself as deeply as possible.

After the initial three-day session with the HGA it will be time to confront the Devils on their own ground and command their obedience. The original script advises first giving instructions to the Devils as to what forms they should appear under. This was presumably to allow the operator's imagination opportunity for constructing those images. After that, those Devil-forms were told which order to appear in before an open window of the Temple, which looked out on a verandah the Demons were supposed to remain upon. The operator was then instructed to reach through that window with one end of his long staff, and the Devil present was ordered to lay one hand (or claw) on the staff and swear an oath of obedience to the Deity as given. Since the staff is a symbolic substitute for the phallus, such an oath would be taken in the traditional Hebrew way on what was believed to be the "Fount of Life" itself, and therefore binding by everything held sacred amongst even the most Evil of entities. This could be considered an unnecessarily dramatic gesture, but since this is a legitimate psychodrama it may as well be played to its curtain line as well as possible.

Therefore, if it could be arranged to have a projector handy that would throw a picture of each particular Fiend at the same spot on the Temple wall as its type-name is called, so much the better, but the important thing is to hold them clearly in the mind's eye, which can be done quite well without the projector once their names and functions are known. The idea behind the Abramelim Project was that sins or failings can be classified into definite divisions having major and minor categories, each under the heading of some specified Fiend. Therefore, the thing to do is call them to consciousness one after the other in their order of seniority, and make it perfectly plain that they have met their human match at last—one who refuses to obey their wicked wills any longer, so rebelling against them as they were supposed to have rebelled against God; and furthermore, one who is devoting the rest of his/her life to an extension of this determination, and therefore they might as well go back to serving God again themselves through him (or her).

As a substitute for a projector with Demon pictures, the twelve different names may be written fairly large on anything that is movable with the end of a staff and the entire contrivance fixed to some point on the Northern wall. Perhaps a circular disc with the names written in sequence, so as to appear in line with a display-slot cut in its cover when its protruding edge is moved by the staff. Anything of that nature will serve well enough, and on the first day only the major four Evil Entities are invoked.

Once the Temple is activated and the HGA is believed present, the operator in the character of his Centerself commands the principal Fiend to appear. After several summons have been given audibly and commandingly, the name of LUCIFER may be made visible and his attention presumed present. The Bearer of Light being Darkness, it is taken as the symbol of non-illumination, which in this case represents willful ignorance or refusal to be enlightened. Such is counted as the most serious of sins since it signifies an *intentional* ignorance and complete rejection of knowledge that might otherwise have advanced reasonable human beings to points a lot closer to perfection than those we occupy at present. The old proverb about none being so blind as those who won't see applies here. So, after carefully considering the probable degree of lost Life-learning caused by this particular Fiend, the operator addresses it as if it were present in person and says something like:

*"LUCIFER, you have prevented me enough times from learning something that could have been vital for my spiritual welfare. From now on, I am going to look for Light in the deepest of Darkness until I find it there. You are not going to stand between me and my enlightenment any longer. . . (*here name the HGA*). . . forbids you to obstruct me in my search for Truth and Wisdom. So stand aside and let me learn what will be well for me to know. Swear on my staff that you will not obscure my spiritual sense of sight again."*

At this point the operator places the end of his or her staff firmly on the name or picture of Lucifer and is supposed to hear the possibly reluctant reply of "I do so swear," or words to that effect. Then the name is altered to that of the second Chief Fiend, when he has to hear an appropriate admonition, which might be:

"LEVIATHAN, you monstrous Serpent-Dragon of the Deep, responsible for all the sins of sexual misbehavior and the Evils that accompany humankind's misuse of what they mean. Denier of the Laws of Love, and blasphemous Being who makes a mockery of all our finest feelings and our most tender thoughts. I will not listen

any longer to your wicked words. Keep your filth and obscene meanings to yourself and bother me no more with beastliness and bad behavior. Sex is something sacred to me, which I only share with very special souls whom I can love and trust with all my heart. Therefore trouble me no more while. . . (HGA's name). . . commands you to deliver up your energy through me unto the Deity we both belong with. Swear this on my staff which represents my procreative power." Here the swearing symbology is gone through again and the name altered accordingly.

With the Chief Fiend of Satan, we encounter the adversary, or the activator, of enmity between everyone alive and the source of whatever makes humankind antagonistic towards its own species or towards other objectives that might prove beneficial to us. Here we have the author of the Hate-principle itself, and so a Fiend to subdue especially. He is the Archetype of whatever goes wrong in life, being the Opponent of Order and Chief Companion of Chaos. An admonition to him could run something on this style:

"SATAN, you especial Adversary of all that is of God and Good, listen very carefully to what I say to you. I, . . . (here give personal name). . . rebel against your rule as you were said to have denied our common Deity. I hereby refuse to serve you any longer in the slightest way, nor make contributions to your Cause that I am conscious of. Whatever hold that you might have upon my purely human nature I will break by every means at my disposal. . . (HGA's Name). . . instructs my Overself in holy matters that will liberate me into LIGHT and so deny you any right to use me for your Evil purposes. I solemnly renounce all Hate with its antagonisms, and I will espouse the Laws of Life and Love alone. Swear upon my staff that you will help instead of hinder me, and let the energy you would have wasted on my personal damnation become blessed by conversion into something that could save us both by ultimately unifying us with the Lord our God."

It is certainly permissible to imagine the Fiends' raising objections to every adjuration and arguing why they should do no such thing as helping any human, but in the end they have to submit, though not necessarily with any particular grace or signs of goodwill. Following the reluctant submission of SATAN, the last of the Major Fiends is summoned. He is BELIAL, the Wicked One.

He represents human inclinations to employ the principles of Evil for the sake of material gains and is possibly the most powerful persuader of them all. It has been said that the love of money is the root of all Evil, which may not be entirely true but is certainly so in a very large proportion of instances; here this adage is identified with the Archfiend Belial, who points out that abandonment of Evil can result in a considerable drop in profits, or probably bankruptcy itself and permanent poverty of a most unpleasant kind. Souls strong enough to resist his smooth sales talk might well reply something in this fashion:

"BELIAL, you who betrays humankind by trading on our weaknesses and exploiting our endeavors to enrich ourselves from all the natural resources of our world, here is one single soul who will not sell himself (or herself) to spiritual slavery within your supermarket, nor yet be caught by your extremely clever claws that reach out to trap me in the meshes of your nasty network. I can discern the difference between dishonest dealings and a fair return for what we have to do to earn our livelihoods upon this earth. So much we are entitled to by all our laws, and I intend to stay within the legitimate limits of my occupation. I will resist your bribes and blandishments to trade with trickery or gain by guile. I believe in honest working for a reasonable and just return for what I do, and I shall refuse enrichment from all doubtful dealings or from criminal commercial conduct. Swear on this staff that you will cease to trouble me with your temptations and so serve the God who gave me . . . (HGA's Name). . . to guide my conduct and safeguard my seekings."

After such an assurance has been received, however hesitatingly, the four Archfiends will have been duly dealt with. They are regarded as being the real roots of all Evil, and they amount to Intentional Ignorance, Senseless Sex, Hurtful Hatred, and Regardless Riches. These destructive energies, it might be remarked, are more closely connected with personal power in this material world at the cost of every principle and ethic governing the good conduct of humankind. That corroborates the Buddhist dictum of "Where there is Self there is no Truth, and where there is Truth there is no Self," although this depends on the exact understanding of "Self." With Buddhism the mere separation of individual spirits from the Primal Power of Cosmic Creation constitutes a Self, whereas Wesoterics tend to see it at distinct levels of manifestation, each with its specific meaning and function. Here we have been dealing exclusively with the control of Underself by Overself through the medium of Centerself via a personification of an alter ego, or Telesmic Holy Guardian Angel, composed of all the best and finest propensities that an aspiring individual may muster in his or her own character.

Subsequent to the summoning of the Four Archetypal Fiends, the Abramelimist should remain an hour or so in the Temple talking to them mentally or audibly, reiterating his or her reasons for dealing so directly with them. Frequent appeals may be made by name to the HGA, who is considered as communicating via the Centerself with the Underself location from whence the Fiends forgather and focus their attention on the human concerned.

After a complete day's encounter with the Principal Evil Spirits and a good night's rest, the following day should be devoted to summoning the so-called Eight Sub-Princes. It might be supposed that having coped with the Chief Devils should be sufficient for controlling the lesser ones, which are believed to be obedient to their superiors, but this extra step is taken purely as a sensible enhancement and implementation of the first. These Sub-Princes are the nominal controllers of what might be termed second-class sins. Propensities that, if persisted in, are likely to lead towards the more serious offenses governed by the first category of Fiends. We are told this subsidiary class of Spirits consists of:

ORIENS, or SAMAEL, which is also written as URIENS, meaning to burn or devour with flame, and ARITON—to delay, hinder, or retard. Both of these associate with LU-CIFER and imply wastage and idolatry. They encourage interest and preoccupation with those spiritual areas that obscure vision of important truths, and that prevent perception of those vital clues that might enable their investigators to perceive fresh light on their paths to Liberation. The next pair are:

ASHTAROTH, meaning assemblies or crowds, and PAIMON, also called AZAZEL, which signifies a goat and implies sexuality and promiscuity. These obviously link up with LEVIATHAN and sexual excesses, or abuse of procreative power. They distract the seeking mind from dealing with Deity by filling it with suggestive thoughts of sex indulgence and desire for inclusion with the "vulgar crowd," from which little that is good may be obtained. Following these come:

BEELZEBUB, the Lord of Flies and Prince of Pests, and ASMODEE, to destroy and exterminate. These clearly connect with SATAN the Adversary, since they encourage destruction, hatred, and whatever may be antipathetic to humankind. Flies are like ill intentions sent to harm and hurt whomever they land on, and they lay their Evil eggs under the skin to hatch later and cause calamities. The last two are:

MAGOT, literally meaning small stones or pebbles, but traditionally, a spirit presiding over buried treasure; and AMAIMON, connected with MAMMON, the God of Money. These clearly associate with BELIAL, the Demon of

Dishonesty and profit gained through peculative practices. Both of these Sub-Princes fill the mind with matters of money and illicit means of making it through theft, drug dealing, crooked gambling, or racket running of any kind.

It should be noticed that this last class of Spirit are those who influence the thoughts of humans, rather than the ones who add that last impulse that impels Evil thinking into Evil doing. That fatal impulse is believed to be given by the Four Archfiends themselves. Nevertheless, it is these Sub-Princes who prepare and condition the consciousness up to the point where it only needs a last decisive touch to rouse its readiness into reality. Unless the Sub-Princes had done their work thoroughly in the first place, the Archfiends could scarcely have expected such a relatively simple subjection to their suggestions. Therefore these particular Devils need to be dealt with very carefully on their special levels of influence. If this can be coped with successfully, the incidence of Evil activities in our world may be reduced considerably.

So once the Temple is ready for action on the penultimate day of its Abramelim employment, the operator should invoke the presence of the HGA and proceed to call the foregoing Eight Spirits into consciousness by the same process as previously, and exact the same oath of obedience demanded of the Four Archfiends. Whether pictures or just plain names are used, this may be produced by any simple mechanism worked by remote control. Each of the Eight has to be addressed individually, their understood functions specified and admonished accordingly, and finally their oaths of obedience exacted after reminders that their Superiors have been sworn likewise, so there are no grounds for complaint by any of them.

After the conventional hour's time spent with these Spirits in the Temple following the oathtaking, the operator should then close it and return the next and final day for the ceremony of what was called "Licensing the Spirits to Depart," and lastly, thanksgiving for the successful conclusion of the whole course. Such are quite normal courtesies that should be extended to any entity, whether human or otherwise. All should be summoned by name, thanked for their attention, and bidden to depart in due order. That is, all except the HGA, who should receive special thanks and be asked to remain in touch with the operator for the rest of his or her life to warn of approaching spiritual dangers, or to avert them if possible. The operator should agree never to summon the HGA by name for any trivial or frivolous reason, but only in cases of genuine necessity. This need not apply to regular sessions of contact and consultation, which might be held weekly in the Temple, and at which anything significant can be discussed freely.

Finally, it would be well to offer ultimate thanks and gratitude to the Supreme Spirit of Life Itself, which caused all this action by Its control of Cosmos and in whose service the Adventure was undertaken. After this is duly done, the ashes in the censer can be scattered on the ground, the Demonic names burned and buried or their pictures put away somewhere they are not likely to be found unintentionally, and the Temple tidied up in general. Lastly, the exhausted but hopefully triumphant operator can sit down comfortably and consider just what he or she has gained from the whole experience.

First, he or she demonstrated by undergoing the entire Adventure that he/she truly realizes the importance of controlling the worst side of him/herself by calling on the best of his/her nature. By using psychodrama to stimulate such a process and put it into practice, he/she *has consciously and intentionally* examined all his/her weaknesses and character deficiencies, acknowledged them, and categorized them by associating them with specific Fiends of recognized and described natures. Those Fiends *per se* may be mythical, but the human faults they stand for are most regrettably real. Refusal to learn from Life, misuse of sex, engenderment of hatred and antipathy, plus the avaricious amassing of money for its own sake because of the social power and position this entails, are all still accountable for the serious Evils we find amongst human beings in all ages. So to call such propensities the Four Archfiends is purely a convenience of consciousness that can be extended to other and less dangerous areas of action. Hence the Sub-Princes, which are the incitements to Evil prior to its actual commission.

Again, personifying and naming one's own "Upperself" as a Holy Guardian Angel is a valuable psychological device for dealing with our undoubted "Devil-drives." Having done this successfully means that with a single code word we can summon everything best in ourselves to cope with Evil and pernicious propensities. That is factually the only way our humanity as a whole has advanced itself over the millenia of our earth occupation: by choosing between Good and Evil, deciding in favor of the former while using the energy of the latter to facilitate the process. The usual difficulty encountered is bringing intentional awareness to bear during specific situations. If that can be done usefully with a single and simple word, that is surely more than a step in the right direction.

Maybe most of all, the individual who has completed the Abramelim course of consciousness has altered him/herself into an energy-converter dedicated to the cause of Deity rather than Devils. That makes him/her into a resistance for the force-flow of Evil, yet a conductor for that of Good. The nearest analogy for this would be an electrical rectifier, which accepts an alternating current input and converts the output into a direct current flow of straightforward positive and negative polarities. It accomplishes such a conversion by permitting only a one-way passage for each half-cycle of electrical energy and allowing them to accumulate at the two opposite poles provided. Thus all the positive half-cycles follow each other in rapid succession towards one pole while their negative complementary half-cycles do the same towards the other. If Good is associated with Right and Evil with Left, then the "righteous" human being is one who sorts them out into their respective channels and lives in a state of spiritual balance between them.

It is this change of Selfstate during the Abramelim Adventure that is of major importance to the individual. Providing that the necessary dedication and attention has been devoted to the undertaking, no one is likely to end in the same state of consciousness they commenced it with. What is relatively surprising are the remarkably few accounts given of actual performances of the ritual itself. Those that have appeared in print seem very ambiguous and somewhat uncertain, and among many occultists the Abramelim Rite has rather a bad name as an unfortunate affair, liable to bring bad luck upon its practitioners and those within their close circles. There is no solid evidence to show how such conclusions could have been arrived at, apart from hints that Fiends might not care for humans who have the temerity to defy them, and therefore would cause such rebels as much trouble as they possibly could. Nevertheless, the more likely explanation is that the Rite must have been imperfectly understood or performed, treated casually, or otherwise mismanaged. Humans have an undisputed right to reject Evil impulses in their own natures that even the worst of Devils would recognize, and the adage that we are never tempted beyond our ability to resist seems to be the sticking point of Fiendish influence—the limits of human endurance.

Just as unendurable pain causes an automatic loss of consciousness and hence cessation of pain, so would overly strong temptation result in refusal to accept it because of obvious impossibility. For example, it would be futile tempting an elderly and arthritic person to achieve an armed bank robbery, however much they might be inclined to the idea. Temptations have to be within the capabilities of those concerned, and seeing that the majority of temptations arise from within oneself or in agreement with some other human being's suggestions, sufficient self-effort can quite well contradict them. Any Self that has experienced the disciplined devotion demanded by the full Abramelim Ritual should be self-conditioned to withstand very heavy spiritual pressures indeed. That may well be the main benefit obtained from the whole operation. The end result should be a strengthened and stabilized soul fully capable of coping with Fiends, from whichever class of consciousness they may come and pour their poison into extended etheric ears. However, if anything goes wrong and they obtain mastery over the operator during the encounter, exactly the opposite would occur, and a much more sophisticated and efficient Evildoer would emerge to swell the ranks of the Wicked Ones. There is always that risk to consider.

Chapter Six

DESTRUCTION OR DELIVERANCE?

Humanity has always been fascinated by and especially drawn to the possibility of its own destruction. Evidence of this may be encountered everywhere. About the earliest incidence traceable is the fable of Atlantis, in which an entire island continent was supposed to have become so wicked that a fantastic flood overwhelmed it in a few days. Whether that was a race memory, or a built-in warning of what could happen today within minutes is uncertain, yet nevertheless a very deep impression of disaster has been made on human awareness as a whole. Mortals always find their maximum focus as identities when they feel most threatened with the loss of themselves. It is the imminence of death that makes our consciousness of life clearest.

From the religious angle, which were the most popular types of sermon? Those depicting the somewhat insipid delights of Heaven, or those describing in detail the horrors of Hell and sufferings of those souls therein? Which news items attract most media attention, the good or the bad? Inevitably the worst news sells the most papers, as every editor knows. There was once an American owner of a minor paper who became so tired of constant calamities in the press that he said to himself, "There MUST be something good happening *somewhere* in this wretched world. In the future I'll look for that and only publish good and helpful things in my paper. That ought to encourage people to buy it." He did so, but went bankrupt after a steady drift of readers of his unique paper went back to the old alarmist but sales-conscious styles of journalism.

The normal human need for a God of any definition makes it necessary to postulate a Devil as a complementary concept. In fact, it cannot be possible to posit either without implying the other automatically. The principle of Good without an equal Evil is just not admissible. Each makes the other's existence not only believable but also meaningful. The ideal course to follow is obviously a central line between the two until they become indistinguishable from each other and eventually merge into a single course of conduct at the end of our evolution. That may take millions of our years, but we have little option in the matter except to facilitate the process as best we can by being aware of it and implementing its arrival by any practical means available to us.

If we stop to consider that every one of us was once an intention of our parents to have sexual intercourse and that such regressive behavior reaches back to the earliest possible epochs of our evolution, we will be forced to admit that intentions alone are responsible for not only humankind but for all biological species. Without them we would not exist at all, and if we extrapolate them into our problematical future we can probably see our species extending to other inhabitable planets in some altogether different solar systems. The question here is, would we take our Gods and

Devils with us, or leave them behind as forgotten fragments of an outworn folk-faith unfit to be perpetuated elsewhere than on this old earth?

As imperfect humans we would have to take both concepts with us in whatever form they had reached by that remote period. It makes no difference to their actual natures, however they might be termed in any human language. They are, and will always remain, the opposite ends of the same energy that enables us to be the separate Selves we are apart from the Infinite Identity we are becoming. We can depersonalize or attenuate those principles as much as we like, disguise or camouflage them by any conceivable means, yet we cannot possibly eliminate them from our natures until they unify as a single Principle of Power supplying the spiritual strength of everyone's existence as a whole Concerted Consciousness. So we are stuck with our division of the Lifeforce into the end alternatives of Deity and Devil for a long time yet.

Of those alternatives it seems to be the Devil that appeals mostly to human nature, probably because his declared characteristics come closer to us than those of God. Briefly, there is more evidence of the Devil in us than there appears to be of God. Think of the various countries that have been founded on rebellion against established rulership, or the many religions that have arisen for the same reasons. Esoteric legend shows the Devil as an ARCH-REBEL because he was said to have disagreed with the virtual dictatorship of God as an Absolute Authority, and so was ejected from Heaven together with his supporting Angels. Whereas he fell to our earth with them and exerted an authority on his own account, hoping that humans would obey him as he had disobeyed the Omniscient One, because they had done the same as himself in the Garden of Eden. Most humans were willing to hear his ideas when these agreed with what they wanted to do anyway, and they certainly supplied him with enough energy to maintain himself in the guise of a Fiend Figure who is prepared to pillage the entire earth for his self-support, offering his faithful followers a percentage of the profits as a payment for services sold. Naturally those who seriously believed their wealth and social status derived from this anti-God ally were quite prepared to set up altars and acts of worship in his honor. Anything in exchange for ambitious advantage.

Whatever personifies or presents the worst of ourselves in some excusable or comprehensible light will undoubtedly prove a most popular creation, as every author, cartoonist, or playwright knows. Villains and wrongdoers are usually a lot more interesting than virtuous and upright types. When Fiends are portrayed as comical characters they become almost lovable creatures, especially if they are taken advantage of or made to look foolish by self-righteous or pious people. This age especially is that of the anti-hero who becomes the protagonist of most modern dramas. Art, music, and literature alike combine to offer us a cult of the Antithesis to whatever was formerly regarded as good, noble, or commendable conduct in human beings. We are being told to believe that people perpetrating the most fiendish atrocities on their fellow mortals for totally inadequate reasons are only psychologically sick souls deserving our kindly sympathy and a rest-cure in comfortable and secure mental institutions. Politicians who would cheerfully murder millions of ordinary citizens at almost the drop of a hat are held up to us as defenders of faith and morals, which few people believe in anyway. We are supposed to be too stupid to see that their real motives would be in support of a failing financial system or in concealing its impending collapse. Arms sales are so profitable that controllable wars must be kept going at virtually any cost to human lives and well-being.

There need be little or no doubt that humankind is

being quite deliberately manipulated by its conscious controllers in the direction of what we have been calling the Devil, namely our worst propensities. Seldom in our previous history have these inclinations been so encouraged or catered to by every commercial enterprise, including that of crime and antisocial interests. Take for example the curious craving for self-destruction mainly among juvenile males. This of course derives from an inherited instinct to limit our species within survivable stocks of the best-bred humans. Therefore young males fight to determine those who will be the fathers of the future race, which the winners must propagate. Among human herds this cannot lead to anything except wars of some kind, whether literal and physical, or substitutes confined to competition in other areas, which of course is far preferable to the first frightful proposition. Nevertheless, this produces football and sports violence at one end of the scale and financial fraud or drug dealing at the other.

Then again, consider our almost abnormal preoccupation with "horror" movies and video recordings portraying every possible combination of circumstances likely to terrify, affront, or otherwise stir the fears and revulsions of ordinary humans beyond their normal boundaries. Only the extent of the wildest imaginations sets any limit to the storylines of these productions. Why should these have become so lucrative and profitable a proposition both to producers and suppliers in recent times? There can be only one real reason: the desperate need for emotional arousal, which nothing but the most shocking and surprising stimuli are likely to evoke from modern humankind.

It is a sad fact, but one of the most serious symptoms of psychosis happens to be a phenomenal loss of emotional feeling or soul-sensations. Subjects may be intellectually quite well aware of what their reactions should be to applied stimuli, yet actually experience absolutely nothing of that nature whatsoever in their own sensoria. It is as if they were suffering from a species of spiritual anesthesia during which the only experience possible is one of helplessness and inability either to make any sense of themselves or to discern much significant meaning in any direction. Even though inner alarm bells may be ringing very clearly in their consciousness, they literally cannot account for their condition or take any practical steps to free themselves from it.

On more than one occasion sufferers from such states in mental institutions have been known to inflict severe physical injuries upon themselves purely for the temporary relief that pain affords. At least it assures them of being alive and proves they are not completely unaware of experiencing their existence. In other words, pain *means* something to them that they are able to relate with as an individual entity. Without meaning life would be senseless, and it is this constant search for meaning and purpose that supplies life with any solid dimension at all. If pain should be the only hope of producing an actual experience, then that must be the last resort against the senselessness of living without feeling.

That, of course, is an absolute extreme of such an unfortunate mental condition, but minor degrees of it are widely prevalent in present-day circumstances. It is becoming increasingly difficult to obtain adequate emotional reactions from modern Western people, far more so than in former times. This is possibly due to the genetic effects of World Wars, plus the constant pressures placed on everyone from all angles, which results in increased resistance from constant overexposure. The fact remains that we do not feel as keenly and intensely as our forebears did, and so to arouse anything like a similar degree of feeling we commonly need some stimulus that touches our consciousness a lot more deeply and closely than it might have done in previous periods.

Since sex and violence (S and V) come more closely to the emotional area of most humans, dealing as they do with the extremities of Birth and Death, those factors have an almost instant entrance to our intentional awareness. They account for continued interest in the Bible for so many centuries, and for the perpetuation of our mythologies dealing with Gods and Devils, since the former are considered creative while the latter are destructive. Normally, humans have an attraction to Life and an aversion from Death, but both are very powerful emotional feelings and are quite capable of reversal according to attitude. Dr. Johnson was perfectly correct when he made his celebrated remark that "Nothing concentrates a man's mind quite so much as knowing that he is going to die at eight o'clock the following morning." He meant that the imminence of judicial execution intensified awareness to an amazing extent.

To a lesser, yet definitely perceptible degree, such is precisely the effect that horrifying and frightening tales have on dulled and blunted senses. They sharpen the mind by sheer force of the fright they are supposed to evoke in the emotions of their audience. This has to be done by shock, since sustained and unvarying application of a terror-stimulus will eventually lose its impact and reduce it to minimum effect. Hence the necessity of making horror movies according to the stylized system of a short and severe shock following a long buildup of uncertainty and suspense. Anyone querying this should take a still photograph from the most frightening sequence of the film and view it for some time while noticing the diminution of its emotional effect. Part of this will be due to visual fatigue and lack of interest because of non-movement, but most of the "fall-off" is a normal product of familiarity breeding contempt.

So the apparent recent increase of interest in horror movies is mainly due to desensitized emotional abilities that require much more drastic stimuli than formerly in order to evoke a reaction. In fact, such a need has always existed while we have been on earth, but our modern means of satisfying it have not been available until the present period. The important question arising is whether "horror viewing" counts as a good or bad experience. Some would say its effect was definitely Evil since it suggests and stimulates such types of thinking in people's minds, which is likely to lead them towards the practice of Evil in reality. This agrees with the idea that thoughts and words are just as wicked as deeds on their own equivalent levels. Conversely, however, it might be considered that the ultimate effect was Good, since having experienced the happenings in the mind already, that could act as a catharsis which would obviate their intrusion into our realms of reality. That is to say, the fictional experience would "get it out of the system," thus preventing any practical performance of the story substituted for the incidents it deals with. Now which of these possibilities appears most likely?

The answer must depend entirely on the type of individual concerned and the class of consciousness connnected with the storyline selected. In one case it would be a matter of accepting the story as a series of suggestions to be followed up with projections of it into enjoyable or interesting experiences; yet with another, the story would be retained on purely mental levels and not allowed to project past the point of imagery into practicality, since it had served its purpose on its own levels. In other words, the homeopathic scheme of using Demons to exorcise Demons is applied. Nevertheless, such treatment depends, as homeopathy does, on minimal treatment and selection of a proper topic. A constant diet of unrestricted horror-stimuli for its own sake is apt to be self-defeating and do more harm than good. Everything depends on who controls what. If humans control the horrors, all is well, but if the horrors control the humans, then God help everyone.

A psychiatrist who was once asked to define the difference between sanity and madness replied to this effect: "It's purely a question of control. Everybody gets impulses to do the most desperate things. Steal, lie, break things up, ill-treat other humans and animals, even murder. That's quite normal. Most people tell themselves not to behave in such an antisocial way and don't. Some individuals, however, can't bear the pressure of those impulses any more and give way to them. That's madness, which is really just loss of self-control, and which may be purely temporary or might be a lifelong affair." It has often been said that the dividing line between sanity and madness is only a hairbreadth in thickness, and that seems to be a fair estimate. Some years previously the aforementioned psychiatrist would have been a priest describing temptations of the Devil, yet unable to say how these might be resisted except by prayers and the grace of God. The psychiatrist, of course, would claim that the Demons were in reality projections of the individual's own inhibitions that needed constructive channeling into alternative expressions. There is no difference except for the way that two men visualize the same truth.

Seeing a truth of any kind is not enough. The observer also has to know what to do with it or how it might be applied for any practical purpose. Here the question is how to gain control of specific spiritual situations. What can be done in order to recondition one's self-awareness into taking command of whatever has escaped from the area of obedience and asserted authority? In other words, to free oneself from unwanted compulsions or restrain one's runaway Devils. Some years ago the late Aleister Crowley worked out a fairly simple system for regulating and controlling his dangerous cocaine habit until he freed himself from it for a considerable period. Whether it would work for anyone else as well as it did for him is a moot point, but it is certainly worth a thought or so in case it can be applied to other areas.

All his system required was first the determination to follow it faithfully for at least a month, keeping a small notebook carried on the person to record the doses and the times at which they were taken plus the real reason for taking them. This last item was vitally important. Under no circumstances must some inadequate remark like: "Because I felt like it" be made. Sufficient time had to be taken for genuine self-analysis and a satisfactory answer. For instance, it would be permissible to write: "Overcome by compulsion because of watering eyes, trembling hands and severe aches in shoulders. Urgent relief necessary from anxiety and severity of withdrawal symptoms." Never must a fresh dose be taken without a small self-inquisition being undergone. There must *always* be some very definite and cogent reason behind each usage of the drug and the circumstances of its ingestion recorded. Here is an extract from Crowley's unpublished diary of 1923 concerning his drug taking:

"I've averaged about three grains of heroin daily since about Oct. 1922 with two short breaks. Friday went to bed about 3 p.m. Vomiting and diarrhea. Complete loss of power in sphincter ani. Dyspnea. Became delirious but under control of will. Slept uneasily at intervals. Treatment inhalation of ether almost continuously. Fifteen grains Luminol. No solid food since lunch. Vomited.

"Saturday. In bed all day. Thoughts gradually gaining form at intervals. Control of sphincter ani still absent but delirium under greater control. Dyspnea worse. Treatment Luminol ten grains and occasional inhalation of ether. Twenty minims of laudanum. It is perhaps a mistake. Food, sweet biscuits and coffee.

"Sunday. Woke early very hungry. All day in bed very tired but mental condition practically normal. Sphincter ani recovering tone. Dyspnea less. Treatment as before but running short of ether so took one dose of heroin. Ate heartily and champagne with dinner. Spasm of coughing towards midnight. More vomiting.

"Monday. Slept from 1 p.m. till 6:30 very calmly and deeply. Woke fresh and strong. No craving. All functions in perfect order. No tendency to dyspnea. Went out and paddled before lunch. In high spirits and full energy. I feel ten years younger."

It will be noted that he described symptoms carefully and what he did to deal with them, but it is perhaps somewhat sad to read his eventual conclusion later in the year: "I am more certain than ever that cocaine is no good under any conditions at all unless in very small doses and very few of them. This prolongs my agony and turns me into a dull, prolix, word cobbler. It was good to get up at 1:05 a.m., I having stopped taking cocaine at 12 and not having taken it at all regularly." Although Crowley could check, control, and even stop himself from taking drugs for considerable periods by his notebook method, he never quite abandoned the habit and died as a registered drug addict, obtaining then-legitimate "maintenance" doses directly from his National Health doctors.

Despite that, his booking system is quite a valid method of behavior control, providing it is practiced properly. First of all, it imposes a voluntary series of conduct checks as a condition for achieving the intended objective. The time has to be checked in order to determine how long it has been since the last occasion. Next there has to be a confrontation with oneself and some genuine justification, not an excuse, sought for indulging in the practice or pursuit indicated. Lastly it must be agreed that the entire responsibility for allowing the action to take place is assumed by the Self in full knowledge of the deleterious effects likely to result. Only when all these conditions are satisfied should the final fulfillment be allowable.

This literally forces the intelligent focal part of the mind to deal directly with the compulsion and admit that although the habit has a bad effect on the individual concerned, it is still being permitted for the sake of some temporary euphoria or other desired emotional experience. That in itself challenges and questions the consciousness, which is knowingly damaging its own vehicle to a possibly serious extent. The simple fact that the book is being used as intended proves that some degree of control is still possible, so in theory it could be increased and extended until it completely covers the life-area now concerned. The book itself is solid and incontrovertible evidence that at least an intention of control exists and has been applied. So it should only be a matter of advancing that control a few notches further.

The next step is to say firmly to oneself: "This will happen when *I* say it can, but not when *it* demands." Then check the time lapses between average doses or occurrences and deliberately extend the period for maybe an hour, making sure to take the calculatedly reduced dose at exactly the specified moment. No sooner or later. This move imposes an intentional control on time and quantity of the objective, which naturally should be recorded in the little book and extended perhaps a trifle longer with each passing day. Providing this can be persisted with, it should come to a point where complete cancellation is possible or a more suitable substitute introduced at an acceptable rate that will eventually replace the original propensity objected to. We do not like being totally deprived of our Devils, as a rule, unless a satisfactory substitute can be found such as methadone for morphine, or a strong peppermint instead of a cigarette.

Humans have always sought soporific, euphoric, hallucinogenic, or mood-altering substances capable of suppressing or changing mental attitudes by chemical means.

However, using these substances is seldom possible without doing any damage to the physical and nervous systems, and some of them can be serious or even lethal, especially with modern synthetic drugs. Most people are now aware of the fatal results obtained from mixing alcohol with barbiturates, yet there must be extremely few folk who have not experimented with some form of consciousness-changing material during the course of their lives, even if it was only with our earliest intoxicant, alcohol. In previous centuries alcohol was often described as the Demon of Drink, and rightly so because it released inhibitions that might have restrained humans from publicly exhibiting the very worst side of their natures, which sometimes resulted in mayhem and murder. Such an extremity, however, was typical amongst naturally coarse and uncultured folk, unaccustomed to exercising much control over themselves in normal times. In the case of people born of cultured stock, excess of alcohol usually caused erratic behavior, confusion of consciousness, and all sorts of stupid and irresponsible activities during which almost anything of an embarassing, painful, or absurd occurrence could happen. Drink is one of our oldest and most difficult of Demons to deal with, although strictly speaking drink itself is not the Demon, but the compulsion to continue imbibing a long way past the danger point. That is where the real Demon hides.

Why, for instance, would any reasonable being want to ingest chemical consciousness-confusers that upset the balance of a mind, fill the awareness with false images, and otherwise obscure clear thinking plus damage the health in the bargain? What is more, the human in question knows perfectly well what will happen yet selects such a course of action in preference to a saner and more sober one. There has to be some very adequate accounting for what would otherwise seem to be insane and self-destructive conduct. There can be only one answer explaining this peculiar problem: sufficient dissatisfaction with one's own Selfstate that urgently demands a substitute condition of consciousness, regardless of how this is obtained or at what cost.

The facts of the matter are that the individual concerned has considered his or her current condition of consciousness and found it so unspeakably unacceptable or actively hostile to all his/her hopes or aspirations that he/she would do absolutely anything to alter it as quickly as possible for even a temporary semblance of something better. To be brutally blunt, his/her focal experience of life as he/she has to face it in this world disappoints and disquiets him/her so much and so deeply that he/she will go to almost any lengths in seeking some antidote that affords only temporary relief from what seems like permanent pressures. It is a classic case of "Needs must when the Devil drives," and it seems as if humans are doomed to enslavement by the Devils of their own choice from whatever category they may be drawn. Yet humans may be dominated by religious or idealistic factors that might be just as damaging if allowed to get out of control. Deity is possibly the most dangerous of all drugs if we judge by the behavior of some "Fundamentalist" faiths at work in our world.

Marx was making a good guess when he compared religion to an opium dream, but he could not have calculated its effects when compared with other drugs he would not have known about in his time, such as LSD or "angel dust." His opium comparison referred to the type of people who are well aware of the social wrongs and injustices of this world and their own miserable conditions within that framework, who understandably invent a religion with a Deity Father-Figure that will put everything right for them in a Heavenly Afterlife, where they will be rewarded for their wretched earth lives with all the happiness they never had here. What is more, those wicked people who made them suffer while they were alive will be made to suffer themselves for such sins in the most horrible of Hells. A sort of tit-for-tat religion that satisfies a very simplistic desire for equal distribution of earnings among all humans so that everyone gets what they deserve in the end. Perhaps it was small wonder the cultured Romans considered Christianity to be the religion of slaves, since it would have its greatest appeal for those of slave mentality who hoped to have the rich and powerful humbled and impoverished, while they themselves were pampered and made prosperous in a hypothetical Heavenworld after death released them from servitude in this one.

Such might have been an opium-inspired sort of Faith, but what of others inspired by altogether different ideals? Marx's own concept of Communism, for example, which abolished official religion of any kind and replaced it with revolution followed by a standard social system based on state control of all resources, including education, and obligatory indoctrination in a purely political ideology that extolled the socialist system alone while condemning all others as inferior and outworn. In effect, Marxist Communism was and still is a social discipline replacing ancient God-concepts with idealized humanity. Since his time it has become a substitute religion in its own right, since it has all the characteristics of conventional religions except for requirements to believe in any supernatural suppositions whatever, including soul-survival subsequent to bodily death. Nevertheless, orthodox Communism has had to make considerable concessions in that respect on account of its many Moslem adherents, who would be most unwilling to abandon their hopes of Heaven with its highly sensual delights.

The prophet Mohammed having seen and understood the disadvantages of alcoholic intoxication, strictly forbade any of his faithful followers to imbibe any of it at all during their earth lives. Yet he was clever enough to encourage drinking after death in a paradise that was one long enjoy-ment of everything imaginable without stint. It was a vast pleasure garden wherein the faithful might indulge them-selves in every sensual practice they pleased. Special wine would be served by obliging long-haired boys, which heightened pleasure to peak points without any headaches afterwards. Gauze-clad girls would offer themselves for sexual services, though the boys would also oblige if re-quested. In fact, the general idea of a typically Muslim Heaven sounded very much like an eternal fornicatory frolic. Except for the men's wives, of course, who were only allowed in on sufferance and acceptance of subservient status. There need be no doubt of male dominance in the Muslim afterlife. To a certain extent this compared with the Nordic idea of fighting and killing each other all day, and then being restored to life by a magic cauldron in order to carouse and caress all night in Valhalla. Never a dull mo-ment there, but who could stand the pace except the most battle-hardened warrior?

Few people would disagree with the historical fact that amazing amounts of Evil have been inflicted by humans on each other ostensibly in the name of religion, though most probably to conceal some much more material motive such as plain greed or profit-making. Sometimes it might really be due to racial differences, but if these could be concealed under a cloak of hypocritical piety, then that would sound a lot better in the ears of believers who want to accept the reputed authority of their Deity for what they were ordered to do by Its appointed officers on earth. Most of modern humankind has outgrown suggestion like that in our times, though there are still those who would readily be stirred to war by the call for a Jihad, or Holy War, directed against some declared infidel. Most modern people of our times, however, are prepared to accept political principles instead of pretending the Deity instructed them to massacre their fellow mortals. Nevertheless, there are still plenty of people left in this world believing that their Deity authorizes them to treat others in very unkind ways. Sometimes they come to such strange conclusions it would be difficult to decide whether this inspiration came from Deity or the Devil.

Perhaps it is best to believe that *both* factors in ourselves need careful controlling if we are ever to evolve into a superior state of spiritual being. Not only the Evil end of ourselves needs to be disciplined and kept within definite boundaries, but it is also highly important that the opposite end of Good should be regulated to match so that poise is maintained as perfectly as possible. The image to bear in mind should be the swinging pendulum of a long case clock with the Devil at the bottom, Deity at the top, Good on the right hand, and Evil on the left. The life-course of the individual concerned is from bottom to top of this mechanism. It should be noticed that the amplitude, or physical distance travelled by the bob, or weight at the bottom, is greatest at its own end and least of all at the top extremity. That means the maximum and most evident movement comes at the lowest or Devil's end of the pendulum, while the minimum motion becomes less and less perceptible at its top extremity. If pushed past that point by the imagination, there has to be a purely hypothetical limit of complete stillness whereat no movement at all occurs.

In order to keep the pendulum swinging perfectly, the applied impulses must be maintained with exactly equal force and rhythm in both directions. This means that when the bob has swung as far as it can to the right and the force of gravity begins returning it centrally, an impulse must stroke its top right-hand side so that the swing to bottom left will be of equal amplitude to the preceding one, and so on. The whole of this action makes a sound mechanical illustration of how to live when motivated by two opposing influences. Take a median line as an ideal course with the energies on either side. Apply them equally and regularly to each side of the median line in sequence, and so continue for as long as need be.

It might be supposed from this that our lives should be a series of consecutive Good and Evil deeds deliberately done to balance each other, but such would *not* be an accurate interpretation. We are dealing with their energy rather than with their nature, and that is the consideration we have to keep in mind. The Lifeforce we are trying to analyze here is ONE, yet it may be applied as a polarized Power to a neutral medium just as individual sperms, either male or female, will determine the sex of a fertilized egg. In the case of our pendulum analogy, we had an exhibition of those three distinct factors in operation. First the neutral of gravity maintaining the median line, then the Deity influence impelling from the right to make the pendulum move leftwards until the counterblow comes from that direction by the Devil-drive, and so the action continues. Theologically it is as if we were being batted between Deity and the Devil like a tennis ball, so that our souls remain with whichever struck last, prior to our deaths terminating the game.

That might have been a good analogy if we were indeed inanimate tennis balls knocked from one side to the other of a net marking the dividing line between Good and Evil. We are nothing of the sort, being living organisms with a will of our own if we care to use it. What we must realize, however, is that since both Deity and Devil are the same identical Spirit in ourselves, speaking from opposite corners as it were, we are bound to listen to them and then decide what action to take and, more importantly, why to take it. At first thought it might seem rather insane to postulate a Supreme Spirit that appears to be a total contradiction of consciousness within Itself, and yet if we think this process through properly, it will be seen that this is exactly what energy amounts to in any means of manifestation.

As itself, energy has to be polarized Power—a flow of force through any field from one extremity to the other and so on in a cyclic continuum. We are here concerning ourselves with the Lifeforce that animates all living creatures, causes consciousness, and is steadily evolving our species towards whatever may be our peak point of development. Now in order to accomplish this directly and, more importantly, *correctly,* It must expose every portion of Itself to the passage of Its Power for as long as it may be necessary to achieve Its entire aims. We ourselves as human beings are individual items (or atoms if that sounds better), which as a whole comprise the field through which that Lifeforce flows, affecting each of us accordingly. We in turn have our effect on It depending on our reactions to Its passage. This will modify Its character by maybe an absolute minimal degree, which nevertheless has a correspondingly altered influence on subsequent human generations, and so the process of perfection continues.

The point here is that total consciousness involves all types of awareness, graded from the most primitive and instinctive of urges to the highest and holiest aspirations of all, plus combinations from every level, forming categories and classes of consciousness by themselves. By and large this polarizes into pro- and anti-perfection awareness, or the anabolic process of building up, sustaining, and enhancing Life, and its opposite katabolic one of breaking down, disintegrating, and negating everything back to components from which fresh combinations may be formed endlessly as Life goes on. Those are the polarities of Life, and they contain what might be called our Mystical Metabolism by which we are in the constant process of being taken apart and put back together again, so that we may exist as separate Selves within the Single Spiritual Self we are becoming. If we consider this carefully and see this Lifeforce as a single Spirit of polarized power, denoted as the Deity of our anabolic extremity on one side and the Devil of our katalysis on the other, we should see clearly enough their interdependence and functional unity.

We can recognize this Lifesystem working perfectly well in our own bodies. A simple intake and output affair with our existence balanced between them. Food and drink in, converted to energy, effete matter excreted; and there is another cycle completed and ready to be recommenced. Each half-cycle is absolutely essential to the other and could not exist if unable to complete itself. Imagine what would happen if either were absent. Total input with no outlet would kill the subject with toxic excess, and with the reverse by wastage and malnutrition. Stuffed to death or starved to death makes little difference if the objective is death itself. It is only the healthy balance between the two that makes a pleasant existence possible, and if this can be accepted in the case of one single human being, it should surely be conceivable in that of a Cosmic Phenomenon in whose "image and likeness" we were reputedly designed.

So why it should have been considered shocking or surprising to suppose that our Deity has a nasty side to Its nature (just as we have) and is attempting to alter this (just as we should), and is factually accomplishing such a transformation *through us*, is rather puzzling. We have had all the hints and pointers towards this conclusion for a very long time, yet confronting such a disquieting fact seemed too terrible a truth for coping with consciously. We dared not impute to Deity any of the Evils we were trying to eliminate from our own natures. For any theologian to imply that God could sin would be more than wicked and blasphemous, it would seem unthinkably impossible—rather like suggesting ice for central heating or using gasoline to extinguish a fire. Furthermore, if it was slander to impugn a fellow mortal, what would it amount to in the case of a God, and what condign punishment might it merit?

Such an attitude did not always exist, and it seems peculiar to the Judeo-Christian beliefs. In prior periods most people who believed in God-concepts of any kind saw them as Powers from whence either Good or Evil might emerge as they intended. Sometimes worshippers saw a Superspirit that was neutral and above both Good or Evil, which came from a lesser spiritual level altogether from whence relatively minor Deities attended to the malignity and beneficence of human beings. Those qualities of character were seen as being entirely in ourselves, while the function of the Gods was to exploit or utilize them as they felt inclined. Some very sophisticated systems, such as Buddhism, did not accept Deities or Devils at all, but attributed everything to the natural law of cause and effect (or action and reaction), which they called Karma. This worked quite automatically with Good and Evil until all actions had been compensated for and brought to a final conclusion at the end of Existence.

All these and many other methods are justifiable ways of regarding the principles of Good and Evil as related with we humans, who experience them for ourselves on earth mostly at the hands of other humans. So really, this overview of seeing Deity and Devil as opposite ends, or polarities, of the same Spirit should not seem so very strange when we look on each other in the same light. What might be noted especially is the evolution of both Good and Evil themselves during the course of our conscious centuries. As our abilities in their fields of action expanded and grew, so did the symbolic Figures that represent their realities keep pace with their progress until they reached their present proportions. From a relatively minor and irritating Fiend starting as a Serpent-Figure, our Devil-concept has developed into a truly terrifying threat of doom and destruction wielding every lethal weapon and artifice he has taught us how to construct. The serpent did not so much represent real wis-

dom as cunning and know-how, or in modern terms, technology without the ability of controlling its application. Our
Deity-concept, which began as an Almighty Parental Power,
seems on the other hand to have metamorphosed into a
somewhat doubtful Being of hesitant holiness and apolo-
getic appearance trying to find plausible excuses for Its own
existence. In other words, we have constructed a far more
believable Devil than we have consciously arrived at a con-
ceivably convincing Deity. Evil has become a lot more evident than Good.

This is probably because we are at last beginning to
appreciate the necessity for what we know as Evil on our
earth, and that all we can do about it practically is alter its
form and adapt with it as painlessly as possible, until eventually it becomes more bearable and we shall at last comprehend its place and purpose amongst us. We might even
discover how to make good use of it and convert it to our
advantage. Looking at Life from an overall angle it is easy to
see how it conforms with the "eat or be eaten" principle of
one living species absorbing another in order to survive.
Most of what we think of as our natural Evils arise from this
source, although strictly speaking they are not Evils in the
true sense of the word, but anti-Life occurrences that hurt
humans very badly. Misfortunes they certainly are, such as
famine, fire, floods, pestilence, and all ecological accidents
like poisoning, being eaten by carnivorous creatures,
drowning, falling from heights or being crushed by rock-
falls, dying from diseases, or any cause that insurance com-
panies describe with surprising accuracy as "acts of God."
Whenever a life-species threatens to overbreed and become
too numerous, some natural cause usually intervenes to cut
down their birth rate by disease, famine, or should all else
fail, plain warfare among the excess population. All such
events or human activities arising in connection therewith
could be considered as arising directly from the Ecology of

Existence to which even Deity must defer. It is not from this category of consciousness, however, that the absolute extremes of antipathy to humans and other forms of Life arises.

They derive from the depths of what might be called anti-Life, in which opposition to any form of Life whatsoever is so intense that not even a solitary cell could exist for a single second if it ever gained access to such an undiluted condition of contra-consciousness. Imagine an aversion to evolutionary existence that is so extreme that it would if possible put the whole process into reverse and "roll it back," so to speak, until total extinction occurred beyond the slightest hope of ever repeating it. This has nothing to do with ordinary death at all, during which individual cells are reprocessed prior to rebirth otherwise. It has to do with the elimination of Life *per se* throughout the entire Cosmos. Which accounts for the marked absence of Life as we know it on other planets in our solar system, or for that matter anywhere else our interstellar probes have reached so far.

Little to nothing is known about this anti-Life force apart from inferential awareness. Sometimes looking cynically on our human race and considering what it has done to this planet, one is tempted to think that whatever might be against our existence would have a lot of justification and plenty of very sound reasons. Moreover, if there should be any kind of intelligence behind the actual workings of anti-Life, it would have particular reason to be concerned with us at this period of our history, when we are clearly within a mere century or so before we shall be able to export our species starwards in search of another planet to infest. Can we be prevented in time? Will anti-Life be able to avert our exit from this world towards another to wreck as we are doing with our present one? That test is something we shall shortly have to face, and it could mean the continuation of our human race or the cancellation of it altogether. Which? Only history can possibly hold the final answer.

So what exactly is this mysterious anti-Life factor? It is certainly not identical with the Satan-Devil who is but a vague reflection of it concurrently with humanity. By our standards, anti-Life is aeons older than our solar system and is a Principle rather than a Power. Perhaps it could be called Infinite Inertia, or even Counter-Creation. Theosophists might think of it as Pralaya, that state of Nonbeing or "Divine Death" into which the whole of Creation collapses at the End of Everything. Although anti-Life cannot truthfully be called Evil, it is definitely a contra-condition we have to struggle against in order to live at all. So let us spare some thoughts for something that neither God, Satan, nor ourselves is likely to survive in the ultra long run.

Chapter Seven

THE ANTI-LIFE ENIGMA

Anti-Life is an ultimate factor that "outdevils the Devil" in the sense that it is not concerned with active Evil *per se*, but only insofar as enough of it might result in the total elimination of all Life everywhere and restoration of the original state of the Universe. So far as we humans are concerned, anti-Life is not so much our intentional enemy as that we are the deliberate violators and disturbers of its lifeless, inchoate, and utterly unconscious condition of Chaos prior to the presumed pronunciation of those fatal words: LET THERE BE LIFE. Since then on this planet, we have become the principal opponent of Chaos, altering everything, ravaging resources, scarring the earth's surface with every sign of our polluting presence, multiplying like microbes, and acting like an invading disease spreading the sickness of our society wherever we go. Ordinary animals Chaos might have coped with grudgingly, but as a species of them humanity was just too much to tolerate. Humans would have to be eliminated. Had humankind known about and taken the advice given to Alice in Wonderland to "Leave *it* alone and then it will leave *you* alone," things might have been manageable, but humanity was a born meddler. Humans would interfere everywhere with everything. By our attachment to the principle of Order, we automatically obliged Chaos to become our eternal opponent, and subsequently Satan acted as its spiritual agent on the levels of our Inner lives.

One way or another most humans have been oddly aware of this invisible "Enemy" since they have been making efforts in this world. Somehow it seemed to interpose its influence between them and whatever they were trying to do so that things went wrong. The one activity it appeared to help them with was war. Humans were the only animals willing to fight organized wars that resulted in considerable death tolls, mainly among young and fertile males, which naturally reduced the population pressure. People were also beginning to suspect that the same agency was responsible for much of the contagions that wiped out so many of them with diseases. Sooner or later they became perfectly certain that some mysterious entity coexisting with them in conditions they could not comprehend was determined to destroy them if it could.

Eventually, humans, being the sort of creatures we are, came to realize that the abilities and effects of our unseen Enemy were not unlimited, and to some extent could be countered by sufficient resistance on our part. So in the end we settled down to an uneasy relationship of conflicting consciousness. We had discovered the pro-Life spiritual ally whom we designated our Deity by all manner of names, while at the same time Its anti-Life antagonist became titled with many different meanings; but the Greeks, who had a word for almost everything, came up in Hesiod's time with the term Chaos, which meant a condition of total disorder to be understood simply as "Space." Not just "Nothing" by itself, but more in the sense of "Meaninglessness," or "Non-arrangement." Theoretically Chaos was supposed to be the residual remains of a previous Creation, out of which our present one was being constructed by the Creative Consciousness using Its pro-Life powers. Put another way, Deity reincarnating Itself for another period of Manifestation. The point at issue here is that true Chaos appears to be the condition that everything would assume if it were not for the imposition of Creative Intention upon it. The opposite state of Cosmos—or Order, Intentional Arrangement, and Meaning—is simply Chaos reversed, or what happens following a fiat of Divine Direction.

The difference between Cosmos and Chaos can be illustrated in a few moments with the aid of an old unwanted china cup. A cracked one will serve admirably. Take such an object, look at it and think something like: "This is a cup that is a useful container for fluids that are to be drunk. If it were not for cups we would have to drink like animals or from our hollowed hands. So they have a lot of purpose for us because of their shape, size, and material. Now I am about to alter all that." Here put the cup on the floor and tread on it firmly once or twice, then look at the resultant mess, continuing to think: "What am I looking at now? A meaningless mess of a few chaotic fragments. There is no longer any use in them. I have destroyed a china cup. Wait! All I have destroyed in fact is a china copy of the cup-idea. Unless I could eradicate every single idea of a cup from the consciousness of every living individual, plus every pictorial or written reference to cups in the whole of our world, I could never destroy that cup or anything else. It is the Idea that is immortal, and as long as that exists, so will an expressed objective representing it. The Idea is always the reality of anything—and everyone."

It could be interesting at this point to consider that

such a commonplace breaking of a household vessel, normally a drinking glass, is a solemn ceremonial act at the end of a conventional Jewish wedding. By it the bridegroom declares symbolically that should he prove false to his marital obligations then may God break him as he has just broken this man-made vessel. Practically he has reduced a perfectly formed and useful object to a chaotic mass of useless fragments—Cosmos to Chaos in a split second—which also demonstrates that what has taken time and effort to construct can be destroyed in less than moments. Maybe a reminder of a human lifetime measured against the magnitude of a Directing Deity. Or perhaps a cynical observation on the fragility of human promises. Certainly a clear demonstration of how Chaos inevitably overcomes Cosmos at the End of Everything.

Now although Chaos in and of itself is scarcely Evil, because that with Good must essentially associate with *Intention,* Evilworkers with an ability to take advantage of Chaos are in a position to cause a great deal more trouble among their fellow mortals than others. To see this point, it is only necessary to ask ourselves which international terrorists could do the most damage to a community—those with hand grenades or those with a small H-bomb? There can scarcely be any argument here, and in fact any nuclear weapon *is* a practical presentation of Chaos. Still, we need not look quite so far in order to see Chaos in action. Since it means disintegration, we have only to glance almost anywhere to observe that in plenty. Maybe as close as an elderly relative, falling leaves, a plant in winter, a rusty nail. A disordered desk. Any sign of decay.

Strictly speaking, Chaos amounts to the natural tendency of all things to fall apart if they are not maintained by an equal or additional rate of Cosmic construction. In an ideal state of Existence, the two energies would equal each other to keep Being in perfect balance. This would mean for example that as each individual died another would be born to replace them, which as we know, does not happen in real life. Consequently our world has become a very overpopulated place that only some kind of drastic destruction or heroic measures are likely to redress. It is more than probable that the present increase of homosexuality among young males is due to an instinctive urge arising in them that acts as a warning against excessive breeding. They are born with an inherited knowledge that once their numbers increase past a certain point they are certain to be slaughtered one way or another. Therefore the only possibility of keeping the population under anything like control is reduced reproduction. That is only possible by two main methods: (a) abstention from sexual practices, and (b) confining sexual practices to infertile channels. Since course (a) is obviously impractical except for an extremely small minority, that leaves course (b), which includes intercourse between heterosexuals using contraceptive methods in which there is always a slight risk of pregnancy, or else between homosexuals in which there is no possible risk of reproduction whatever. It should be remembered, though, that there are risks of venereal disease with all types of intercourse.

Homosexuality on a large scale could be classed as a Chaos phenomenon, since it implies the deterioration and breakdown of natural order among humanity. It can scarcely be classed as an Evil *per se* unless a deliberate intention of harming anyone is involved. Although it is symbolically Satanic on account of its anal connection as a receptacle for the spermatic Life-fluid, that symbolism is invalidated if other forms of connection are used. There is a true story told of an American sergeant who was court-martialled for the military crime of sodomy and awarded a stiff and brutal sentence, then was asked formally if he had anything to say against it. The man simply indicated his rows of medal ribbons and said quietly, "My country gave me these for killing men I didn't even know. Now it gives me fifteen years imprisonment for loving just one man I knew very well and cared a lot about. I only want to know one thing: WHY?" That question has never been answered satisfactorily.

It is purely the almost automatic linkage between Chaos as a disintegrative influence on life and the physical function of excretion that brings the Devil into the picture at all. Our concepts of Cosmos and Chaos are not identical with those of our Deity and Devil or Good and Evil, although they are to a great extent parallels along much larger and longer lines altogether. Our organic and intelligent type of life is only one single phenomenon within the multimanifestation of energy we consider our Universe. Cosmos and Chaos are, so to speak, our "outside" factors at the very edges of what we believe constitutes our Existence, and they are for us complementary Counterforces—Cosmos keeping everything together and Chaos taking it apart. "Inside" them as it were, come concepts closer to ourselves that we see as Entitized Energies of Deity and Devil connected with what we know as the principles of Good and Evil.

It is one thing to think about such almost unbelievable energies from a philosophical and abstract viewpoint, yet quite another to appreciate and realize in a practical manner exactly what they mean to people in ordinary terms. For making personal relationships, the best thing is to think: "Cosmos is the Energy that keeps me together as the individual I am, while Chaos is the lack of it that lets me drift downwards into primordial pieces." We are probably familiar with the commonplace phrase: "He let himself go all to pieces" or the injunction, "Pull yourself together." Almost as if anyone were made of many parts joined together by elastic that could be tightened or loosened at will. Such a mechanical supposition makes an excellent illustration of the Cosmos-Chaos condition as applied to an ordinary human. The pivotal point between the two principles is Intentional Focus.

This is experienced by first imagining oneself as consisting of many loose parts connected together by elastic cords of consciousness in a condition of easy tension considered normal. Then apply the "pull yourself together" technique by focusing awareness as sharply and keenly as possible at the front of the brain. It should feel almost like a physical "snap" as everything seems to come together in a concentrated point of power. Next do the "going to pieces" process by relaxing the focus and tension so that everything seems to flow from the back of the brain into a helpless heap of incoordination. If possible, assist the output acceleration by feeling and accelerating it with intention. Repeat the cycle rhythmically for several efforts. This combined exercise may supply only a simulated experience of the Cosmos-Chaos concept, but it will at least be a practical participation with the actuality.

It is now only necessary to imagine what would happen if the influence of Chaos reached a much higher potential than that of Cosmos. A continual leakage and loss of a steadily deteriorating Lifeforce beyond reach of recovery by immediate Cosmic ability. At usual levels of disintegration the katabolized end-effects of Creation are caught and put back into circulation as it were by commencing currents of Cosmos. We can easily see the normal process for ourselves in our own environmental ecology, especially in the workings of any good sewage farm where the wastes and poisons of urban humanity are converted to the chemical constituents on which so much of future farming depends. If on the other hand the Chaos current responsible for keeping the balance of Life within reasonable bounds on our earth were to suddenly exceed its flow by an abnormal amount, then we should be in serious trouble.

Let us take the illustration of our world being like a reservoir with two connecting pipes. One pouring fluid in (Cosmos) and the other letting it out again (Chaos). So long as those two conduits are kept in reasonable balance with each other the state of the reservoir will be reasonable too. Should either of them fail notably in function, however, the condition of the reservoir will be badly affected. Either its resources would be drained away before replacement became possible, or an oversupply of of unusable additions would be poured into this planet unexpectedly and unallowed for. Since we live on so many different levels of consciousness and culture, such an unbalanced condition could apply on some or any of those levels to the ultimate detriment of all. In recent years one special factor has entered our environment that already has, and for the future most probably will, increase the Cosmic-Chaos discrepancy. This novelty is nuclear energy.

Although this phenomenon has always been with us to a natural extent, it is now here to an unnatural one ever since it became possible as a man-made effect. Nor do we know for an absolute certainty what its long-term effects are likely to be. We can make some educated guesses that its genetic and associated health hazards will not be favorable— with forecasts of increasing cancers, birth deformities, and as yet unknown horrifying threats to our Existence on this earth. So far, nobody seems to have made any sound speculations concerning the spiritual ramifications of increasing the presence of nuclear energy amongst us, but these are unlikely to be beneficial. From immediate observation it would seem that all our worldwide nuclear experimentation appears to have connected us closer to the Chaos factor than we should be, and if present trends continue at the same rate we shall be heading for some most unpleasant happenings in our future history.

Just as the civilization of humans on this earth has been

marked by definite "Ages" indicating special stages of technological progress, such as the Stone Age, the Bronze Age, the Iron Age and so forth, we should bear in mind that during the last century we have entered several of those Ages simultaneously. For example: the Motor Age, the Air Age, the Plastic Age, the Computer Age, the Electronic Age, and the Nuclear Age. Never have we entered so many Ages in so brief a period, and there might be some doubt concerning which could claim priority of place for nominating our current era. However, if that dubious honor should go to whichever could claim a maximum effect on the most human lives, it would have to be the Nuclear Age, since this single factor will have the most permanent effect on the greatest proportion of people, the vast majority of these being yet unborn.

So in this post-nuclear period of our Nuclear Age, we shall have to struggle very hard to control the Devil we have raised by our modern magic. Every Age evokes its own particular Devils from the pits of its past, and we have definitely raised one of sufficient potency to make all the previous ones look like mere children's bogies. Maybe the most frightening factor of all is that we shall eventually need the full force of this Fiend to facilitate the final exit of our species from this planet altogether. Meanwhile we will have to adapt as well as we can to what we cannot possibly disinvent. Nuclear energy is with us to stay, and in the end it may prove to be our end in itself.

Since a principal problem of our present world is overpopulation, what is most likely to happen when it reaches "critical mass," as it is bound to do within a calculable period, is that governmental authorities will have no other option except to destroy large numbers of each other's population by the most practical means available, which naturally indicates nuclear warfare on some kind of scale. In fact there is every reason to believe that this is exactly what will happen. At very top levels the actual controllers of the major countries are likely to hold consultations with each other in order to decide where, when, and to what extent warfare should take place in order to reduce their populations to more manageable proportions. In effect they will say to each other, "I have fifty millions too many while you have seventy. You kill my fifty while I kill your seventy, after which we get together, sign all the needed pacts and agreements and start trading once more. Neither of us should have unemployment problems for a while anyway."

Let no one suppose that their particular brand of politicians would be averse to such a program if they believed economic or political necessity dictated it. Since time immemorial wars have been considered a fairly normal way of population reduction, and they are likely to continue for some time yet, more especially if scientists can devise means of limiting the effects of nuclear explosions to, say, a few thousand deaths within a specified area. Of course there are other methods of reducing populations, such as compulsory euthanasia at an agreed age, prohibition of birth by either abortion or infanticide, or compulsory contraception with very stiff penalties for contravention. Possibly the best system would be the voluntary adoption of a contraceptive program until a birth rate became reduced to a satisfactory level, but unless this could be enforced by legislation of some sort it would not work very well.

There is another way of keeping a population in control that would obviate the need for wars neatly: compulsory vasectomy on a large proportion of males. Instead of preventing breeding by killing off surplus males, why not de-fertilize them in the first place and turn off the tap at the main, so to speak? Granted this would raise all sorts of problems as to selection etc., but it is a most practical proposition for population control. Sooner or later humans will have to consider this seriously unless we are willing to accept the awful alternative of world warfare. Sterilization should certainly be applied to the obviously unfit, such as congenital idiots, and eventually the civilized world will have to accept population restrictions in one form or another if our race is to remain on this earth with any degree of comfort. Otherwise the rat-quotient will apply.

This developed from a psychological experiment in which rats were added to a limited space slowly and singly. As their numbers increased the rats showed increasing signs of tension as they became more closely crowded together. Their toleration for each other lessened proportionately and perceptibly as their proximity to each other increased, and as the final rat was added to the rest the whole lot of them seemed to go suddenly mad, becoming a violently panicking mass of creatures tearing at each other frantically with teeth and claws while uttering fearsome screams and cries of utter terror. Each individual rat was engaged in a life-or-death survival struggle with all the others. This "last straw breaking the camels back" type of experiment demonstrates that each living creature needs a definite "living space" area around itself for safe and sane survival, and if that should diminish past the safety point there will be a "critical mass" explosion. In other words, the principle of Chaos as Space is a vital necessity to Life when provided in correct proportions.

The vital factor with all our concepts is harmonious balance between their extremities—the ideal Middle Road. We need the Cosmos-Chaos concept in order to deal consciously with our Existence, our God-concepts for showing us what to do rightly, our Devil-concepts to teach us what wrongs to avoid, and our Life/anti-Life concepts for coping with living and dying. How we interpret all these is purely a matter for individual understanding, but unless we can come to some sort of terms with them we shall never be able to obey that all-important injunction of Delphi: KNOW

THYSELF, and its updated variation: BECOME AS THOU WILT WITHIN THEE. If we are truly to undergo all the experiences necessary for evolving and perfecting our human species, then obviously these will have to consist of both Good and Evil ones as understood on our levels of Life.

The question is, why should the Chaos-factor be trying to get rid of us from this earth? Strictly speaking it is not, but we just happen to be inimical to it by the very nature of ourselves. Looking at what appears to be the normal condition of an average planet such as Mars, for instance: it is lifeless, barren, and disorganized. So far as may be known we are the only inhabited planet within heaven knows how many light-years, and we have no evidence of any civilization comparable to ours elsewhere in the whole of Existence. Only our inherited genetic memories and the laws of probability tell us otherwise. So far as Chaos is concerned we are intruders, invaders, and most certainly despoilers of its original conditions, and in our attempts to produce some kind of order amongst ourselves and throughout the world in general we have automatically incurred what might be termed its antipathy. That is to say, it is not so much ourselves that Chaos opposes as our alignment with Cosmos and imposition of structures, patterns, and purposeful arrangements everywhere on this earth, and especially in our currents of consciousness. Within this century alone, we have implanted these as electronic impressions into the very ambience, or aura, of our earth in the form of every radio and TV program existing, plus the entire range of telecommunication and radionic frequencies emitted from almost everywhere in one continual if normally inaudible cacophony.

Although we were originally supposed to be ground dwellers confined to earth's surface, our recent conquest of the air has resulted within a few brief years in a considerable proportion of the world's population living permanently in the atmosphere. Anyone who has lived close to a major international airport and watched the huge airliners arriving and departing regularly—some five hundred and more people at a time for twenty-four hours a day—can vouch for this fact. Furthermore, the percentage of casualty figures for air travel is so slight as to be almost insignificant. Added to this, the average expectation of life has considerably increased while the mortality rate is decreasing accordingly. Infants who because of physical defects should never have lived after birth are now kept alive and maintained in community care for many years. All these anomalies are typical of our present period, and unless some corrective controls are applied they will certainly have some serious effects our civilization. Chaos is not a factor to be trifled with or ignored. Neither is it one to invoke with impunity.

With Cosmos we are dealing with Life and all it stands for, but with Chaos we are dealing with Death, and preferably permanent death at that. Temporary death may be a necessity for us here, or how else would any further life be possible? At the same time Chaos is a "take apart" inertia that applies to more than biological factors. Chaos is opposed to all forms of order and organization where or whenever evident. That means not only our physical bodies and the dispositions we have made in this world, such as roads, railways, agriculture, cities, and the rest of our civilization, but also our constructions of consciousness like art, music, literature, mathematics, thinking processes, and whatever links one thought with another to form processes of intelligence. Pure unmixed Chaos is automatically inimical to any form of Order.

So what value can Chaos be to us and how should we handle it? Properly employed, its most useful purpose is for taking things apart so that Cosmos can then reconstruct them into something better. We need Chaos for reducing our apparently inflexible and immutable forms of thinking into their irreducible particles, so that they can then be recycled into greatly improved developments of what is essentially the identical Idea. To a great extent this process might be described as being the Mills of God, which may grind slowly, yet they grind exceedingly small. With the Death-phase they grind our ideas to residual impressions that are so attenuated that they become no more than ancestral and genetic memories from previous incarnations. From these, plus what we gain from contiguous sources of consciousness, we have to reconstruct our relationship with Life in this world again, but with one rather remarkable exception: the numerical system remains intact.

The unit of everything and what can be done with it have remained a constant of consciousness ever since humans combined one thing with another. The value and comprehension of one, two, and three are exactly the same now as they were ten or twenty thousand years ago. True, we may have found out a lot more to do with them and all sorts of different ways of relating them with each other, but their fundamental meanings for us remain unchanged since we first became aware of them. Counting on fingers and toes is common to all humanity, and for the vast majority of humankind this inherent sense of numeration conveys nothing beyond an awareness of quantity or mass, with the unit being themselves, while everything else gets classified into "bigger than me" and "littler than me" categories, the former being usually associated with apprehension, and the latter with tolerance or affection.

Such a sense of numeration is the most likely one to "carry over" more or less intact from one incarnation to another, and the Qabbalists started a scheme for consciously associating a primary Life-principle with each of the first ten digits. They tried this in the hopes that eventually an inherent awareness of this connection would tually an inherent awareness of this connection would become a permanent integer of human genetic inheritance, and from that might be rebuilt the structure of their spiritual strivings, or at least a conviction that there really WAS some kind of connection between numbers and spirituality *per se*. The specific associations between numbers and principles defined by the Qabbalists were extremely definite and fundamental, being: (1) Highest and Best, (2) Masculine-type consciousness, (3) Feminine-type consciousness, (4) Mercy and Compassion, (5) Strictness and Stringency, (6) Balance and Harmony, (7) Victory, (8) Honor, (9) Fertility, (10) This Kingdom of Creation. That is to say, ten basic ideas of Being connected with undoubtedly sound spiritual states. If those could survive the Chaos process intact, then they might prove to be the seeds from which an altogether finer generation ought surely to arise.

Seeing that a numerical system is our absolutely primal method of creating Order (or Cosmos) in our thinking consciousness, it certainly seems somewhat strange that any of it should survive a processing by Chaos. The probability is that mathematical exactitude can be contorted by the Chaotic and anti-Life purposes with equal precision as anything needed by the Cosmic polarity of Power. We should remember that it was mainly mathematicians who made nuclear energy available to humankind in the first place. Without the minds of people like Einstein, Meitner, and Oppenheimer, nuclear energy would not have become a practical proposition for a very much longer period. Moreover, it is mathematicians again who will have to calculate the necessary formulae that will eventually take our species away from earth to survive elsewhere.

We should also bear in mind the intimate association between our monetary systems and our numerical one. Probably sheer greed and the compulsion to amass more and more wealth is responsible for greater Evils on earth than can easily be calculated. At one time this was naturally a matter of physical possessions, but now it extends to enormous economic empires of acquired interests on international scales of importance. The movement and manipulation of money around the world decides the destiny of whoso authorizes this action, plus probably that of their friends and associates also. In fact, now that "computer crime" has become a reality amongst us, the money market has become unreliable, and forced inflation at an almost incredible rate is about the only hope of staving off the inevitable crash for as long as possible.

The entire Chaotic principles of modern finance are beautifully set out in the second part of Goethe's famous *Faust*, which relatively few people ever seem to read nowadays. The storyline here is that Faust and Mephistopheles have come to the court of an Emperor whose realm is on the verge of bankruptcy, and he is offering fantastic rewards to anyone with some practical suggestions for solvency. Mephisto of course has all the bright answers, which he puts forward through Faust, who naturally wins every prize. First he inquires who owns all the buried treasure in the country, and when the Emperor replies that as Ruler he, or the Crown, does, Mephisto goes on to ask its total value, whereupon the Emperor confesses himself utterly unable to even guess at it. Probably many millions he guesses. Mephisto then asks whether this buried treasure would be enough to redeem the nation's debt if it were all dug up and converted into cash, and the Emperor says no one would doubt this for a moment, and is Mephisto suggesting that they get a team of dowsers working on such a project right away? Here Mephisto and Faust put forward their mind-boggling (at that period) suggestion.

No, he says, leave the buried treasure exactly where it is, but issue promissary notes on it which state that any buried treasure found and presented to the Royal Treasury will be redeemed at current value as estimated by the Exchequer. Then set those notes in circulation and hope not many people ever turn up at the Treasury to claim their stated value in specie. After hesitating awhile to digest this audacious idea, the Emperor decides to try it out and it succeeds beyond his wildest dreams. Everyone accepts the idea and the paper notes circulate around everywhere. First the Army is paid up to date and the General-in-Chief announces happily: "Arrears of pay are settled duly, the Army is enlisted newly; The trooper's blood is all alive, the landlords and the wenches thrive." Later the Lord High Steward continues the tale: "Twas scattered everywhere like wildfire blazing as currency, and none its course could stop. A crowd surrounds each money changer's shop, and every note is there accepted duly, for gold and silver's worth—with discount truly. Thence it has spread to landlords, butchers, bakers. One half the people feast as pleasure takers. In raiment new the others proudly go, the tradesmen cut their cloth, the tailors sew. The crowd 'The Emperor's Health!' in cellars wishes, midst cooking, roasting, rattling of the dishes."

In other words, the whole set-up was one gigantic "con." There was nothing back of all that printed paper except blind belief in the existence of a problematical treasure, which might have been purely imaginary anyway. That is precisely the situation in our world of the present. Take a dollar bill and look at it. All the wording states is "This note is legal tender for all debts public or private." Nothing else. British notes say, "I promise to pay the bearer on demand the sum of" and then follows the figure-value of the note and the official signature of the Chief Cashier of the Bank of England. Other currencies have similar statements. Because every rational person is prepared to believe in the validity of government-backed printed paper, the system works and everyone involved with it seems satisfied. The plain fact is that money *per se* is a pure invention, and is kept going solely because people dare not disbelieve in it for fear of completely disorganizing their whole structured civilization.

Originally money was valued by weight of its own pure metal. That is to say, the specific weight of any metal was its value, gold being the highest, silver next, and copper least of all. This soon became far too awkward to handle practically, so agreed systems of relative valuations were eventually in general acceptance. For a long time, however, people depended on portable valuables such as finger rings, neck torques, bracelets, and the like, which they could sell by weight to raise ready cash. The first forms of paper money were banker's agreements which acknowledged that valuables received by one branch might be paid out at another elsewhere, less an agreed amount deducted as a service charge. Apart from fraud, financial crime in early days was limited to clipping minute amounts of metal from valuable coins (which milling the edges prevented), debasing their metal with a percentage of cheaper metal, or illegally stamping a false coinage from altogether imitation or inferior metal. Once paper money became possible, however, forgery became a highly lucrative if hazardous profession.

Now that actual money is virtually nonexistent apart from computer calculations geared to plastic credit cards, one might suppose belief in it would weaken, but factually just the opposite has happened. Ever since money became more and more of a concept in its own right and less of a solid commodity, so to speak, its importance seems to have taken on an almost spiritual dimension to the majority of humankind. Yet in itself it is no more than humankind's mutual belief in each other's material resources expressed through a system of symbology acceptable to all, whether as printed money or as pure figures exchanged through an electromechanical international hookup. When we think of the magnitude of this worldwide concern connected with a common numeration, it becomes quite clear why Qabbalistically minded people were so anxious to attach some spiritual figures. If only we could treat those exactly as we treat money, exchanging them amongst us profitably and enriching ourselves through experiencing them in our lives, we might soon become much better people. Perhaps one day some ingenious Qabbalist will devise a means of doing that and manage to link it with an international network. That could produce some very interesting effects, such as people being born with an inherent sense of connection between commonplace figures and matters of Cosmic importance.

Together with mathematics, a sense of music frequently survives the Chaos-Death experience, though very rarely in a sophisticated form. It is interesting to note the influence of Chaos in most so-called "modern" music. All attempts in favor of what was formerly known as melody have been scrapped in favor of atonal arrangements of what seem a lot more like "pseudo-sonics." Normally there are only three elements to most modern music—a twang from an electronic guitar, a thump from a drum, and a howl, yell, honk, screech, whine or moan from a greatly amplified vocalist. Although there are reputed to be meaningful words contained therein, it would not matter if there were none at all. Only the noise seems significant, providing it is continual and cacaphonic, guaranteed to prevent or distort any deliberate attempt at ordered, intelligent thinking.

Among previous generations it was believed that such types of sound summoned the Devil, and in country districts they would gather around and make what they called "rough music" outside the home of whoever they had selected to be bedevilled. They usually chose a dark night and made as hideous a noise as they possibly could with household and agricultural utensils, combined with every kind of vocal expression that seemed offensive, such as excretory and vomitory noises. Occasional insulting slogans might be thrown in, plus sundry bays and cockcrows. The rattling of a poker against a gridiron was supposed to be a special Devil summoner, especially if accompanied by goat-like bleatings (in view of his reputed appearance in the shape of that animal). Once they felt they had aroused the Devil's interest sufficiently to deal with the object of their dislike, they dispersed to their own homes. Nowadays they would only have to leave an amplifier behind them shriek-ing the latest song-hit. The modern "music of Chaos" sounds quite normal to those whose nature it reflects so closely.

There is considerable argument concerning whether the Chaos factor should be associated with the Devil or not, since its essential nature signifies disorganization and the elimination of life, especially among humans, whereas the Devil indicates direct antagonistic opposition to us for the sake of obtaining our energy in order to enhance its own existence. Hence one might suppose that the principle of Chaos would automatically need to eliminate the Devil with everything else, which would indeed be the case if humans ceased existing. Nevertheless, the Devil, as the anal function of the Cosmic Being we know as "God," is act-ing in a pro-Chaotic fashion, since he is breaking down human beings into what amounts to spiritual feces, which will later be excreted from the Cosmic Corpus altogether. Therefore the Devil can legitimately be regarded as an agent of Chaos to that extent, since he serves the same end for a percentage of the profits. Nevertheless, the end-effect produced by the Devil (spiritual excreta) can equally well serve Cosmic purposes, because that is also a valuable product for fertilizing the growth of fresh and useful ideas, which are likely to advance our development towards Deity. However, since there is no *intention* whatever involved, neither Good nor Evil may be assumed, and either may be the outcome of Cosmic or Chaotic influences.

So in reality Cosmos and Chaos are inseparable ends of the same energy, although they can be approached from either extremity. A good illustration of this would be a large bar magnet. If a small section were broken off from near the North pole, that would then have a dual polarity of both a North and a South pole. This process could be repeated as far as possible until the magnet was broken down into extremely minute fragments, each of which would still have both poles present. With each breakdown, however, the pieces of magnet would be proportionately reduced in power according to the actual mass of the portion concerned. With a magnet each individual molecule has bipolarity, and as bulk increases or diminishes, so does the total strength of the mass vary while the polarities remain unchanged in nature. A single-poled magnet is an impossibility and we might think of the mass of humanity in that way. Each individual is a bipolar creature capable of combining with others so as to increase field strength without altering polarity, *providing those poles are aligned correctly.*

The first principle of magnetism indicates that "like poles repel, unlike poles attract." If we apply this to humans, it would mean people would be attracted to each other at their dissimilar polarities, thus forming an infinite number of small closed circuits, each absorbing its own energy, so to speak, and leaving almost no surplus for achievement of other effects. Those with intentions of combining energies for definite purposes would need to align themselves so that their similar polarities were deliberately brought together and directed towards a commonly agreed end, although this would be subject to the requirements of rhythm and alternation. Therefore any change of group polarity would have to be concerted if it was intended to be effectual elsewhere. Individual polarity orientation is continuous and perfectly normal, altering as circumstances necessitate.

Although Cosmos and Chaos are diametrical opposites, they have bipolar natures like everything else. Thus the plus (+) of Cosmos is the minus (–) of Chaos, while the + of Chaos is the – of Cosmos. Following these observations it might be assumed that the + of Deity and Good complements the – of the Devil and Evil, so the + of these latter does likewise for the – of the former. At a glance, we have:

OUTPUT+		0		INTAKE–
LIFE	Cosmos	0	Chaos	ANTI-LIFE
LOVE	Deity	0	Devil	ANTIPATHY
	Good	0	Evil	
INTAKE–				OUTPUT+

So in order to attach him/herself firmly to either set of principles, a human would first have to choose between them and then join up according to polarity. For example, if the Chaos side were selected he/she would need to connect his/her intake-negative side to its output-positive, and vice versa. This would mean a maximum exchange of energies between participants, and the same would be true for the Cosmic side of the scale if we reversed the application. At an exact midway point the polarities of the principles must surely stroke a balance between themselves, and that would be the best theoretical course to pursue. To do this successfully, the two polarities have to be held so that they have an equal influence on the soul with minimal lateral movement, while progress is being hopefully aimed at the Cosmos+ and Chaos– end of the scale. At the neutral point, however, a fall might be more rapid than a rise, and considerable care is needed to keep the course as straight as possible. In fact, this was why it was referred to in the Scriptures as the "Straight and Narrow Way." It was usually so difficult to maintain that only a few determined humans ever managed it competently. The majority of us continue swinging between the two extremities from one incarnation to the next, hopefully hitching ourselves a fraction higher with each Life experience, or else slipping a bit backwards as we miss our mark and have to start again below the level we might have reached had we been just a trifle wiser.

It might be supposed from this that we would be facing a very dull world wherein Good consisted of doing no Evil and Evil amounted to doing no Good. A most unlikely proposition for the forseeable future, since that situation argues a condition of consciousness virtually Nirvanic in nature, and most normal humans are naturally somewhat closer to Evil than they are to Good. Nevertheless, with the advance of evolution a significant proportion of us are indeed making obvious efforts towards those tendencies in ourselves by at least aiming away from Evil and Chaos. At the same time we have to remember that a definite percentage of humanity are calculatedly choosing the Evil Way as a polarized path, purely for the sake of greed-gains at the expense of fellow mortals foolish enough to allow themselves to be exploited for such purposes. Anyone doubting the seriousness of this situation need only consider the probable effects of an adverse virus entering their system and multiplying its influence by spreading its species as widely as it can. It might be well to remember, though, that this is exactly what we have done ourselves in this world, and who can doubt the results we have had here?

Both the physical and spiritual systems have built-in immunity factors designed to deal with such pathogens under normal conditions. A learned rabbi recently gave it as his opinion that the Jewish people in particular might be likened to the white corpuscles of the blood, whose singular task it is to sacrifice themselves for the sake of the Being whose blood they belong with, by counteracting any dangerous invaders and overcoming them while dying in the struggle themselves. That is a most profound and significant saying with many more than surface meanings. It ties in with the Sangreal Concept and clarifies it to a considerable extent. That may be the overall plan of Nature, but the deadly disease of AIDS is interfering with it on physical levels, and there is normally some spiritual equivalent to match all our physical propensities. In this case the chances are that the spiritual type of AIDS preceded its material manifestation by several generations. It is definitely a disease of degeneration, and symptomatic of what we might consider the "Satanic Age," since it aligns with Chaos very convincingly. We can only hope that its compensatory factor is in the process of development at present, but at the same time it should be pointed out that the cure for a physical disease does not automatically signify its cessation in spiritual dimensions. Nothing but an intentional and persistent alteration of polarity patterns is likely to do that.

Ultimately we are compelled to the conclusion that Existence itself consists of energy oppositions that cannot exist alone and apart from each other any more than a single-ended stick can manifest itself. Which might bring fresh meaning to the famous Zen koan, "What is the sound of one hand clapping?" The appropriate answer to this should be to clap one hand vigorously against the thigh or any adjacent surface. The koan does not necessarily specify that one hand should be clapping against another one. That would only be a superficial implication, and esoterics should always learn to think more deeply than that. Strictly speaking again, there should never be such things as terminal conclusions, but only "way stations" that have been reached by extensions of consciousness up to that point. Any genuine mystic will readily admit that all his or her so-called conclusions are only temporary halts along his/her perpetual pathway, and from each one a further arrival point should be focused into view.

Therefore, although we may see things in a totally different light than that of our ancestors, we are still looking at the same problems and live on the same planet, however much we may have altered it. Food is still food whether we buy it in a supermarket or carve it off the carcass of something we killed ourselves. Homes are still homes whether in caves or condominiums. Clothes are still clothes whether animal skins or acrylic. Birth remains birth and death has always been death. We still know fear and anger, love and hate. It is mostly our social attitudes that have altered by our adapting with each other, and the most noticeable changes have occurred chiefly during the last century or so. We no longer view our Gods and Devils as we did formerly, preferring instead to think of them as natural forces rather than personifications of these; although, such an attitude on our part makes not the slightest difference to the actual character of the energy in question, but only to ourselves who are dealing with it. Since this gives us an extended and increasingly advanced insight into the areas of our investigations, we might as well ask ourselves here exactly what the concepts of Deity and Devil mean to modern humankind, or, more advantageously, what they could mean to those who are bold enough to push their Inner perceptions past several sticking points. Even the merest peep at possibilities could be well worth our considerations.

Chapter Eight

SATAN THE SALESMAN

The chances are that humankind believed in Satan a long time before believing in God. Malevolence seems so much more obvious than Benevolence in this world. The interesting point is why humans should ever have believed in any spiritual factors behind Life at all? Life beyond Death for instance—what could possibly convince anyone of that? They could see for themselves the corpses of their kindred rotting away until nothing but bones remained, and common sense alone would tell them that such was the inevitable end of everyone alive on earth. So what would have put any ideas of disembodied existence into their heads at all, and furthermore develop these into one of humankind's deepest and strongest convictions completely contrary to any reasonable suppositions or probabilities? There can be only three possible explanations: First, the constant arrival of fresh-born people to replace those who died; second, some psychic ability among survivors that enabled

them to sense their departed companions' continued existence in a strange state of "otherness"; and thirdly, an
inherent instinct that somehow we all were little lives living
inside one Great Life.

Such an instinct most probably arose from "cell consciousness," or an awareness among bodily cells of being
individual units which in association with each other com-
prised a single and far superior type of creature. As any
modern schoolchild should know, our bodies consist of
multimillions of living cells, each species having its own
particular function and life-cycle. By the use of the word
"consciousness" here, only its most basic level is implied in
the sense of instinctive awareness, which is to be differen-
tiated from intelligent, constructive thinking. Thus whatever lives at all is conscious to some degree, including plant
and microscopic life, although to an extremely minor degree as compared with ours. It is possible to considerably
lesser extents that consciousness could continue through
the mineral kingdom as well, attenuated to a remarkably
distant degree from ours on those remote levels.

To illustrate this point in particular it is only necessary
to consider an ordinary corpse of any kind. We say this is
dead, yet what we really mean is the cessation of its coordinating intelligence. From the purely cellular viewpoint a
corpse is very much alive, and its decomposition is nothing
more than all those microscopic lives breaking away from
each other and attempting to rejoin their original elements.
To preserve or embalm a so-called dead body, we literally
have to kill it with powerful cell poisons so that it will retain
something of its original appearance whilst its substance
becomes converted into something inert and inactive. For
example, ancient Egyptian mummies were preserved by
converting what was once human tissue into leather, the
skin remaining intact around its bony framework. Anyone
doubting the faculty of consciousness in cellular tissue

might remember that brain cells are only highly specialized ones evolved from simple ordinary cells, which form the basis of all animal life on earth.

We might bear in mind that earlier humans were far more emotional and sensitive than most intellectual moderns. They depended on feelings and experience rather than reason and reliance on recorded statements by other humans. Reading and writing did not exist, so they were limited to listening to the speech of their companions or the noises of Nature, from which they had to make what sense they could by means of their imaginative faculties. It is likely that dream dramas contributed a great deal to their repertoires of inward experience, from which confused memories of these might occasionally be mixed with objectively gained impressions. Early humans learned about Life in very hard ways and often with the greatest of difficulties. We have to remember that most livelihoods were gained by two main methods—mobile hunting and grazing, or static agriculture. The former grouping tended to be fast-thinking since they were concerned with speed of mobility, while the latter grew more accustomed to the seasonal pace of Nature. So together with their considerable inbreeding they became notoriously slow-thinking and averse to innovative ideology, even though their grain-rich diet considerably enhanced their capabilities of consciousness.

Nobody can say precisely at what point the concepts of Gods, Devils, or any kind of Superspirits entered the consciousness of humanity, but it must definitely have been in prehistoric times and long before humans became literate beings. The likelihood is that so much could and did go wrong with affairs of this world that people kept looking for something or someone to blame for all their afflictions, and not finding any human cause to lay this on, postulated an invisible enemy who must surely be responsible. Quite apart from natural misfortunes such as earthquakes, floods, landslides and brushfires, there were endless personal mishaps to endure: strange sicknesses and accidents to self, family, or friends; children and animals dying; crops failing for unknown reasons; valuable properties getting broken or seriously damaged; losses of all kinds occurring; and inexplicable events happening in a chain of circumstances that might have been comprehensible if they had been deliberately arranged by some extremely powerful enemy, but scarcely otherwise. Since no human existed who seemed capable of causing such calamities, there had to be some non-human originator who was certainly ill-intentioned so far as human beings were concerned.

Those abused humans were only too well aware of the damage they were capable of doing to each other due to dislike, hatred, revenge, and similar feelings of antipathy. Since it seemed evident that their Universe was acting in a comparable manner against them of its own accord, it was presumed that the Universe was motivated by the same, or at least equivalent, sentiments to theirs. Nobody today can be certain what those early people called this occult oppresser in their times, but since primitive speech imitated natural sounds it might be guessed that name would not be unlike our SaTaN. S for the hissing of a snake to infer an Evil hidden enemy, T to imitate spitting, and N for the grunting of a defecating person. The total to convey a warning combined with dislike and disgust. Spitting at each other has always been a sign of antipathy among humans, while defecation signifies the utmost in rejection because it indicates the final expulsion of unwanted matter from the human body. It is possibly from this that the legend of Satan's expulsion from heaven was born.

Once they had something to call this calamitous power, humans considered ways and means of making favorable relationships with it. They had soon discovered methods of dealing with human enemies they could not conquer physically. Their most practical way was to buy them off with valuable presents or services and make the best possible bargain they could. True that any such truce might not last very long before renewed demands would be made, but even temporary suspension of hostilities meant a welcome respite for war-weary warriors and afforded opportunities for procreating fresh fighters and restocking depleted supplies. If such peace-bribery worked with fellow mortals, it might work with intangible influences as well. So, since the strongest suspicions were that this mysterious Satan manifested most clearly through the underground fires that excreted from earth, occasionally leaving liquid feces of flaming matter that solidified into a strangely lit stone, it would be scarcely surprising if awed humans acknowledged the presence of this terrifying manifestation of Satanic supremacy by contributing a mortal life or so for its consumption. The probabilities are that such primitive anti-human Powers were the first acts of public religious worship known on earth.

How long it took humankind to realize that this unknown influence was not entirely antagonistic to the whole human race but had a helpful side as well is very uncertain. Our fabled knowledge of Good and Evil certainly did not come with a single bite from the forbidden fruit in the Garden of Eden, but from long and hard-earned experience of Life itself. By the time that we had any definitely established codes of conduct, most of our discovered Deities were believed to have bivalency of influence, blasting or blessing their adherents according to their deserts or for whatever seemed an appropriate reason. In fact, it was not until the concept of Dualism became popular that the idea of separate Gods specializing in Good or Evil began to gain much ground; and that was mainly in Persia with its Zoroastrian concepts of Ormuzd the God of Light, and Ahriman, Lord of Darkness, who was said to be Chief of the Cacodemons, or Evil Spirits, their title deriving from the Greek *kakos*, meaning anything bad or wicked. By that period definite theologies were becoming fairly well established around the world, with many similarities and differences of opinion both uniting and dividing them. For example, fire-worship, which is still practiced among the Parsees of India, is reputed to be the world's oldest organized religion extant, tracing its history back to the Stone Age. Zoroaster was reputedly the main reformer of this religion some three thousand years ago. Nevertheless, for modern Parsees the Fire-element means nothing Evil, but the Power of Life itself. To them it is so sacred that they will not pollute it by cremating their dead, but still use the oldest method of corpse disposal—by leaving them to be eaten by birds and insects in a reverential and acceptable manner inside their cemeterial "Towers of Silence."

Apart from the Cathars of Europe, who regarded Satan and Jesus as being twin brothers, we should consider the parallel of Osiris-Set in the Egyptian pantheon, where the same relationship applies and was probably the forerunner of the Cathar concepts. Although details were different, the fundamentals were much the same. Both Osiris and Jesus were humans promoted to God-status after their deaths. Set, or Typhon, murdered his brother and was subsequently regarded as the author of all Evil, and he was represented as an odd mixture of crocodile and wolf. He is usually depicted as waiting in the Judgment Hall of the Dead by the scales weighing the heart of the deceased against the feather of Truth. Should the result be condemnatory, the heart is thrown to Set, who devours it and removes the damned soul to his underground Lake of Fire. An identical scene is sometimes shown by Christian ideographers, except that the Archangel Michael is weighing souls in a balance while the Devil lurks close by for any rejects. A splendid example of this can be seen on the surviving Tower of St. Michael's

Church on Glastonbury Tor, Somerset, England.

According to Christian Scriptures, the main encounter between Jesus and Satan is supposed to have taken place during the self-sequestration of the former in the desert. It was then a relatively common practice among shamen and those intending to devote their lives to their Deities and spiritual services to their fellow men. They would wander out into a wilderness like the scapegoats, fasting and meditating in hopes of finding some Otherworld Being who might confirm their purpose and possibly convey a definite message of confirmation from the Supreme Spirit or other high authority. Their fasting and exposure to the elements would tend to sensitize them hallucinogenically after a prolonged period of sleepnessness and salt-free nourishment. There would have had to be some water available, of course, but small amounts of this are usually present in desert places for those who know where to dig for it. Such a survival ordeal was a very ancient custom amounting to a practical initiation among self-dedicated holy men.

In the case of Jesus, there are only three recorded temptations, which presumes he must have told the story himself since he was alone. First he was prompted to convert common stones into bread and eat them, which would have been the natural wish of a hungry man, but Jesus countered this with a Scriptural quotation. Again he seemed to be at a high altitude observing the world, and felt he was being offered all its many kingdoms in return for worshipping the Devil, whose unquestioned right to bestow them on whoever he pleased Jesus never denied or disputed. This time he used a phrase ambiguous to modern ears: "Get thee behind me Satan." Satan understood it perfectly, because in those days it was an euphemism for "I shit upon you." That is to say, Jesus was identifying with his proper significance. On the final temptation Jesus had the experience of seeming to be on a topmost pinnacle of the Temple at

Jerusalem, and this time it was Satan quoting Scriptures at Jesus, suggesting he should leap into the air and let angels carry him to the ground miraculously. However, Jesus kept a steady enough head to counter this idea with another Scriptural admonition when Satan "ended all temptation and departed from him for a season." A temporary rather than a permanent absence.

The interesting part of the story is that Jesus made not the slightest effort to deny or contradict Satan's claim to rulership of this earthly realm, nor did he use his own words to cope with the Satanic situation. Later (John 14:30), he said to his faithful, "Hereafter I will not talk much with you, for the prince of this world cometh and hath nothing in me." It seems there was then a current belief in the Devil's supremacy on earthly levels. Certainly the Scriptural phrases employed by Jesus were familiar formulae for averting Evil in his day, and so were numerous charms and amulets existing then. It was obligatory, though, that he should face whatever trials he might meet with the strength of his own resources alone and deal with them as best he knew how. The fact that he had emerged from his ordeal with his mind reasonably intact and unscathed by marauding or vene-mous creatures for the whole forty days would be taken as proof of his successful shamanship. Buddha spent his days of isolation under his Bo tree also, and legends are full of instances concerning solitary periods of privation culminat-ing in spectacular spiritual triumphs. Possibly one of the most dramatic was told of the Norse God Odin, whose name means "Wind," or "Spirit." Wounded by his own sword he hung grimly on to the World Ash-tree, Yggdrasil, until after nine days and nights he fell, and found the sacred Rune alphabet that enlightened all initiated individuals.

This encounter with the Devil or its equivalent was, and still is in a different form, an absolutely essential part of what is usually called "initiation." That is to say, a sort of "inspection test" to find out how suitable individuals are for the type of life they propose to lead. No average employer would hire anyone without applying some kind of test to discover the capabilities of that person for doing the work required, and some of such tests can be very elaborate and time-consuming because they are aimed at estimating character as well as technical skill. For example, it would be useless employing an accountant, however skillful the man was, if he were thoroughly dishonest and meant to rob his employers of all he could. That would be entirely counter-productive. So just as all different employments have appropriate suitability tests, so distinctive classes and grades of humans have theirs, and probably intimate exposure to the direct influence of what might be termed the Devil is about the toughest test that a highly developed soul could face and come out well from. To be submitted to the severest strains by one's own worst propensities and survive them intact is a character determinator of the most positive kind.

Since the best way to test anything is to subject its weakest part to a considerable overload and then observe its general behavior, so should the Satan factor reveal the individual weaknesses of anyone by concentrating at that particular point. For instance, at the recorded temptation of Jesus it revealed that his especial weakness, apart from ordinary and temporary needs of food, was an intense desire to be acknowledged and recognized by a large number of people, coupled with a craving for the spectacular. Otherwise those would not have been the characteristics selected by Satan. Even though he survived the Satan-tests satisfactorily on the surface, it is doubtful if he ever fully overcame those traits completely in his lifetime, or he would have lived in quite another manner without attracting so much public attention to himself.

Jesus certainly adopted the revolutionary idea of returning Good for Evil and loving enemies who offered only hate. At Luke 6:27-8, he says "Love your enemies, do good to those who hate you, bless those that curse you, and pray for those who treat you spitefully." To take that advice literally means that Satan the Devil should be especially prayed for. In Judeo-Christian beliefs, who was humankind's worst enemy? Surely the Devil? Who was supposed to behave spitefully and ill-treat people? The Devil again. Who was reputed to hate humanity worst of all? Once more the Devil. Properly speaking, those who worshipped him with all the wickedness they could think of did him the worst disservice possible, because such behavior condemned him to remain in his Hell eternally. Those brave enough to attempt liberating him with loving forgiveness by sensible and careful spiritual procedures could indeed call themselves true Christians, since they would be following out the most arcane advice Jesus ever gave. He said later: "Love your enemies and do good, hoping for nothing in return and your reward will be great, for you will be children of the Highest who is kind to the unthankful and the evil."

With those words Jesus was telling his disciples that the correct treatment of Satan should be from a very exalted and idealistic viewpoint. Nothing but an absolutely overwhelming love can really overcome or absorb hate and antagonism, but it has to be a *wise* love proffered in a sensible spirit so that it will prove effectual and evoke the most favorable response. Furthermore, it would require phenomenal patience and perseverance in its offering, because the ultimate absorption of Evil is likely to be a very prolonged affair of maybe several millenia more. Those interested in the salvation of Satan must be prepared to extend their altruistic attention for many incarnations without any hope of reward or return except perhaps unkind or offensive ones. Jesus did warn them from personal experience to expect nothing if they insisted on attempting such a spiritual self-sacrifice. He ought to know how to deal with the Devil, having done so himself at the closest quarters.

Without any Satan-stresses at all we could not hope to achieve really solid survival strength at any of our levels. With no physical resistance our bodies would not develop properly, and all muscle exercisers are some kind of weight or spring to be pulled against rhythmically. In a comparable way, the element of Satan in Life makes an invaluable spiritual exerciser if and when adapted for our needs and never subservient to our wants, which can only be illusory conditions tempting us into cooperation with them anyway. We are apt to use and think of that word "tempt" very carelessly, as if it were something on the end of a line, like bait set out for a fish, which it is in rather a different sense. Literally it means "to try or attempt anything," but by sheer usage it has come to mean persuade into Evil courses. However, a much more modern interpretation would be the term "sell" in the sense that everyone would understand entirely. A salesman has come to signify a highly trained person whose function it is to organize a commercial transaction between a selectee and his principal, who supplies the product sold, and for which the salesman receives a percentage. In other words, he is an appointed agent whose job it is to transfer money from his selectee to the principal he works for. Exactly how he does this is entirely his own methodology which he may have learned from anywhere, although usually from a commercial school normally advocating extremely elastic ethics.

Thus the salesman's job is to extract money from people whether or not they really want to part with it. This has to be done by means of his mind and pure powers of persuasion. The only thing he is not allowed to do is produce a pistol and demand the money by sheer threats. Otherwise he is free to use whatever inducements he pleases, and many salesmen rise to very strange heights of suggestive pressures. They sometimes have to create demands where none previously existed or make an otherwise unsaleable item a popular commodity. They must somehow break down the strongest resistance to their product and find a market for it in the most improbable places amongst the most unlikely people. Anyone can sell things people want to buy anyway, but the real art of the salesman comes in selling others what they do not particularly want and are uncertain what to do with once they buy it. That is how the art of the salesman and the skill of Satan become almost synonymous, except that most humans act as their own Satans.

So it could be useful to think of Satan as a supersalesman rather than merely a tempter, because Satan does not give anything away for free except "come-ons" that are scarcely free because they are always calculated in with the end price, which is not payable in money but in sections of oneself so to speak—the literal ownership of human beings exchanged for money and advantages, or whatever may be demanded. We do not live in this world for nothing, and barter is the system we have chosen as a convenience to live by, which is normally fair and reasonable except when unfair pressures are applied and dishonest means adopted to make totally unentitled gains. In the old days, knowing this was simple enough. Physical objects were stolen or people plainly ill-treated. There was usually something to know about or particularly to talk about when Satanic events took place in our world. Nowadays one of the few guidelines left is expressed by an old adage: "In Nature's shop, take what you want—and PAY!" Providing anyone is prepared to part with whatever is demanded in return for requirements, there will be no shortage of commodities while Satan controls the stock cupboard. He is the most competent salesman in Creation.

Even if the Energy we know as Satan had not existed when we came to this world, he (or It) would definitely be existing after all these millions of years spent in expressing immeasurable amounts of consciousness throughout all our self-spaces. The reality or otherwise of Satan is purely a semantic question. The reality of our own awareness of him is only arguable with reference to intensity, degrees, effects, and the usual concomitants. Furthermore, that awareness has been responsible for making or modifying every single artifact in the world, and for coping with every kind of concept that the mind of humanity is capable of originating or communicating. The spaces around and within ourselves are crammed with different sorts of energies, some of which we know about and can utilize, like magnetism and electricity; yet who would be rash enough to deny absolutely that yet unknown and intangible influences might exist right under our very noses, so to speak, awaiting discovery by some inquisitive and inspired investigator?

Because the Satan-energy does not speak to us in human language does not mean it is either nonexistent or that we can ignore it with impunity. Satan talks through instincts and emotions as well as flashes of sometimes surprising intelligence, although he nearly always harps on the same old message. Each human being is urged to exalt oneself at everyone else's expense, disregard all finer feelings as stupid and unnecessary sentiment, firmly reject and deny any ideology suggestive of spiritual subjects as being unscientific and unworthy of intellectual people, plus accept the gospel of dialectical materialism as a background to all behavior and outlooks. As an alternative, some particularly severe and sadistic religion may be suggested wherein all other opinions will be condemned to the hottest of Hells, and sinners of the slightest sort subjected to the most terrible sufferings. Whatever appeals to the worst instincts of every human being. With some it will be avarice, with others sheer cruelty, with others again desire for domination and conquest. All have their own favorite feelings, except that Satan does not call them so, but rather regards them as skills and abilities of the most splendid kind. Most humans would agree with him once they discover what those accomplishments can bring them.

There is no doubt whatsoever that a successful sinner needs to be a highly intelligent and well-informed individual. Brutal, senseless, and obvious offenders are likely to be apprehended by the police and temporarily imprisoned by the laws of society as punishment for being stupid enough to be caught. Had they listened to the apocryphal story of a lawyer detailing his fees it might have been different. This legal eagle was said to have stated: "Mister, for telling you what you can do safely inside the law and get away with it, my fee is fifty dollars, but for telling you what you can do outside the law and *still* get away with it, my fee will be two hundred dollars." Which is why criminal consortia hire their own legal departments just like any other corporation or business enterprise. Neither would they dream of employing unskilled or untrustworthy people to carry out their instructions. Then again, really well-established criminal concerns would have their own pension and hospital funds for dealing with insurable contingencies such as imprisonment, family care, bribery of officials and the like. In fact, there would most probably be a legitimate business to cover the activities of such a large secretarial staff, with only an absolute minimum of them aware of any clandestine activities.

In a similar fashion, we have become so used to seeing what was formerly regarded as wrongdoing in a totally different light from that of our forefathers that we can seldom distinguish Good from Evil, and now frequently have the greatest difficulty in distinguishing between Deity and the Devil. The question is whether we ever did, or if we were simply hanging on to ideological frameworks that have become totally outdated. Our once reliable criteria, which formerly felt so rock-solid and dependable, are becoming more ephemeral and tenuous, however we try to handle them. All our collections of consciousness and thinking systems exist to be altered at our convenience or retained for the same reason—namely, that we cannot think what else to do with them. Original and constructive thinking is a lot rarer than might be supposed, and the majority of humans would rather do a day's work of the hardest physical kind than cope with a load of complicated concepts for five minutes.

What the average intelligent human being subconsciously seeks is a species of self-belief that is utterly beyond the slightest possibility of doubt, query, argument, or discussion whatever. Some single point so absolutely unquestionable that it just *has* to be what or how it is indicated, particularly in relation to the believer him/herself. This forms a sort of kingpin or central concept around which everything else can be hung or attached, as it were; yet at all costs it will remain intact whatever else disintegrates. Time and time again humans may be reduced to such a solitary faith-factor, which might amount to a solitary "I AM," yet that alone would be sufficient to rebuild everything if the worst came to the worst. All the great religions have their own such formulae. A Christian will say, "In the Name of the Father, Son and Holy Spirit"; and a Jew, "The Lord our God is One"; a Bhuddist, "I take refuge in the Norm"; and a Muslim, "In the Name of God the Compassionate and Merciful." Others may put it whichever way they like, such as "I'm ME," or just "Oh God." Perhaps the most commonly used expression among males in English today is the ubiquitous "Fuck."

Oddly enough, this Icelandically derived expletive was not originally meant as any kind of an obscenity at all, but as an expression of life-faith and self-belief. With a single forceful expulsion of breath it fulfills all the conditions of the preceding paragraph. Etymologically, it is presumed to come from the "Futhark" combination of runic symbols signifying a Male-Female force of sexual generation and fertility. The implications behind this one brief word are fantastic. Firstly, it signifies that the utterer acknowledges the act that brought him into bodily being through every ancestor, and thus pays tribute to them also. It is an invocation to the Lifeforce Itself in Its most intimate form. A statement that the speaker is aware of his own Life-purpose to extend himself through this act and become another individual. An admission that this will eventually reincarnate him and is therefore his hope of ultimate evolution. An appeal to the one certainty behind Existence that will cause Life and not Death. Although none of this may be considered consciously while the word itself is being uttered, the utterer will be aware of its sense on very deep levels of awareness. The built-in taboos on saying it in the hearing of a woman are of extremely old origins. This was not because the word was considered particularly offensive in itself, but mostly because it was believed to lose its special "virtue" if the female sex treated it casually. It was mainly fear of losing sexual potency that confined its use among males for so long, although among polite circles it became considered coarse and unmannerly to use explicit sexual terms in mixed company, and so the usage declined. We still have totemic influences in our civilization, and with some tribes until recently it risked death for men and women to see each other's sacred sexual fetishes.

In fact, concealment or minimum revelation of sex details is one of the strongest aphrodisiacs known to humankind, while continual nudity is exactly the opposite, as most moderns are well aware. This is the natural curiosity in our human makeup: an insatiable desire to know more about what lies under this or behind that and especially why anything should be semi-concealed anyway. This constant search for sensation-satisfaction is a major, if not nearly the central, point of our being alive at all. It is literally a continual need to experience Existence by every possible means. Our drive TO BE in whatever way or form we may meet with it. That is, after all, our chief necessity in Life. The overwhelming compulsion to be informed or assured of our identities by everything we encounter, whether of a material, mental, or spiritual character. This is normally an automatic process that we take for granted, because we seldom step back far enough from ourselves to discern any fine division lines between ourselves and our senses.

Most mystical systems advocate practicing exercises aimed at exactly such an awareness, or focusing on this distinction between one's actual identity and whatever declares it by contrast. Sometimes we are told that if we were words written in black letters we would need to be read against a white background, or if in plain white, against a black background. By implication, whatever we seek is clearest and plainest in contradistinction to its opposite, and so we shall be most conscious of anything when it is brought up against its diametrical opposite. Hence the concept of God is appreciated closest when considered against Satan, and the latter when seen against God. We can truly say the two concepts are really ONE and should always be taken as different ends of the same Entity, or opposing polarities of the same Power, providing each is understood to be a bipolar Being, and never as God and Good being purely positive while Satan and Evil are entirely negative. Once we remember the reversal of polarities, that will cover the general field of thinking.

So if we ever intend to evolve, and there is not much point in staying alive unless we do, it is not enough to sense whatever we should evolve *towards*, but perhaps more importantly what we are evolving away *from*. Only in that way shall we gain a sense of purpose and direction in life, without which it is meaningless. The driver of any ordinary vehicle has to know both where he has come from plus where he is going, and more importantly *why*. Everyone knows that much, and yet millions will live from one end of life till the other without any sound appreciation of why they exist, what they exist for, or what they ought to do about it. Endless creeds, suppositions, systems, and methodologies have been invented or proposed since our civilizations began. We are still inventing them and will most probably continue doing so until the end of Time. All have been useful to some, yet none of them to all. Eventually each individual soul will need to select whatever comes closest to its own consciousness and construct a self-system from that. Given a common point of evolution, all those multimillions of apparently separate systems should mesh perfectly, like every part of a single body—cell by cell, nerve by nerve, and muscle by muscle. WE WOULD BECOME ONE BEING, and not only that, WE WOULD KNOW WHO WE ARE.

As yet, of course, we are still in the process of reaching that point and no one knows our most probable period of arrival there. So many factors prevent or decelerate such a happening, the principal one of which is Satan, or that part of ourselves which we might call anti-evolutionary. It is not in Satan's selfish interests to evolve from any spiritual standpoint, though it is highly desirable from a purely Devilish angle that our technology develops as fast as it can. Real Evil needs *efficiency* more than most things, and an incompetent Evildoer is virtually a contradiction in terms. Tolerance and forgiveness are unknown words in the Satanic vocabulary. So much more can be done by intelligent and materialistically minded people than by wooly-minded pseudo-spiritual types who drift dreamily along from one delightful fantasy to another while accomplishing very little of anything, such as the "tepids" who made Jesus feel sick whenever he thought about them. How often has it been said, "The greater the sinner, the greater the saint" without perhaps seeing the full significance of that remark?

So-called saints and sinners are the same sorts of humans, with the only main difference between them being one of reversed polarity—the saints being Deity-attracted and the sinners Devil-attracted, or an attraction to opposite ends of the same Entity. In either case there is considerable energy expended, consciousness applied, and emotion experienced. Only the intention or motivation differs diametrically. If that could be changed around, the character of the individual would alter from one category to the other, as sometimes, if rarely enough, happens. Normally, since the variation from notable sinner to notable saint is the most dramatic, that is the change which attracts the widest publicity, although the opposite can equally well occur. It is the suddenness that is remarkable. Anyone altering polarities steadily and slowly very rarely invites much attention, while those actually born with Satanically set propensities seldom cause any serious alarm or surprise. It is much more usual these days to blame unfavorable environments or inadequate education for evidence of inherent Evil, yet nevertheless there can indeed be genetic causes for what was once called the "bad seed." Should such a one be born in what could be called "suitable soil," then we have the most dangerous of Devils amongst us: incarnate ones.

Those are souls who are quite naturally dedicated to Satanic service from birth and have been so probably for many incarnations. They are the real "Elite of Evil." They may never take part openly in any kind of official Satanism for the whole of their lifetimes and may even profess some particular religion should they be required to do so, though there is not a great deal of point in such a pose these days.

Proclaiming themselves as Satanists publically would be about the most stupid thing they could do, and no "bred in the bone" Satanist can be suspected of stupidity. They learn to live exactly like a trained enemy agent domiciled in whichever country he or she is employed to destroy, secretly and solidly loyal to one authority whilst acting against the interests of another. Living completely double lives successfully, owing to an inherited instinct directing their activities and inspiring their thinking.

Sometimes these people can be detected when they are very young children, mostly by a strange look of age and occasionally unexpected malignancy in their eyes, coupled with surprising intelligence and possibly unusual incidents of cruelty. Otherwise they behave normally enough. Their inherited allegiance to Satan was what the Christian Church called Original Sin, and the baptismal service was aimed at exorcising the Demonic influence, especially in the cases of those born into influential families, who would be likely to affect the destinies of many when they became of an age to do so. This does not seem to have been noticeably successful with a great many historical characters, however. It was, and still is, the understandable ambition of truly Satanic souls to become born into families where they would automatically inherit great wealth and positions of power in our world, thus being enabled both to carry out their missions and to satisfy themselves at the same time. It would not be difficult to think of examples throughout human history. The whole of our tragic tale is full of them.

Not that such a story is one-sided. Its opposite is equally true, with highly developed souls of a totally different nature incarnating for the reverse reason among beneficent and kindly people concerned with the welfare and prosperity of their kinsfolk. We have always been this peculiar mixture of Good, Bad, and Indifferent people—confined to no one race, religion, or particular grouping, but spread all over the world in relatively balanced proportions, yet recently coming closer and closer together because of communication link-ups. The one noticeable difference between the Goods and Bads on earth is that the Goods have proclaimed their purpose publicly and have organized systems of religion for officially recognizing this, whereas the Bads have openly done nothing of the kind. Apart from a few and recently formed "Churches of Satan," which seem little more than the usual profit-making concerns, there is no obvious organization of Satan in existence that anyone would be welcome to join and find friendship with like-minded brethren. One wonders why. There would be nothing illegal nowadays in acknowledging spiritual allegiance to the Satan-concept, providing no constitutional laws were broken while doing so.

It is reputed that here and there families exist that still keep up an unbroken tradition of Satanism in their own intimate circles, which have never been permitted to practice openly, even to the present day. This is most probably untrue, since the possibility of keeping such a thing secret for centuries would be one in multimillions, especially in modern times. Yet the Angevin rulers in Europe were noted as the Devil's Brood on account of their descent from a notorious ancestress, the wife of Fulk Nerra, a tenth-century count of Anjou.

The legend went that Fulk returned to his castle from an unidentified journey with a surpassingly beautiful wife of unknown origin, named Melusine. She bore him four children and was an ideal wife in all usual respects except that she had one strange peculiarity. She seldom attended Mass, but when she did, she always left before the actual Consecration. One Sunday her husband secretly ordered four of his knights to kneel close to her and prevent her from leaving at the last moment. They tried, but Melusine tore herself free, grabbed two of her children and flew straight out of a window never to be seen again on earth. As a daughter of the Devil she naturally dared not face the presence of Christ in person. So the story goes, anyway. King Richard the First strengthened it by saying of his own family: "From the Devil we came, and to the Devil we will return."

The chances are that the Plantagenets earned their nickname through their famed Evil tempers and the likelihood of a Pagan influence in their immediate background. Many have made unjustified claims to Satanic connections because of Pagan relationships and the fact that most Christian missionaries looked on all forms of Paganism as being Satanic, whereas Paganism has no more of an exclusive connection to Satan than other religions. There is a Satan *element* in all religions, and probably more so in Christianity than most; but since Satanism is essentially reversed Deism, it can scarcely be identified with Pagan principles, which recognize both Good and Evil alike as appertaining to one and the same Being.

If in fact sincere Satanists are those who feel an obligation to follow the concept of Satan with some form of religion, they will have to adopt some philosophies and practices comparable to those of their fellow humans who devote themselves to a Deity Figure. At one time it was supposed that Satanic gatherings were simply groups of people intending to ridicule and insult the official Christian Church by making a mockery of its practices with ridiculous, absurdly acted parodies. There could be some truth in this, but many a mock "Black Mass" has come badly unstuck and invited a genuinely Evil entity to attend its performance, as some experimenters have already discovered on more than one occasion. To genuine Satanists, however, their object of worship does not resemble an ugly imp but a strikingly beautiful young man, albeit of a particularly hard and uncompromising appearance. He does not die on their behalf, but it is their task to see that enough humans die for his benefit. He is the Patron of the Powerful and the Lord of Lust. In short, he is all their own worst personal propensities personified. What else could he possibly be?

At one time among Satanists it was considered justifiable to pay worship in an ordinary Christian Church, providing one altered the sense of the Lord's Prayer by slight and hopefully unnoticed changes in its construction. The Satanically revised version went:

"Our Father which wert in Heaven, hailed by thy Name. Thy Kingdom come. Thy will be done on Earth yet not in Heaven. Give us this day our daily bread and forgive not our trespasses if we forgive those that trespass against us. Lead us into our temptations and deliver us to Evil. Amen."

Just sufficiently similar to the authentic version to pass as a mumbled imitation, yet with the total meaning completely changed in direction. There was also the popular belief that the normal Lord's Prayer said backwards was a certain summoner of His Satanic Majesty. Given the same concentration of effort and intention, reciting a railway timetable backwards would have had the same effect.

Nowadays, however, Satanists are no more devoted to ceremonial religion than are the majority of other human beings. Besides, all the perverted practices and sexual abnormalities, which formerly they might only have found in genuine Satanic Temples, can now be located in exclusive private clubs with enormous membership fees. So if participation in sado-masochistic orgies was their only real incentive, it is purely a question of having enough money and knowing the right people. Just as it is possible to be a devoted Deist and practice every principle of Good without belonging to any established religion whatsoever, so is it perfectly possible to be a Diabolist and practice all the principles of Evil without being a registered member of any Satanic organization. It is also possible to believe in both

Principles combined in a common Consciousness, whereof human beings are capable of partaking to a proportional degree. Such would seem to represent about the most rational approach to the problems of psycho-spiritual power in our present times.

It has been well said that the Devil is God as understood by wicked people. In other words, they have their own reasons for deliberately aligning themselves with Evil in contradistinction to Good. Suppose, however, that God and Devil were both seen as the same Being, existing to evolve Itself, as humans do, by working on the worst of Its nature and steadily transmuting this over the multimillenia into a supernal spiritual condition of consciousness. Suppose that all living creatures, especially ourselves, had particular and specialized parts to play in this incredible process, and that until our mission of humankind was finished and fulfilled, our Universe could not be considered complete. What if the Deity we had mistakenly presumed perfect was in reality someone like ourselves, but on an unbelievably vaster scale of Existence—living as we are, and for the same purpose—self-perfection, and struggling like ourselves to deal with Its own type of Devil? Suppose that all we worked for the Good helped this process forward, while everything we thought and did for the Bad had the opposite effect and delayed or interfered with our incredible Ultimate? It might be well to remember the Biblical text: "So God created man in his own image, male and female created he them."

If there are any solid grounds for such presumptions at all, their implications are almost beyond comprehension, but they do form a very practical platform from which to appreciate the general construction of our Cosmos—a Deo-devil of Energy that, theoretically, resembles the cells of our own bodies. Should we find this difficult to grasp, compare it with the idea of a single body-cell trying to figure out what sort of individual controls the mass of meat it lives amongst, if it even suspects that such a Being exists at all. Just as the behavior of our consciousness influences our entire beings, so does the Cosmic Consciousness of the Deodevil affect us accordingly, conjointly making up our whole interrelationship throughout all Existence. From now on we might as well term this Supreme Superconsciousness our Deodevil and regard It, like ourselves, as a God-Satan seeking Its Unity as an Ultimate in Its course of Completion. What we have to decide is whether to help this process by consciously initiating It ourselves, or to hinder this so far as we can by polarizing our portions of Its power in the direction of the Devil.

By doing that, we would be acting in a somewhat similar fashion to infective microorganisms in a human system, the end result being a diseased or disordered Deity. This swiftly summons the required antigens to cope with the cause, as indeed they do at the cost of many microbic lives, and a condition of health will then be restored to the spiritual system. A deliberate preponderance of Evil will result in a sick or ailing Deity, which then has to employ the immune factor to deal with the unwanted state and bring it back to normal balance. Health for an ordinary human or a Deity means just the same thing—a condition of poised polarity or "wholeth" (where the popular modern term *holism* derives from, which signifies complete treatment on all levels simultaneously). So any marked disturbance of this harmony in either direction will result in corrective measures being applied.

This happens if the overbalance occurs on the Good side of the scales, too. It can be possible to have too much of a good thing in the sense of our progress rate accelerating past its normally safe peak, which seldom occurs in Nature. This does not call for the commission of extra Evils to compensate for such an unusual discrepancy, but it does mean that the rate itself needs retarding somewhat so that its overall status comes close to equable proportions. There was a lot more than mere wit behind St. Augustine's famous prayer, "Lord make me good and pure and holy—but not just yet, Lord! Not just yet." He knew only too well his own capabilities of alteration and suspected that the Deity might also be liable to the same Laws of Life on a totally different time-scale and terms of fulfillment.

So here we have the purpose and function of human-kind defined as one of cooperation with our Deodevil fulfilling Itself and all Life as the Entitized Entity and Energy of Existence. Whoever we are, and whatever we think, say, or do is part and parcel of this astounding program, however we title this or attempt to consider it consciously. In fact, it does not make a lot of difference except to ourselves whether we do or not. The subconscious and genetic levels of our lives are operated by instinctive and inherent types of awareness that are almost independent of intentional, con-structive thought processes. This is only because it has taken us millions of years to acquire such an ability. Orig-inally it took us our whole lives being conscious of the sim-plest faculties, such as breathing and eating, in order to learn those abilities at all. Gradually, after innumerable life-times, humans developed control over consciousness until increasingly larger and more abstract areas of awareness became transferred to the involuntary part of ourselves. *This process is still continuing,* and has a long way to go yet before it is anywhere near its end. By extrapolation, any intelligent individual should be able to hazard a guess in the likely direction of its eventual outcome.

From a purely mystical viewpoint, our primal Life-task is to participate in the spiritual scheme aimed at altering the Devil into Deity—past that polarized point into a Being beyond anything we might ever imagine. This could be considered as the evolution of God into What and Whoever It was meant to be at Its conception. So far as we are concerned, this should be a reciprocal action requiring an indefinite period of conscious concern, for an untold number of incarnations, which need not worry us a great deal since we cannot curtail them. All that can be said with any certainty about the likely amount of time required for Deo-development is that this will take just as long as it needs. It may be comforting to bear in mind the Biblical passage that speaks of a thousand years in the sight of God being less than a summer evening, which is very brief in Middle Eastern latitudes.

We shall not accomplish any of this by denying, denigrating, or otherwise dismissing the Devil-concept with contempt or derision. It is something we must acknowledge in ourselves and treat as untapped energy capable of conversion into a useful and profitable product, which can then be supplied to Deity as needed. We have reached our present point of civilized culture on earth by discovering the use and value to us of everything, reducing raw materials to marketable products which become exchangeable commodities. If we can do all this with ordinary material objects, then surely we might do the equivalent with metaphysical matters and abstract affairs. We have been taken in by Satan's smart sales talk for so long, and it is about time we started selling *him* for a change. Perhaps Deity might be glad to do business with us. There was once an amusing little verse which went:

> "The Devil, having nothing else to do,
> Went out and tempted Lady Pettigrew.
> My Lady, acting on a sudden whim,
> Instead of yielding, turned and tempted him."

It is simply a question of reversing a reversal, which should straighten out even the most crooked line.

Chapter Nine

"WHO SUPS WITH THE DEVIL—"

When the old-time alchemists spoke of their "Great Work" or Magnum Opus, it was sometimes uncertain whether they meant the literal transmutation of base metals into gold, or their own moral transformation from bottom to top of the spiritual scale. How many had the least inkling that this last procedure also implied the improvement of our common Cosmic character is very uncertain. The prevailing doctrine of their period was that Deity must be perfect and all lesser qualities lay entirely with the Devil. To even hint that God might not be the absolute acme of perfection would be a blasphemy too horrible for contemplation. Yet such was an attitude of mind built up by the Christian Church, though without foundation from anywhere else. The God of Israel as presented by the Hebrew Scriptures made no pretenses to perfection. He could be angry, vengeful, intolerant, humorless, exacting, and exhibit other autocratic idiosyncrasies that are seldom admired for their amiability and sympathetic nature. It could have been that the Church was trying to postulate the perfect Deity by inventing a theoretical ideal of such a Being, and they could not characterize It too closely for fear of imposing senseless limitations on It. If so, they made a very poor presentation of this picture, because it did not seem to move the people's minds or imagination very much.

It is possible that in our Western Esoteric Tradition only the so-called magicians had any notions of what they were doing when they got the idea of controlling Demons with angelic agencies and making them work for ambitious humans. These magi might not have hit on the best methodology, but the fundamental scheme for obtaining energy from our most Evil propensities in order to evolve the best and most beneficial part of ourselves was indeed a very feasible notion. In principle, the general proposition of harnessing Hellish horrors to serve the Heavenly hopes of our humanity was a very sound one. Once the fundamental idea itself started to circulate in the mentality of humankind, its progress would be almost automatic, even if it would take an extremely long time to appear as a practical projection in this world among us. Think how long the idea of flight for humans took before the first human foot left this earth—literally thousands of years at the cost of many lives. Yet today we are casually stepping from one continent to another for the sake of whims, and tomorrow we shall be planet-hopping with the same nonchalance. If only we could manage our metaphysical affairs with the same success as our material ones, this world would be a very much better place to dwell in. Everyone knows that instinctively, yet how many humans contribute towards this awareness consciously and constructively? Not nearly enough or in anything like the correct way, otherwise we should be much closer to our target than we are at the present period.

So that should surely be considered the most magical Magnum Opus we could possibly undertake: to continue the task of evolving our Deity by doing the same with ourselves, because it amounts to the identical achievement in the end. So long as there is a trace of the Devil left in us it will remain in our Deity as well, because both are the same Being seen from opposite standpoints. Their reality need not be questioned because they (or IT) are as real as we are, but the details of their whats, whys, hows and everything else have to be constructed from our creative imaginations, since we have no other tools to use. The Chinese have an old proverb which says that whatever the mind of a person can conceive must exist somewhere and somehow, because otherwise it could not have been conceived at all. There is definite truth in this, providing we do not impose limits of time, space, or circumstances. We have been thinking of both Deity and Devil for thousands of years, but have made in our minds the sort of Deity we wanted, rather than the sort which would want us. In the case of the Devil, we have made what we well deserve, an enemy within ourselves.

Voltaire was right in saying that if there were no God it would have been necessary to invent one. He meant that we need some factor with which to relate our developing good qualities through the millenia, and we might as well call that "God" as anything else; and of course the same is true of our Evil propensities, which are so much in evidence that there is no possibility of concealing or denying them. All we can do is to admit and then try to modify or transmute them into something preferable. We have been accomplishing this tremendous task extremely slowly over the last few centuries, but now that our rate of civilization seems to be speeding up so rapidly, we shall need to increase our plodding perfection-pace considerably in order to stay spiritually level with our technological advances, if indeed we may hope to keep anywhere close to them at all.

It may seem a strange thing, but Western visual art, which has always been strongly opposed to displaying the Supreme Spirit except in purely symbolic forms such as a right hand, overseeing eye, or a dove for the Holy Spirit, has a whole collection of Devils and Evil Spirits—all portrayed as ugly and hideous monsters, which are usually a mixture of bat, goat, and serpent. They frequently show faces where their buttocks should be, or close to their lower abdomens. This is typical of our readiness to recognize the worst of ourselves as humanoid, while we only acknowledge the best possibilities as symbols of what might be. A probable exception might be the images of Jesus and Mary portraying idealistic images of Male or Female Archetypes. The majority of other religious systems depicted hosts of different Deities all with their specialities, much as modern Christians formulate a pantheon of saints in their place. However, in common with Judaic custom we tend to reject visual ideas of Deity while forming clear, if extremely unflattering pictures of our Devil. Few people nowadays would see the Devil-picture as other than earlier caricatures or cartoons symbolizing natural nastiness. A much more accurate form of Devil-depiction in modern terms would be the familiar mushroom-shaped cloud of a nuclear explosion, which may indeed become eventually recognized as acceptable symbolism.

Yet the human mind, having a limited reach, normally needs some kind of focal point to hold before it can cope with abstract concepts such as Deities and Devils. The Jews have their Ark and Scrolls of the Law, the Christians their New Testament and Sacramental Elements, the Muslims their Koran and Mecca, the Buddhists their Bodhisattva figures and so forth, while the Hindus have their Vedantas and Pantheons of Gods—all appreciable material foci for calling up their entire connected ideologies. A sort of "start here and expand indefinitely" scheme. A very clear one too, providing it can be seen how the process works. Some simple physical symbol is chosen to represent an entire spiritual system, and then its various ideological components are connected therewith, one by one, as they are consciously considered. Something like the whole complicated mass of the Qabbalah connecting with the single mathematical Tree of Life glyph. Or the doctrines and philosophies of Christianity linking with the Calvary Cross. When properly programmed, the original symbol acts as an access code does for any computer scheme. It provides a starting point at which to open up an entire area for investigation if followed up with a careful search-system. It might be wished we had some common symbol for both Deity and Devil so that we could set up a convenient summons-signal. In fact we already have one that is recognized universally and has been well known for thousands of years. It is simply—*MONEY!*

What else could possibly be so perfect a bivalent symbol for both Good and Evil as money? It is a common means of accomplishing either or transcending both if pushed far enough. We all know the oft-repeated truism about the love of money being the root of all Evil, but we also know the amazing amount of Good that can come from its correct usage. Money is probably the only symbol known to humankind that can combine the natures of Deity and Devil so adequately and accurately. Even its function as a medium of exchange between people is truly symbolic, because in this case it can signify the most important transaction of all times: the Devil's need for Deity's nature, and Deity's need for the Devil's energy. The problem is that neither side is particularly keen to deal with each other directly, since they are of opposite inclinations; so it is up to we humans to act as agents or salesmen, handling the proposition as attractively as possible in order to advance its taking place when and wherever practical. The difficulty is that we ourselves are the price the Devil is demanding, and so what we are seeking will be acceptable substitutes.

If only the problem were as straightforward as this analogy, it would be a lot simpler to solve, and yet the fundamentals of it are all there. Isn't this what we are trying to do with ourselves for the whole of our lives? Decide between alternatives and make up our minds which way to direct available energies? Construct a course of consciousness between birth and death that will amount to something appreciable in the lives and affairs of those who are connected with it? In other words, to make some kind of mark on the recording tape of Time that says, "I am so and so and have been here doing this and that, and therefore remember *me*." In effect, to impress oneself and one's individuality indelibly into the essence of Existence itself, so that a "Me-mark" will remain there forever. Deity, Devil, and humankind have that interest in common. We simply serve the idea in different ways, and money is only a means of obtaining that service.

The Devil-end of our Deity shows us how easy it would be to gain money by dishonest means and gratify all our greeds, providing we are prepared to be ruthless and disregard our fellow creatures to an extent where we would cheerfully sacrifice them all to gain our immediate ends. In return for this, however, his price would be ourselves for conversion into what amounts to fuel for his further activities. The Deity-end of our Devil, on the other hand, offers us eventual integration with Itself if we would be willing to follow a code of conduct that allows for the accommodation of all other Life-orders within its range. If our Deodevil were one huge and hungry Being and we were food provided for Its nourishment and enjoyment, we would either be converted into interesting and intelligent energy at one end or be reduced to excrement and expelled from the other. Possibly both, according to the proportions of Good and Evil in ourselves.

What we have to remember is that the Deity does not make us Good nor the Devil make us Evil. We make ourselves what we are during the course of our evolution no matter how long this may take. The important thing is our methodology, because whatever that may be, it will certainly be one with which our Deodevil is experimenting Itself. Our average way of working is firstly to examine options in all directions, then decide how far we propose to go in any of them, consider our chances while examining alternatives, and lastly to initiate whatever action we have calculated should achieve the end in view. In being guided to this "execute" point, a number of related factors will come into play, such as past experience in similar situations; opinions of others; comparisons with existing codes of conduct; cultural, educational, and ethical standards; genetic instincts; and a whole host of modifying intellectualizations that may or may not affect the eventual projection of power along a definite line of consciousness. This entire process between instigation and accomplishment could take less than a split second or several thousand of our years, depending on the nature or scope of whatever it was. Since it will obviously take multimillions of humans quite a long time to make any significant impressions on our Macrocosm, we might as well each make our individual contributions as clearly as we can with as much effort as we may manage.

This seems a terribly slow way of achieving change in our Cosmic tradition to secure our spiritual safety, but it is the only certain method, because the basic truth is that until the majority of humankind decide to Deify themselves beyond the risk of reverting to predominant Evil, we cannot consider ourselves completely clear from risk of further worldwide damage and deterioration. To a considerable extent we could actually contain many expressions of Evil by affording alternative areas of action. For example, the warlike violence of young males could be released in the controlled arenas of football fields. The avaricious and acquisitive instincts of predatory people could be offered outlets in gambling or ordinary profiteering. In fact, apply that conversion principle to the whole huge field of Evil and we have perhaps the perfect answer: THE IDEAL WAY OF DEALING WITH EVIL IS TO COMMERCIALIZE IT. Sell Satan in small pieces or large lumps to eager buyers, providing he is sold as a processed package having a minimum ill effect. The same actual amount of Evil (or anything else) reduced to minimal quantities and spread over an extensive area can be contained quite comfortably. A whole gram of cyanide that would slaughter, say, a hundred people in seconds, could be administered quite safely to a million during the same period. That is the most practical principle to adopt.

In fact, if we think of the problem in terms of our Deodevil, we should see this as comparable with the way Its Devil-end is steadily converting itself into Deity—more or less by dissipation, distribution, and diminution—otherwise, natural wastage. It may sound strange to say that our God is growing older, yet in effect that has been happening, and with age comes experience and therefore better judgment. It would be pointless speculating on the probable age of our Deodevil in relation to that of average human lives, and yet it might be useful to bear in mind that even the slightest thoughts will affect that incredibly immense Awareness to the extent of our own existence therein. Each single one of us may not move It any more than a fish disturbs the ocean it swims in, but that movement will theoretically remain impressed in that Sea forever. So all of us can make meaningful contributions to the sum total of our common consciousness.

Once, humankind used to believe in ideal states of

Heaven or Hell as places where the souls of Good or Evil people associated together and practiced either quality to their heart's content. This meant that all the Good people treated each other well and enjoyed themselves, whereas the Evil ones made each other miserable by treating each other in the worst way they could imagine. Our ordinary human world was regarded as a mixture of both these, wherein we determined which predominant category everyone fitted into so that we might sojourn in our appropriate areas when we died. A neat and tidy idea. Many must have thought what a splendid scheme it would have been had we been able to divide the whole earth into similar territorial divisions. After all, Dante portrayed his Hell as being arranged in circles of categorical sinners. All the liars and untruthfuls in one group, all the sex offenders in another, blasphemers in another, and so on. Outside the main gate was displayed the fatal notice: "ALL HOPE ABANDON, YE WHO ENTER HERE." Suppose we modernize this a little and visualize our Hell hand-out as reading: "BE AS WICKED AS YOU WANT. KILL, CHEAT, LIE, BURN. TORTURE, STEAL, GRAB ALL YOU CAN GET. *BUT DON'T HOWL WHEN IT ALL HAPPENS TO YOU*—WITH ADDED INTEREST!" One wonders just how long any experimental penal colonies of such a nature would last if they could be set up somewhere on this earth.

Suppose, purely for the sake of speculation, that World Government were an accomplished fact, and all definitely Evil or antisocial characters who refused to reform were provided with some section of the world to live in where there were no laws of any obligation to abide by definite codes of conduct. Inside this section they would be perfectly free to do exactly what they liked to and with each other, but if they attempted to escape or set a single foot outside their designated area, they would be executed immediately. What would be the most likely outcome of such an undertaking?

Results would be highly predictable. After the initial massacre and mayhem, with survivors banding themselves into gangs whereof the strongest claimed rights to the most favorable territory, the more intelligent ones would be working out ways of getting what they wanted by whatever trickery or deceit they thought might be imposed on the others. As with any kind of pack-creature, leaders would emerge spontaneously and dominate the main mass perforce of personality, imposing their intentions as they saw fit and only modifying them if absolutely expedient. Once they had succeeded in establishing their required rules, offenders and other dissidents would be treated very severely and made horrifying examples of. The "New State of Evil" would eventually become an autocratic dictatorship with a constantly challenging chain of office-seekers, all intriguing and angling every which way they could think of for positions of power and advantage. Hierarchies would become established and relationships made. Eventually this "New State of Evil" would become a reflection of what it had broken away from, with all regulations enforced for the protection and profit of its most powerful people. Human herds have a built-in association pattern regardless of their moral motivations.

It is not so easy to speculate on what a society composed entirely of fundamentally Good people would be like, because if there were no opposition to anything there would be insufficient motivation or challenge to human abilities. Consequently little would be likely to get done in any real direction. In fact, the main use and purpose of Satan in any scheme of Existence is to present us with perpetual problems for satisfactory solutions. Without them we would scarcely make a great deal of progress. It is only by overcoming our obstacles that we exert enough effort to evolve ourselves in the direction of Deity, so it is really our reaction against Satan that drives us Godwards. So Satan has that much significance in our lives, and without him we would often be lost for our sense of direction. Perhaps the old fairy story might be called to mind of the baby princess whose many Fairy Godmothers attended her baptism and bestowed every possible blessing on her, until an older and wiser Fairy arrived and said, "My poor child! The best thing I can give you is a little Sorrow." Whereupon the baby's family drove the Fairy away with execrations for ill-wishing their delightful daughter. Yet subsequent events proved that the more experienced Fairy Godmother had hit on the one factor needed to complete the girl's character with genuine inner grace and beauty. There is often more solid spiritual truth to be found in simple familiar fairy tales than in tome after tome of the most complicated philosophy.

So a Heaven without a single trace of Satan would be somewhat of an uneventful condition, but one wherein Satan was welcome—with a converted nature, polarity, and possibly a changed name to match—would certainly be an interesting proposition if such can be imagined. In that guise he would act as a stimulant and spur to ingenuity and inventive ability. There has always been a legend that Satan will be the last one admitted to Heaven after the whole of humanity have been successfully saved. That would be due to his fulfillment of obligations to act as their tempter and tormentor during their earthly existence so that they might develop themselves through suffering and sad experience. As we know well enough in this world, there are plenty of unpleasant jobs to do, such as performed by sanitary and sewer workers, morticians, prison officers and the like, that are of considerable importance because without them we could not maintain our standards of civilization. To a certain extent Satan can be compared to such valuable functionaries on a spiritual scale—he has a purpose and a place in the Grand Design of things, and therefore deserves a more fruitful fate than total dismissal in disgrace after having done such a dirty job successfully for so long.

One point we have to remember about the hypothetical Heavenworld is the apparently contradictory dictum that "a thing is not just because God wills it, but God wills it because it is just." Does that mean that some higher Principle than Deity must decide what justice is before it can be duly done? Not at all. Deity and humanity alike know what real Justice is: a balance, an equalization, a replacement of poise, and a correction of any incorrect condition. It means, especially, righting a wrong or realigning an unwarranted displacement. In short, compensatory action, or in Cosmic terms, Karma. The essential meanings of Karma and Justice are identical. So before any type of Justice can be done, an injustice must happen or an error made so that a correction becomes possible. Therefore, if we make the errors Deity cannot very well decide exactly what would correct them until they are actually made. It was not Divine Will in the first place that any errors or injustice should ever be made anywhere, but nevertheless humanity *did* make them, and so *our* wills were responsible—not God's at all. Karma was invoked automatically because this is ultimately a self-correcting Universe—the Justice of anything does not come about because of the Will of God, but because the wrong itself demands justification. In effect, the Devil demanding Deification. It might sound extreme to say Satan was seeking salvation, but the innuendo is there all the same.

In effect this has been happening very slowly and steadily ever since our concepts of Deity and Devil began, and we ourselves are the media that have been effecting such a Cosmic change by our alterations of awareness and developments of self-determination. The truth is that whether we accept each other or not, we all affect each other's existence by the simple fact of sharing it together in whatever condition we happen to be. Since our development determines the nature and extent of our Deodevil, we might as well agree to adapt ourselves in conformity with the ideology IT affords our attention. Of first and primary importance is to recognize the process as one taking place in ourselves and to intentionally assist this in any way we can. Realize that we are converting our "Devilselves" into our "Deityselves" by our deliberate alteration of Evil into Good. This gradual system of transformation we should appreciate at present by contrasting its modern forms with those of the past, such as ancient sack and pillage changing into modern taxation and profiteering, old time brigandry altering into modern marketry and so forth. Intertribal warfare turning into multinational takeover bids, for instance. Whatever we once did purely by crime we can now do perfectly well by commerce, so why expend energy needlessly?

Possibly one of the worst spiritual Evils ever accomplished was the setting up of a Satan-concept in secret and keeping it as an exclusive emblem of the vilest and most brutal behavior possible among humankind. To a large extent there was a parallel situation in that some sections of humanity created a Deity-image of such stringency that IT (or they) would condemn a little girl, for example, to the hottest of eternal Hells for the theft of two dollars from her father's wallet, which so preyed upon this particular child's mind that she threw herself out of a window and killed herself. Also, in former times it was a custom amongst God-fearing people when their young children "sinned," by telling a lie or committing a small theft, to deliberately hold the tip of the child's little finger in the flame of a candle until the child was screaming with pain, and then after withdrawing the finger and applying a dressing to the burn, recite the following moral injunction: "My Child, if you cannot stand the pain of one tiny candle on the very tip of your smallest finger for the shortest time, how will you ever endure the flames of hell over the whole of your body for ever, and *for ever*, and FOREVER?" Granted, this was a reduction from the earlier Church custom of burning heretics alive in order to supposedly save their souls, but it was certainly a continuation of something that might exist even today in isolated instances.

So long as Satan was still seen as the Evil (yet slowly improving) end of God in Which (or Whom) we were all concerned, there was plenty of hope for us; but when Satan began to be viewed as being entirely separated from Deity, utterly irredeemable, and an implacable enemy of everything to do with evolution, then that was indeed what he became for us and has remained ever since. We have the Christian Church to thank for that in the first place, because it more or less originated such an outlook. By isolating Satan in the way it did, the Church practically promoted him to become the president of an exclusive club of Evil, which admitted increasingly advanced Evildoers with much more power than previously, almost unlimited wealth, and of course attitudes to accord with their social and cultural status. Once they intentionally and consciously set all those advantages to serve the cause of Evil, that dedication made them Satanists *de facto*, whatever else they might have termed themselves otherwise.

There is no real need for ceremonial initiations or any so-called "Black Rites" to make a Satanist, any more than official membership in a Church makes a sincere Deist. The acceptance of Evil as a way of life, with full knowledge of what it involves and taking sole responsibility for the voluntary performance of its practices, constitutes true Satanism in its own worst essence. Those who make that commitment could be called professional Satanists, especially if they make their livings thereby; whereas others who prefer the thrills of belonging to a secret cult should be classed as amateur Satanists, who nevertheless fulfill a useful function in the Hierarchy of Hell. If they really enjoy the pageantry of perversion and the acting out of their inmost and nastiest inclinations with authentic materials, who would prevent them, providing it was all done in private with totally willing partners? In fact, one is tempted to wonder which had the worst effect in our world—a few carefully concealed murders and bestialities, or multiple massacres, tortures, and wholesale thefts openly carried out by people with political interests, who gave thanks to God publicly afterwards. It is a moot point.

Exclusive Satanists, however, are about as rare as exclusive Deists. The vast majority of humans are neither, acting sometimes in the interests of one concept, sometimes in the interests of the other, and often for no particular reason that they can think of at all. Nevertheless, every single thing they activate counts towards the unimaginable total of a Consciousness that will at last triumph with THE TRUTH OF WHAT IT ALL AMOUNTS TO. Because none of us living now will be present in our current bodies at that Happening does not mean that we need do nothing to help achieve it. Every generation owes an obligation to the future as a debt it has inherited from the past. It is time to take up ours and see what can be contributed towards its repayment. Being neither saints nor sinners, but just the usual mixture of both, we might as well try the old trick of speaking to ourselves as if we were God, which amounts to the same thing as speaking to God as if It were us, and say something like:

"Listen Deodevil, whom I used to think of as God, I know you have the same problem of duality that we humans have with Good and Evil. What is more, it probably has the same solution. For instance, I would like to do Good, but I need the energy of Evil to work with, and so do you. So I am suggesting that we alter the actual nature of our Evils in such a way that it becomes bearable by ordinary people and stimulates enough resistance to allow us to cope with it comfortably. I know well enough that this will take a

tremendous time in terms of my years, so all I ask is that my tiny contribution to this change will be acceptable as an addition to its mass momentum. This is what I am now offering: From henceforth, every time my mind meets money under any guise, I shall be reminded of our common problem and intend its sure solution so that ALL have satisfaction. Whether this will be a split-second thought or a long and careful consideration, I shall be sending its energy in your direction. So take it and combine it with all similar supplies from everyone and everywhere so that eventually we all will come to an identically ideal conclusion.

"Just as our currency can be converted into whatsoever terms we want, so I believe our Evils are capable of changing into altered forms of opposition that we can well find fortitude to bear with benefit. Please arrange our Evils by installments well within our spiritual incomes, and do not make demands on us we cannot meet. Bankruptcy brings no benefits to anyone concerned with currency, so please take care that we are solvent and can live within our means effectively. If we can work this in our mortal world by means of common commerce, how much more should its equivalent be possible on subtle living levels whereon Consciousness itself is currency? For centuries humankind has dreamed about every possible kind of panacea: the touchstone that turns lead into gold or poverty into wealth; the Holy Grail that heals all illness and turns Evil into Good; a magical conversions factor that would change wrongs into rights just by its application. Surely, wouldn't the most remarkable of these be Devil into Deity and past that point into PERFECTION, whatever that may be?

"I believe this miracle may be managed not in moments, but certainly within millenia. Just as the total wealth of our whole world consists of one small coin indefinitely added to another, so does the Consciousness of Cosmos amount to tiny thoughts and items of awareness added to infinity forevermore. I am only able to send my fair share, which I will do most willingly as I am minded by the means of money. I know it has been said we cannot serve God and Mammon alike, but it has never been said that we may not

make Mammon into a most valuable servant of God, if not always a very faithful one. So why not try and do the best we can with this idea? Here is what I'll do myself: Whenever I meet money in whatever way, I'll think of Deity absorbing and altering the Devil into Itself simultaneously. For a flashthought I'll code that consciousness as DEVDEI, pronounced "DEV-DAY," and signifying the DEVil into DEIty with every implication and attached consideration possible. When opportunity allows I'll make it more with meditation, treat it as a topic for discussion, or else enlarge it any way I can. I will make this my Magnum Opus, my Holy Grail, my Panacea. For a minimum effort it will make a maximum of meaning, which I hope to understand with my uniting in the Ultimate."

However such sentiments may be condensed or expanded, that is the gist of what has to be dealt with between human individuals and the Deodevil. Furthermore, there would not be much point in thinking or saying them without at least attempting to *do* them in some practical or demonstrable fashion. Even a simple action such as taking a handful of change from a purse or pocket, looking at it while thinking "DEVDEI," and then returning it, would be practical. Any promised meditations must be done, and all transactions that were previously done without any special spiritual significance ought to be given that slightly increased inner importance which this extra thinking will add to it. Less than a second will suffice in most cases, but a little practice will be needed if greater proficiency is to be obtained. It is suggested that a few coins be held in the hand, although a bankbook or credit card would serve the same purpose, and thinking in this manner:

"DEVDEI. DEVDEI, DEVDEI. I am holding in my hands and mind the symbol of what living in this world means for most of us. With it I can do all sorts of things both Good and Evil. Hence for me this is the sign of Deity and Devil, both together as a single Being. I believe that Deity is an Entitized Energy as we are, in the process of

perfecting Itself by altering Its Evil into Good and then transcending both into a spiritual state of being beyond all guesswork. Therefore to me this money is a sign of such a highest Happening, and a certain hope of its occurrence at the end of this Existence. So I am coding all this consciousness in the single word DEVDEI, which will mean to me the Devil changing into Deity, or Evil into Good, and every time I say or think it, such is the significance which it must bear for my beliefs. So DEVDEI. DEVDEI, DEVDEI." A few sessions of this nature should imprint the message indelibly in most minds.

Now there would not be very much point in addressing ourselves to the Deity-end of the Entity without having something to say to the Devil-end of It as well. This is where the Christian Church has been making a sad mistake for many centuries. It formulates a great deal of fulsome and flattering prayers in the direction of Deity, but only a few rather rude remarks made in the direction of the Devil, mostly by way of exorcism. Assuming even the least infernal intelligence, this is surely a somewhat stupid attitude to adopt. Granted there is neither need nor obligation for any flattery or complimentary behavior at all, but neither is there any call for rudeness or gratuitous offensiveness. Direct approaches to the Devil could at least be kept within customary civil limits. A little common sense should convince anyone interested that *if* it is possible for a Deity to "hear" prayers, in the sense of contacting the consciousness of a devotee and responding in some way, then it should be equally possible for a Devil-Being to do the same thing from an expectedly opposite angle. Therefore an approach to Satan may be made somewhat in this fashion:

"Listen Satan, I know perfectly well who and what I'm talking to—all the very worst of my human nature and of every other soul's who ever lived or will live in this wicked world for as long as it lasts. I'm calling for your attention to my mind and soul, so hear this carefully. I mean to change myself and my whole nature so that

I become an altogether better being entirely. This means I have to alter all your Evil in me and adapt its instincts—first to satisfactory substitutes, then to better beneficial happenings, and finally beyond those limits altogether into Endlessness Itself. I am urging you to seek the same solution by a parallel path.

"I also know quite well that you are most unlikely to accept advice from any one mere mortal, so I am not expecting this. However, if and when multimillions of us share a similar idea and subsequently give it our strongest support, you must admit that would make a maximum of difference to your attitude. It would have to. In fact, during the many millenia we claim to have been civilizing ourselves, your attitude has altered and is still doing so. You are accepting our alternative offerings of Evil, and the scheme is spreading almost everywhere. Money is our main means of making Evil milder and more bearable by feeble folk. We can and will work wonders with it, but it is a double-dealing media, working well as much as ill. Everything depends on whosoever handles it. In this world you buy with money what you will, and so it is the equal sign of Good or Evil. It is all a matter of intention, or WHAT WE WILL. You cannot compel us into Evil courses any more than Deity can drive us into Good ones. We know that in the end we shall become beyond them both, for humankind maximally matures along the Middle Path of Progress.

"We also know that we need goading into Good, and you are very good at goading by itself. Then, too, we humans are very perverse people. What happens if and when you try your most to make us Evil and malicious, and instead we use the energy you send us for helping humans? Could you trust us to be wicked with it every time? You know how unreliable we humans are. How far would you depend on us for anything you needed desperately? Would you really be stupid enough to put your whole existence in our hands, supposing that were possible? You know the average human answer to all questions of probity, it goes like this: 'I don't know. I might or I might not. I'll see how I feel when the time comes.' We do not believe you are idiotic nor indeed the least bit foolish. To the contrary, we credit you with cleverness beyond believing. Besides, experience alone has taught you not to count on anything we say or do.

"You have a name as the Father of Lies, which means the author of untruth. What could possibly be more untrue than human beings that vary more than any weather vane they ever made? A lie is something told with the intention of misleading or deceiving, and of possibly concealing things from those who have the right to know them. Otherwise known as a falsehood, or a false hold, meaning an inaccurate grasp of anything. For us, the truth is whatever we want it to be or think it is at any given moment. How could minds like ours ever appreciate what real TRUTH is anyway? So if we cannot believe anything you say, you certainly could not accept whatever we said. Our largest liars are most highly paid as politicians and mass-media makers. We defy you to be more deceitful or duplicitous than they are.

"As we are evolving, so will you. The old, crude creature we once feared so much is now a sleek, sophisticated Satan of the smartest sort. A fashionable Fiend indeed, with all accessories and whatever indicates your status and significance. Where you once held a common pitchfork you now hold a nice, new nuclear device. This of course makes a much more powerful persuader than your ancient weapon. On the other hand you will know all about the Mexican standoff, where two brigands are each holding a loaded pistol at the other's head, and neither dares to press a trigger for fear the reflex action of the other will result in his own death. Why should we be frightened by the threatened horrors of your Hell when we have now invented worse ones of our own on Earth?

"So Satan, can we come to a commercial understanding? In our world open enemies will trade with one another secretly, while slaughtering each other's soldiers and civilians without mercy. Behind hostilities, commercial deals continue in those neutral zones both combatants keep clear for business purposes. Centuries ago a Roman writer remarked, "Whoever loses a war, it's never the bankers," and that is even truer now than when he wrote it.

Therefore even if we should remain official enemies, can we not compromise upon our trading interests? We could at least exchange ideas or seek for something mutual which would neither benefit nor hurt a single soul and which therefore might be workable with common consciousness."

Looked at along such lines there would be no reason for noncommunication with our Satan-Spirit as such. There would naturally be constant need for caution and for continual care to be taken to avoid all traps of every sort. The initiative would always have to lie with the instigator of such "Satan-sessions," and no information or knowledge gained from them could be taken as accurate or reliable in the slightest, but merely as something interesting to be examined later in the light of subsequent experience. The concept of Satan, although treated antagonistically, is nevertheless to be considered one of consequence and importance, deserving automatic respect and diplomatic treatment.

There is nothing whatever to be gained in treating our Satanselves as though they were stupid, unimportant, tiresome, or insignificant imps. There is even less point in trying to pretend they do not exist or have no noticeable reality. To the complete contrary, they have considerable significance and should be taken very seriously indeed. The fact that we are evolving very slowly out of their former influence does not allow us the liberty to treat them with hostility or contempt. Taken as a whole, our Evil instincts are still enormously powerful and could quite well destroy the civilization it has cost us so many millenia of suffering and misery to build up in this world. That is a painfully obvious fact that should not need much intelligence to see clearly enough.

So there is no advantage in trying to deny the Devil in our own natures or in pretending that Christian baptism alone banished it forever, however much that may have loosened its grip. Apart from anything else, the principle of the Devil is bound up with our basic self-preservation instincts, and its impulsive promptings could preserve our earthly lives on more than one occasion. To put it bluntly, we *need* the Devil for what it can do, BUT we do *not* need the Devil in its present spiritual structure. The greatest necessity is for a complete change of nature in both the Devil and ourselves. Exactly how this will take place is somewhat uncertain, but all the energies of evolution will have to play their part. Changes of consciousness will positively have to happen, and it is here that influences like religion, culture, and esotericism will be most valuable and have their greatest effect. So will genetics and medical science, which are likely to improve our qualities of breeding and capabilities of consciousness. Whatever assists the advance of humanity towards its Ultimate is bound to help us all forward, if by only a single step.

Might it not be said that there is some danger in dealing with the Devil? Indeed there will be, quite as much on a different level as if we were handling nuclear energy, but the point is that we are dealing with the Devil anyway—subconsciously. Surely it would be better to confront and cope with it consciously, with awareness of all the risks, than allow it to continue unchallenged its insidious work within us. Doing nothing would be sheer stupidity on our part. No human with a spark of real intelligence ought to let the Devil in themselves run their whole lives without a single word of protest or objection. That would indeed be spineless and weak-minded almost beyond belief. Even a rabbit squeals when pounced on by a predator. We might as well say *something*, even if that is only "HELP." The more highly intelligent our Devil is, the more dangerous does it become. We cannot hope to compete with it in that field alone. However, there is one thing the Devil cannot possibly do, a field of action in which we can outclass him every time. THE DEVIL CANNOT *LOVE*.

By that one word is meant very much more than merely sensual pleasure, and certainly more again than silly, sentimental pseudo-spiritual feelings for something outside human ability to actually experience. Real love is the free and unconditional offering of an entire soul for inclusion with that of another entity. In purely commercial terms, a merger of mutual interests for the benefit and promotion of both, or at least the intention of this on the part of one party. We might say it would answer the definition of love to be a human self sincerely seeking completion by finding the fulfillment of all its spiritual deficiencies in the same Source.

That is the reason Christians were given the unheard-of advice to love their enemies or those they regarded as such for any reason. The ultimate of this meant that Deity must love the Devil strongly enough to seek fusion with It as a single Spirit of mutual polarities. This might also have meant in modern terms that we should be seeking nuclear *fusion*, rather than the present nuclear fission, for the supply of energy. Fusion brings together while fission breaks apart. Once our scientists can devise a practical and economic system of using fusion instead of fission for nuclear power, we might hope for a happier relationship between our Deity and Devil.

It might be reasonably queried how anyone could love the Devil. The answer lies in an old adage, as answers often do, that "God loves the sinner but hates the sin." Of course neither we nor God could love the Devil *as he is*. But for what he was reputed to have been, and particularly for what we would wish him to become in the end—an intrinsic part of Deity Itself—yes, that aspect of the Devil we can and should love. As he was once and will be again. How often do we see a human example of this in real life between husband and wife? One partner ill-treating the other shamefully and often brutally, while the abused individual not only endures this stoically but almost appears to invite such ignominy, claiming to love their tormentor. They often say, "He (or she) wasn't like this when I first knew them," and believe such a happy former state could be achieved again. If we like to think of our Deity-Devil situation as being comparable with such an unfortunately common domestic problem on a Cosmic scale, that would serve as an analogy.

Therefore, there seems to be no sound reason why an alternative type of Satanism should not spring up in modern times, wherein Satan is looked on as a temporarily detached part of Deity whom his earthly protagonists are hoping to restore Heavenwards so that we may all be happy together once more. There are endless legends to this effect that could well be collected and made into a marvelous myth to form the basis of an entire spiritual system. Satan could be shown, like ourselves, to be a victim of his own worst faults, from which only we humans could liberate him by conquering our own. Which is fundamentally true enough. That alone should make an interesting philosophy to follow up and expand. It is true this could create a sort of Satanism counter to the currently believed popular picture, but reversing a reversal should certainly set everything as straight as it ought to be.

The deciding question is this: Why should Satan remain a permanent, fixed, and altogether immutable emblem of Evil—exactly the same now as he always was and impossible to vary by the slightest degree? The *principle* of Evil may be all those things, but its forms, intensity, effects, and all its other active attributes are as subject to the same laws of variation as anything else. Therefore it is only reasonable to suppose that Satan himself would alter with them. The medieval Satan is not the same as his modern descendant, because Satan always inflicts the Evils of a present period, and these have altered down the ages, however much they may yet connect with those of the past. So our present need is for a contemporary concept of Satan that will be seen for what it really amounts to in modern minds. That may be a lot more frightening than anyone would suppose, but at least we would realize just what we were up against in ourselves.

Once having clarified the concept satisfactorily and accepted its purely provisional structure, the problem arises of what to do with it. If a proposal is made to employ it in any esoteric spiritual practice, then this should be laid out along the lines previously suggested: the focal Satan-figure not to be taken as any kind of a Master or Chief Controller, but more as One to be watched and considered with extreme caution. Certainly as Someone to take into account with every possible care and safeguard applied. For example, there must be plenty of fellow-humans whom one would gladly do business with or meet socially in public, yet would never invite into one's home or intimate circles. There is another old saying: "Who sups with the Devil will need a long spoon," the implication being to adopt a proper distance and always keep a correct attitude. That advice should be carefully heeded and no opportunity allowed for exploitation of weaknesses or the taking of undue advantages. All the general rules that apply to the care of dangerous psychiatric cases or convicted criminals are quite valid in dealing with any aspect of the Devil. Relationships must be firmly restricted within limits where control can be maintained at all times. Otherwise there is bound to be danger.

It has been well said that "Eternal vigilance is the price of freedom," because that is the main consideration where all deals with the Devil are concerned if we are to remain free from his elaborate entanglements. We need to be constantly on the watch if we do not intend to be caught by simple and trivial tricks that would not deceive an alert child. Once reasonable safeguards are settled properly, the main program can be set up, which would probably be mostly experimental in its initial instances. For example, there could be quite a lot of discussion and idea-gathering at first, or possibly prayer sessions for the easing of Evil into alternative expressions of energy that are more tolerable than those we know at present; and in the meanwhile, supplications could be made for sufficient strength to survive the Evils we endure on earth today. Then could come the summoning of Satan, unto whom we would make our meanings plain and perfectly determined beyond any shadow of doubt. Following this could come a declaration of love for the Satan that *was* and for what we hope he *will become* in our mutual far-off future. Maybe some singing and dancing suggesting such an effect, or whatever else might seem appropriate for this "New Look" type of Satanism.

There would most probably be a lot of objections that such would not be real Satanism at all, and neither would it be in the eyes of non-Satanists, who can only see the topic from a single limited viewpoint colored by the popular press and sensational journalists. It could be mentioned that non-Catholics exist who refuse to recognize Catholics as Christians and firmly believe they worship the Virgin Mary instead. In the light of that misunderstanding it is easy to appreciate how Satanism can become confused in people's minds. There is no question of it being totally Evil in one sense, yet leaving this alone to become indefinitely worse would be more than serious, it would be fatal. An absolutely new type of Satanism is needed in the only form that makes any sense in our world today, and never for a single second must the main motivation be lost sight of—the restoration of Satan to his primal condition and prestige as a Son of God. He was then described as the most beautiful of Beings, who was cast out of Heaven for his refusal to acknowledge humanity as a masterpiece of God's work.

Frankly, looking at humankind as we once were and mostly still are, could he really be blamed? Thinking of ourselves drifting in the direction of Deity including Satan, as we should pray we will indeed become in the imaginable future, a different picture presents itself. Factually we are in the course of painting that picture right now, and what we are doing at present is outlining its eventual appearance.

For too many centuries we have been sending nothing but disparaging and denigratory thoughts in the direction of the Devil, and none of these have helped anyone in the slightest way. Surely isn't it about time we started altering our ideas into something more spiritually valuable? For example, thoughts that might be most practical in the process of not only returning Satan to the Deity he belonged with in the first place, but also of doing the same for ourselves by a parallel path. According to best beliefs, the former cannot be completed until the latter is accomplished. Those beliefs also tell us that Satan's original name was Lucifer, or the Bearer of Light, which of course is Darkness; yet the Light he was reputed to bear brought us Knowledge, and it always will. If his particular Light showed us what *not* to do or be, that is at least half our salvation problem solved, and if for the other half concerning what we *should* be and do, we need Deity to tell us, then together we shall BECOME AS WE WILL BE—*ONE.*

It is probable that human beings have thought a lot more about Satan than they have about God in the course of our civilization, but how often have they ever thought useful or constructive things? Possibly very seldom, and certainly not nearly frequently enough. One of the strange beliefs on the Satan trail was held by the Russian cult to which the notorious Rasputin belonged. This was expressed by their watchword, "Sin for Salvation," and their argument was that if Jesus came into the world expressly to save sinners rather than the just, then without sin there could be no salvation, and therefore one should sin as much as possible in order to be granted such a grace. Rasputin did as much as he could for the cult's reputation, and presumably he might be termed a martyr for its cause, but humans have always found ingenious excuses to shelter their fondest frailties.

Therefore, there seems to be every reason why a complete re-think on the subject of Satan and all the mystical meanings attached thereto would make quite a valuable contribution to modern consciousness. It would not be so much of a reverse trip back along the way we came, but the straightforward continuation of an immense Cosmic Circle, returning us to our starting point somewhat higher than its previous point on our spiral scale of evolution. It seems scarcely likely that such research would culminate in a campaign with banners waving before it with "SAVE OUR SATAN" emblazoned thereon, but a serious reappraisal of Satan's character and all his modern attributes would be helpful to the more thoughtful part of humankind, who would be capable of comprehending fresh approaches to ancient topics. It is frequently by re-digging in ancient archaeological sites that entirely new and sometimes very striking lights are uncovered from what we formerly thought was totally exhausted soil. The fresh finds simply needed intelligent interpretation.

It might be made a rule by religious people of all Faiths that they should never think of or pray to their Deity without sparing at least a minimal petition for the salvation of Satan synonymous with their own. He, we, and Evil are all bound together by very strong cords of consciousness, but if ours can be loosened then so can Satan's, and if our Evils can be converted into acceptable commercial terms and made more amenable to all concerned, then so can his. If we ever hope to reduce Evil into negligible proportions on this earth, until it becomes virtually eliminated as a feared force, then such could happen to Satan also when he regains his original position. Nonreligious people can partake in the same program by seeing the idea of Satan as a symbol for all the undoubted wickedness in our world and then willing its alteration and amelioration with their whole minds, if they do not believe that they have any souls. Such an effort is bound to add up with the total.

Well over a century ago, Thomas Barham, the author of *The Ingoldsby Legends,* wrote his version of invoking the Devil as a short poem in the form of a tale told about Cornelius Agrippa. His ideas of the Devil and ours could well coincide, so it would not be amiss to retell it here. The presumption is that a young student of the magical arts is requesting his master to invoke the Devil *in propria persona,* and the master is slightly hesitant to do so, but in the end proves quite equal to the task and performs it adequately. This is the story:

> 'And hast thou nerve enough?' he said,
> That grey old man above whose head
> Unnumbered years had rolled,
>
> 'And has thou nerve to view,' he cried,
> 'The incarnate Fiend that Heaven defied?
> Art thou indeed so bold?
> 'Say, canst thou with unshrinking gaze,
> Sustain, rash youth, the withering blaze
> Of that unearthly eye,
> That blasts where'er it lights, the breath
> That like the Simoom scatters death
> On all that yet *can* die!'
>
> 'Darest thou confront that frightful form
> That rides the whirlwind and the storm
> In wild unholy revel?

The terrors of that blasted brow,
Archangels once, though ruined now
Ay—dar'st thou face the DEVIL?'

'I dare!' the desperate youth replied,
And placed him by that old man's side
In fierce and frantic glee.
Unblenched his cheek and firmed his limb.
'No paltry juggling fiend, but HIM!
THE DEVIL—I fain would see!'

'In all his Gorgon terrors clad,
His worst, his fellest shape,' the lad
Rejoined in reckless tone.
'Have then thy wish!' Agrippa said,
Then sighed and shook his hoary head
With many a bitter groan.

He drew the mystic circles bound
With skulls and crossbones fenced around.
He traced full many a sigil there
And uttered many a backward prayer
That sounded like a curse.
'He comes!' he cried with wild grimace,
'The fellest of Appollyon's race!'
Then in his startled pupil's face,
He flung—an EMPTY PURSE!

There must be more than a few people who agree
entirely with this definition of the Devil, and yet it would
have been equally true had the purse been a completely full
one. Satan always holds the strings, whatever a purse contains. If there were such an institution as the Bank of Bad-
ness, there would be no prizes for guessing whose signature
would be appended to the notes as Chief Cashier! Here it is

especially tempting to modify the foregoing poem slightly so as to bring it up to date with a minimal alteration of the last verse so that this will now read:

> He drew the mystic circles bound
> With skulls and crossbones fenced around.
> He traced full many a sigil there
>
> And uttered many a backward prayer,
> Sounding like souls long lost,
> 'He comes!' he cried, 'Watch this who can,
> Behold the Evil end of Man!'
> Then caused his pupil's brain to scan
> A Nuclear Holocaust!

Perhaps a last major point to bear in mind is the incredible energy and power contained by the Satan-concept. If the same amount were totally transferred to the Deity-end of our Entity, an almost unbelievable change would occur within our Cosmos. The sheer quantity of energy expended on Evil by every human alive on earth alone is virtually incalculable. That probably explains the great attraction Satan has for certain souls who hope to purloin a share of that power for their own purposes, even knowing that such an advantage can only be an ephemeral one, because in the end there is no such thing as free power and it must all be duly paid for. They would do well to remember that the Devil is a natural profiteer, and his prices come very high in human terms. It is only the God-end of him that gives anything away, and frequently that is no more than good advice, which is seldom taken any notice of anyway. Nevertheless, and as we should know, energy is convertible into all sorts of alternative expressions, so if Satan supplies the energy, why should humans not put it to whatever usage they propose?

Wickedness, *per se*, is a natural inclination of most human beings. So if humans have an overpowering and compulsive urge to be wicked in our sense of the word, why not let them release those urges in carefully controlled ways that would not cause any great harm to other humans or do irreparable damage inside their immediate area? Moreover, it might be contrived that thereby they would teach themselves valuable lessons as well. Additionally, they should suppose that they are committing all sorts of crimes and Evils, whereas they are really being no more than a nuisance, and mostly to themselves. In other words, sell them acceptable substitutes for Satan that will satisfy their craving for his company.

A tough task, maybe, but surely not beyond solution by human ingenuity. An ersatz Evil? Why not? We have invented perfectly serviceable substitutes for about everything else, which are in common use amongst us. It could come down to a question of salesmanship and persuasion on a massive scale before people could be pressured to purchase synthetic sins rather than real ones, but such has been done in other areas already, and the scheme only needs planning and application as well as adequate financial backing. We should not, however, expect any subscriptions from Satan for any project calculated to compete with his thriving business, though he might put in a bid at a later period for a takeover when he saw it was likely to succeed.

What all this really amounts to is easing ourselves out of Evil rather than trying to cut it clean out of our characters as if amputating an entire arm. To borrow the serpent analogy again, we could compare our evolvement of Evil to the process of shedding a complete skin at convenient intervals instead of casting it all at once. Does this sound impractical and impossible? So did heavier than air flight once. Almost everything is assumed to be impossible at its inception as a pure idea, and it is only after many years of thought and maybe some experiments that the average human mind as such is willing to admit the potential of any project put before it. The whole of our history is crammed with instances of ignored ideas that subsequently proved very successful. So the suggestion that Satan can be converted into something of especial spiritual value should not be surprising to those who are aware of this already and are trying to make it work in a world that has become uncertain of what "spirit" may mean.

A long time ago, Michael Faraday, the inventor of the dynamo, was giving a public lecture on the subject with the help of a small model he was demonstrating. At the end, a lady in the audience asked the question: "Could the lecturer please tell us the practical use of his pretty little toy?" Faraday replied politely, "Certainly, madam, providing you can tell us the practical use of a newborn baby!" Unfortunately the lady's reply, if any, does not seem to have been recorded. So let us no longer see Satanism solely as an utterly "beyond the pale" belief of our most depraved and degenerate types, but also as an attempt to restore the Satan-image—not *back* to its original position with our Deity, but *forwards* to its final future, where ALL of us may meet as ONE in

PERFECT PEACE PROFOUND.

And that is the only sort of Satanism worth working for in this world!

STAY IN TOUCH

On the following pages you will find listed, with their current prices, some of the books and tapes now available on related subjects. Your book dealer stocks most of these, and will stock new titles in the Llewellyn series as they become available. We urge your patronage.

However, to obtain our full catalog, to keep informed of new titles as they are released and to benefit from informative articles and helpful news, you are invited to write for our bi-monthly news magazine/catalog. A sample copy is free, and it will continue coming to you at no cost as long as you are an active mail customer. Or you may keep it coming for a full year with a donation of just $2.00 in U.S.A. ($7.00 for Canada & Mexico, $20.00 overseas, first class mail). Many bookstores also have *The Llewellyn New Times* available to their customers. Ask for it.

Stay in touch! In *The Llewellyn New Times'* pages you will find news and reviews of new books, tapes and services, announcements of meetings and seminars, articles helpful to our readers, news of authors, advertising of products and services, special money-making opportunities, and much more.

The Llewellyn New Times
P.O. Box 64383-Dept. 273, St. Paul, MN 55164-0383, U.S.A.

•   •   •

TO ORDER BOOKS AND TAPES

If your book dealer does not have the books and tapes described on the following pages readily available, you may order them direct from the publisher by sending full price in U.S. funds, plus $2.00 for postage and handling for orders of $10 and under. Orders over $10 will require $3.50 postage and handling. There are no postage and handling charges for orders over $100. UPS Delivery: We ship UPS whenever possible. Delivery guaranteed. Provide your street address as UPS does not deliver to P.O. Boxes. UPS to Canada require a $50 minimum order. Allow 4-6 weeks for delivery. Orders outside the USA and Canada: Airmail—add $5 per book; add $3 for each non-book item (tapes, etc.); add $1 per item for surface mail.

FOR GROUP STUDY AND PURCHASE

Because there is a great deal of interest in group discussion and study of the subject matter of this book, we feel that we should encourage the adoption and use of this particular book by such groups by offering a special "quantity" price to group leaders or "agents."

Our Special Quantity Price for a minimum order of five copies of *Between Good and Evil* is $29.85 Cash-With-Order. This price includes postage and handling within the United States. Minnesota residents must add 6% sales tax. For additional quantities, please order in multiples of five. For Canadian and foreign orders, add postage and handling charges as above. Credit Card (VISA, MasterCard, American Express,) Orders are accepted. Charge Card Orders only may be phoned free ($15.00 minimum order) within the U.S.A. by dialing 1-800-THE MOON (in Canada call: 1-800-FOR-SELF). Customer Service calls dial 1-612-291-1970. Mail Orders to:

LLEWELLYN PUBLICATIONS
P.O. Box 64383-Dept. 273 / St. Paul, MN 55164-0383, U.S.A.

TEMPLE MAGIC
William Gray
This important book on occultism deals specifically with problems and details you are likely to encounter in temple practice. Learn how a temple should look, how a temple should function, what a ceremonialist should wear, what physical postures best promote the ideal spiritual-mental attitude, and how magic is worked in a temple.

Temple Magic has been written specifically for the instruction and guidance of esoteric ceremonialists by someone who has spent a lifetime in spiritual service to his natural Inner Way. There are few comparable works in existence, and this book in particular deals with up-to-date techniques of constructing and using a workable temple dedicated to the furtherance of the Western Inner Tradition. In simple yet adequate language, it helps any individual understand and promote the spiritual structure of our esoteric inheritance. It is a book by a specialist for those who are intending to be specialists.

0-87542-274-8, 240 pgs., 5¼ x 8, illus., softcover   **$7.95**

THE GOLDEN DAWN
by Israel Regardie
The Original Account of the Teachings, Rites and Ceremonies of the Hermetic Order of the Golden Dawn as revealed by Israel Regardie, with further revision, expansion, and additional notes by Israel Regardie, Cris Monnastre, and others.

Originally published in four bulky volumes of some 1200 pages, this 5th Revised and Enlarged Edition has been entirely reset in modern, less space-consuming type, in half the pages (while retaining the original pagination in marginal notation for reference) for greater ease and use.

Corrections of typographical errors perpetuated in the original and subsequent editions have been made, with further revision and additional text and notes by actual practitioners of the Golden Dawn system of Magick, with an Introduction by the only student ever accepted for personal training by Regardie.

Also included are Initiation Ceremonies, important rituals for consecration and invocation, methods of meditation and magical working based on the Enochian Tablets, studies in the Tarot, and the system of Qabalistic Correspondences that unite the World's religions and magical traditions into a comprehensive and practical whole.

This volume is designed as a study and practice curriculum suited to both group and private practice. Meditation upon, and following with the Active Imagination, the Initiation Ceremonies is fully experiential without need of participation in group or lodge.

0-87542-663-8, 744 pgs., 6 x 9, illus., softcover   **$19.95**

MODERN MAGICK
by Donald Michael Kraig
Modern Magick is the most comprehensive step-by-step introduction to the art of ceremonial magic ever offered. The eleven lessons in this book will guide you from the easiest of rituals and the construction of your magickal tools through the highest forms of magick: designing your own rituals and doing pathworking. Along the way you will learn the secrets of the Kabalah in a clear and easy-to-understand manner. You will also discover the true secrets of invocation (channeling) and evocation, and the missing information that will finally make the ancient *grimoires*, such as the **Keys of Solomon**, not only comprehensible, but usable. *Modern Magick* is designed so anyone can use it, and is the perfect guidebook for students and classes. It will also help to round out the knowledge of long-time practitioners of the magickal arts.

0-87542-324-8, 608 pgs., 6 x 9, illus., softcover   **$14.95**

MYSTERIA MAGICA
(formerly Volume V of the Magical Philosophy Series)
by Denning and Phillips
THE INNER SECRETS REVEALED: The Secret Symbolism of the Aurum Solis is given to you for the firt time! The Gates to Knowledge, Ecstasy, and Power are opened to give modern man powers undreamed of in past ages. For those who would know the Meaning of their lives, who do know that we are more than simple machines, who believe—and would experience—there is Beauty and Love in the Universe. No matter what your level of ability in Ceremonial Magick, this is one of the most important books you could ever own. Bringing together the best of the magical systems of Egypt, Ireland, Pre-Columbian America, the Mediterranian, Northern Europe and the Middle East, the authors lead us into new and profound areas of Magical Work. Knowledge is power, and the knowledge presented in these pages is some of the most powerful ever published.

MYSTERIA MAGICA offers you essential and profound magical knowledge, authentic texts and formulae of the Western Mystery Tradition which have hitherto been hidden in inaccessible libraries, in enigmatic writings, or in rarely-imparted teachings passed on only by word of mouth; and, in addition, it contains ample sections showing you how to use all that is disclosed, how to give potent consecration to your own magical weapons, how to build rites on the physical and astral planes with word and action, sound, color and visualization, to implement your own magical will. Here are secrets which have been guarded through centuries by an elite among popes and rabbis, adepts and seers, dervishes and mages. Here, explicitly set forth, is knowledge by which the mystical priesthood of Egypt wielded true God-force through millennia, thaumaturgist in establishing bonds of knowledge, love and power with their chosen deific force however named.

0-87542-196-2, 450 pgs., 6 x 9, revised edition, illus., softcover   **$15.00**